The Globetrotter's Get-Gorgeous Guide

Outskirts Press, Inc.
Denver, Colorado

The Globetrotter's Get-Gorgeous Guide

DIET and BEAUTY SECRETS of Travel and Beauty Pros, Traveling Executives and Celebrity Travelers©

Foreword by Samantha Brown of The Travel Channel

The World's First Beauty Book For Traveling Women!

Come aboard for this Tour of Beauty!
It's *Allure Magazine* meets *Travel + Leisure Magazine* meets *Born To Shop.*

DEBBI K. KICKHAM

The Globetrotter's Get-Gorgeous Guide
Diet and Beauty Secrets of Travel and Beauty Pros, Traveling Executives and Celebrity Travelers
All Rights Reserved.
Copyright © 2010 Debbi Karpowicz Kickham
www.GorgeousGlobetrotter.com

Outskirts Press, Inc.
http://www.outskirtspress.com

ISBN: 978-1-4327-5982-7

Outskirts Press and the "OP" logo are trademarks belonging to Outskirts Press, Inc.

PRINTED IN THE UNITED STATES OF AMERICA

Praise For

THE GLOBETROTTER'S GET-GORGEOUS GUIDE:
Diet and Beauty Secrets of Travel and Beauty Pros, Traveling Executives, and Celebrity Travelers

It's the world's first beauty book for traveling women:
Allure Magazine meets *Travel + Leisure Magazine*
meets *Born To Shop!*

"If Debbi's book makes me look as good as she does, I'm buying it! So many women travel today and have no idea how to stay fit and healthy. I only wish her book was published years ago – it would have saved me from gaining and losing 25 pounds."
Jennifer Stein
Editor and Publisher, *Destination I Do Magazine*,
www.destinationido.com

"At last! A practical how-to beauty book that comes from the trenches. We are the road warriors, and we've got the scars and beauty marks to prove it. Instead of using travel as an excuse for letting down your beauty and exercise regime, this book helps you streamline and benefit from other beauty-minded women who keep fit despite the obstacles."

Diane Sukiennik
Editor, Food and Wine Access, www.foodandwineaccess.com

This book is dedicated to my wonderful, loving, and handsome hunk of a husband Bill, with whom I always travel First Class – even when we go in Coach.

Here is a man who greets me every morning telling me how much he loves me, how beautiful I am, and what a lucky man he is. He makes every day a joy. Is there any better way to get up every morning?

My favorite places to go? Hawaii, Paris, Canyon Ranch, Bora Bora, any luxury hotel, and best of all, inside Bill's hug.

Table of Contents

    The Top 10 best-ever low-calorie snacks to travel with. Calorie-fighting
tactics on the fly. Rules to solve diet dilemmas when traveling anywhere.
Canyon Ranch tips for traveling. Top 10 tips to staying fit-and-trim
while traveling, so your exercise routine doesn't take its own vacation.
Ten snacks less than 100 calories.

Acknowledgements

I could not have written this book without the support and friendship of so many wonderful people.

First, I wish to thank my wonderful husband Bill, who has supported me in this endeavor, in every possible way, from the moment I came up with the idea for this book.

Julie Bernstein, I totally appreciate your reading and editing my manuscript in its early stages. Your comments and suggestions were right on!

Sally Shields, author of *The Daughter-In-Law Rules*, you are the reason I am self-publishing, and your generosity and friendship with contact information, every step of the way, are deeply appreciated. We are bound to be best friends forever.

Marybeth Bond, author of 11 books, including *50 Best Girlfriend Getaways in North America* – your great assistance with sponsorship information, as well as your interview for the book, was a terrific asset.

Gloria Attar, thank you for your wonderful edits, comments and suggestions for every chapter. It was a pleasure working with you.

To the beautiful Helen Powers – thank you for taking my huge, heavy unfinished manuscript with you when you traveled to model in Hong Kong. Your comments, support and friendship are much appreciated.

Carolyn Sheltraw, thank you for your award-winning design efforts, which you used to design the interior of this very book!!

To Alex Safar of Salon Acote – all of my best wishes and gratitude for your interview information, and for keeping my hair looking fabulous and "TV ready" all the time. All of me, and every hair on my head, thanks you!

To Rin Kurohana – thank you for your two adorable illustrations, of the biplane used for all of the Callouts, and for the cute little blonde in the Mercedes convertible.

To all of my interviewees – thank you for your assistance, information, and support for this book. I couldn't have done it without you!

Foreword

BY SAMANTHA BROWN
OF *THE TRAVEL CHANNEL*

As a woman who spends her professional life traveling the world as a host of numerous TV shows on *The Travel Channel,* I am delighted to write the Foreword for *THE GLOBETROTTER'S GET-GORGEOUS GUIDE* – a uniquely informative and valuable book for any and all women who travel frequently, whether for business or pleasure.

I love the title "Get Gorgeous" because as women who travel frequently know... beauty and health on the road is something you have to actively work towards, since it most certainly isn't going to come to you.

The world of travel today can, simply put, be a brutal one. The airport alone holds all the pleasantness of a Boot Camp. I've never been but I'm pretty sure, after the hundreds of times I've had to hop on one leg with my boarding pass stowed in my mouth while removing a shoe with one hand and my laptop with the other, that this might qualify me for some kind of Army maneuver. Then there's the plane ride itself, which after a well-needed nap, creates a rat's nest of hair and mascara taking its own trip down your cheeks. You're left looking less business woman and more lead singer in a Punk band. Debbi knows it's hard out there. And she wrote this book for you.

When Debbi first filled me in on her idea for her book she told me something that I couldn't quite believe, but realized was true: That while there are innumerable books on the market about beauty, and separately, many books about travel, not one book has been published on these two subjects before this, which combines information on staying healthy, fit and beautiful while meeting the rigorous (and as I've described torturous) physical demands that today's travel requires. This is the first beauty book for travelers!

THE GLOBETROTTER'S GET-GORGEOUS GUIDE is a treasure-trove of secrets to help you stay beautiful while traveling. You'll find under-the-radar beauty tips and diet and exercise tricks. Tried-and-true methods to put your best face and figure forward – when the rigors of traveling put all that in reverse. This book is your passport to domestic and international beauty, and it can help you travel so that your diet, exercise and beauty routines don't take their own vacation (or get lost with your luggage).

What I love most about this book is that it's been tested not in scientific laboratories by mice on treadmills but out there in the real world: These are real women, true female road warriors: executives, professionals in the beauty and travel industry, as well as celebrities who, on their own version of a science-lab treadmill, logged the miles on planes, trains and automobiles, who have stayed in five-star hotels down to one star; whom have gazed down at the menus of award-winning chefs and up at the neon-lit boards of fast-food joints. To sum it up they have figured out how, when life hands you Economy you always give 'em First Class.

Then there's Debbi herself – a beauty and travel expert who has spent years compiling tactics, tricks and little jewels of tips that have now amassed into a gold mine of information. She understands firsthand how women are traveling more now than ever for business, as well as how statistics show women are the decision-makers 80% of the time when it comes to family travel. These two trends have fueled explosive growth in the travel industry. For example, the numbers of women who travel at least one night away from home has reached such a peak that at some hotels today, they have created "women-only" floors offering upgraded beds and linens, lighter menu options, nicer soaps, and (my favorite) better lighting in the bathrooms. Finally. Those fluorescent lights make everyone look like they've been stricken with food poisoning! Add to that the explosion of beauty products on the market, and the ever-present demand for diet information, and you've got the "perfect storm" that makes this book so timely.

As someone who has traveled professionally for over ten years and away from home on average 200 days a year, this book was a revelation and taught me things I didn't even know – which I will take with me on my travels.

So fasten your seatbelts – you are ready to take off to being frequent-flier fabulous!

Paean to Pulchritude

(IN OTHER WORDS, LET'S HEAR IT
FOR FEMININE BEAUTY!)

BY DEBBI K. KICKHAM

(I've always been besotted with beauty, cosmetics and travel, so read on, and let this poem capture all the great things that are to follow in the pages of this book…)

I've always wanted to be a beauty –
Like you. Or why not just a real cutie?
At the sweet, tender young age of seven
Nail polish and lipgloss were Seventh Heaven.

There I was, with pink bow in my blonde hair
Plus Evening in Paris scenting the air.
And thus began my own beauty saga
Before Madonna and Lady Gaga.

I went on to Tinkerbell, then Tussy
(When I was much too young to be fussy).
Then I met my bestest friend L'Oreal
Which clearly has been my own special pal.

I rarely leave home without eyelashes curled
And pouty lips from my friend Cover Girl.
But – it's funny how some men also know
Ultimate secrets, to offer a glow.

Men like Charles Revson and Charles of The Ritz
Had their particular, great beauty hits:
Classic Lipsticks like Cherries In The Snow
And special serums that go with the flow.

Make no mistake, though; I often am seen
With Nivea, Jurlique and Maybelline.
My little face always wants more, more, more,
Of Chanel, Guerlain and "J'adore Dior."

Avon calling is also just the thing
With which to have a fine cosmetic fling.
By heaps of freshener, toner and lotion
You get a 'natural' look – I've an ocean.

With a dusting of powder, gloss and rouge
I can create my unique subterfuge.

I look in the mirror and with a glance
Capture myself in my own special trance.

Take it from me – you can always look great,
On every journey. You'll travel first-rate
And make every part of trips you travel
A beautiful trek where you won't unravel.

Just follow my advice, and try the creams
That will fulfill your best cosmetic dreams.
Pack gorgeous goodies, with skirts, shoes and pants
And you won't be sorry on Swiss or Air France.

You'll eat, sleep, exercise and look your best
In transit, on buses or just Northwest.
This book is written to show and unfurl
Travel and Beauty – the best of both worlds.

Introduction

The seeds for this book were planted one night in Thailand, after a heavy three-hour dinner that ended at 11PM. *"Yikes,"* I thought. *"I need to exercise."* I was traveling on a rigidly scheduled press trip, to write about a slew of Thai spas – and, as is common with so many travelers, my personal dieting, exercise and beauty routines took their own vacation. I wound up doing step aerobics for a half-hour *in my bathroom*, which had a walk-in shower with three steps leading down to it. At the time, I wondered, *What the heck do other female travelers do to exercise and diet when they are overcommitted, overtired and in an overcrowded room?* After that, it became my mission to ask every woman I met, who traveled for business or pleasure, *How do you stay thin on the road? How do you battle the bulge? What do you eat in transit? What do you do when there's no gym?* I was also curious: *What are your favorite beauty products? What mascara and skincare do you swear by? How do you help yourself to feel good when you travel?* With these questions and a million more, to flight attendants, travel agents, makeup artists, traveling executives, beauty queens, and many more women, ***The Globetrotter's Get-Gorgeous Guide*** was born. Following my own beauty-diet-exercise routine ***when traveling*** – and finding out what other women did – became my mission. I'm a size four, 109 pounds, and 54 years old – and believe me, staying fit and ever-attractive doesn't come easy to me – I have to work at it like everyone else. I count calories, measure my food, exercise as much as possible and do all I can to stay motivated – ***especially when traveling.*** If I were only a few inches taller (I'm 5'4") I could eat a little more every day, but alas, that's just a dream. To stay slim, and to fit into all the lovely size-four clothes in my closet, I have to restrict calories every day, and especially when I'm navigating the globe. Trust me when I tell you – I'm always ready for a snack – or my next meal. Every bite I enjoy is a mini-celebration. And every year it gets harder and harder to stay so slim. I also just don't have the bouncy energy that I once had as a kid. I always have to push myself to get to the gym. I can't say that it's the highlight of my day but I'm always happy when the exercise hour is over.

Here are just some of my strategies. I eat anywhere from 1,200-1,400 calories per day. Yet I never feel deprived, because I love to eat healthy. I walk three miles a day, usually, no matter where I am in the world, whether it's Walla Walla or Bora Bora. And yes, I also allow myself a little treat, every Saturday night, for about 300 calories – three pieces of really excellent chocolate with a chocolate-hazelnut praline. Or Nutella smeared on a slice of diet bread. I eat it with my eyes closed, with a rapture akin to a shipwreck survivor who's been stranded on a desert island, and is enjoying her first meal in months.

I sure as heck don't want to have even a little pork on the hoof. I'm sure you feel the same way too, and I'm here to share some of the ways I and many of my travel and beauty colleagues work to maintain – and decrease – their **net girth**! And let's face it – having too much weight on your bones definitely ages you, so you're apt to look at least 10 years OLDER than you really are. Who wants that?

This book is for you:

- ◆ If you're always seeking ways of 'undoing the chewing' – especially when you're traveling.

- If you desire exciting, creative and "under the radar" ways to look good and feel great when you're on the road – when beauty/diet/exercise routines typically take a back seat.

- If being thin and beautiful is one of your priorities, or one of your goals, and you're looking for a boatload (or for that matter, a carload) of new-found motivation and inspiration that you can take along everywhere you go.

In other words, my hope is that no matter what your method of transportation – train, plane, boat, bus or car – this book will help keep you from falling off the wagon.

Two other factors inspired me to write this book.

A recent story in *USA Today* showed that women comprise 43% of business travelers and that in 2010, women were projected to spend some $125 billion on travel. In fact, women make 80% of travel decisions! With more and more women traveling for business, and even for pleasure, the time was right for me to create a book that would address their diet and beauty decisions when on the road.

The second other factor has to do with the rapidly expanding cosmetics and beauty market.

Revlon and Cover Girl used to be the only game in town; nowadays, beauty products are exploding onto the marketplace faster than you can say, "*Sephora.*" Local companies selling small-scale manufactured beauty products, many made with regional ingredients, are a growing part of our nation's economy. At a time when large companies are sending manufacturing overseas, small soap, cosmetics and candle companies are keeping Main Street alive and helping families build wealth on their own terms. Why are artisanal products such a hit? "Nowadays people want unique products they can't get on every street corner," says Donna Maria Coles Johnson, founder of the Indie Beauty Network, a trade group that represents nearly 1,000 companies and maintains a social network of over 6,000 manufacturers of soaps, cosmetics, candles, aromatherapy products and fragrances. (www.indiebeauty.com).

Furthermore, "Consumers are tired of the Big Box stores which not only threaten small manufacturers, but which also offer plain old boring products. People want to buy from people they know; from people who contribute to their local community," Donna Maria says. "It's astounding. I started the Indie Beauty Network in 2,000 with a handful of small companies, and today, they are popping up all over the US and the world!"

The internet has also helped turn many hobbyists – concocting lotions and potions for fun – into bona fide small businesses, fueling the growth of the economy in general and the beauty industry in particular. "Ten years ago people made products mostly for fun," she adds. "But today, as more people seek to own and manage a successful business of their own, small scale cosmetics manufacture has become an attractive business option. Besides," she says. "Everybody buys cosmetics, and it's a market that continues to grow."

So there you have it – the dynamic duo of beauty and travel that makes me believe that *The Globetrotter's Get-Gorgeous Guide's* time has really come. I wrote this book to be a combination of *Allure Magazine*, *Travel + Leisure Magazine* and the *Born To Shop* shopping guides. I have written what can only be described as **the world's first beauty book for traveling women.** This is the book I always wanted to read, ever since I first became a travel writer in 1984. If you read this book, and can approach your excursions with an open mind, an attitude of gratitude and an appreciation for different cultures, you're going to have a wonderful trip.

One more thing – because I've been an editor for more than 30 years, I always use AP style, where you use the person's last name on the second reference. However, to convey to you the spirit in which I have written this book – providing trusted advice to girlfriends, from other girlfriends, and myself – I wanted to use a first-name basis. It's quirky, I know. But everyone I interviewed divulged their best travel secrets, just as a best friend would, and that it what I wanted to do as well.

Lastly, I designed this book so that you can read it right through from Chapter One, or skip around. If you're beauty-obsessed, you might wish to start with Chapter Eight, Quest For The Best. Or if you're embarking on a cruise, by all means read Cruise Control, Chapter Five before you do anything. You get the idea. You can skip around chapters with confidence, knowing that you won't miss anything.

So pack your bags, fasten your seatbelts, and get ready!

It's going to be a great ride – and thank you for joining me on this special journey.

Safe travels,

Westwood, Massachusetts
March, 2010
www.GorgeousGlobetrotter.com

CHAPTER ONE

Eat Petite

Yikes. It happens to the best of us. You put on that form-fitting pencil skirt, or your favorite pair of silk slacks – and they're a little tight. I hate that feeling. In fact, my mission in life (along with being a blonde with no roots) is to avoid that feeling as much as possible. I can't say I have the ultimate answers – but I do know what works for me. And maybe, just maybe, some of my techniques and strategies will work for you.

So here are the two million-dollar questions inside this challenge. I believe that being thin, especially when you're traveling, and not gaining weight, boils down to asking yourself two questions:

Try It, You'll Diet!

Top 10 Snacks For Gorgeous Globetrotters

My criteria for these smart snacks? They have to be delicious, crave-worthy, and low, low, low in calories. My credo is that nothing tastes as good as being thin and sexy feels, but with these smart snacks, you really can have your cake and eat it too!

1. **Powdered peanut butter** – The world's best-ever diet food!! On diet bread (35-40 calories per slice). Or a 90-calorie raisin English muffin.

2. **Sunsweet Prunes** – make the Sunsweet swap! Or **Figamajigs.**

Do I want to **EAT** whatever I want?

Or, do I want to **WEAR** whatever I want?

For me, the answer is just that easy. You **cannot** do both. You must make a conscious choice. And since I love to wear beautiful clothes, **wearing** whatever I want always wins out. Even when it's hard. Even when I am seriously tempted by delicious and fattening foods. Like Nutella. Pasta in pesto sauce. Nacho Cheese Doritos. Or anything covered in chocolate. (When I eat my last meal, it will be three things: Nutella, Nutella, and more Nutella. Covered in Nutella, if you get my drift.)

These two questions have helped me enormously and perhaps they will help you too. What is YOUR CHOICE? Make a conscious choice, and it will help you to keep your eye on the prize, when it is most likely to be diverted – when you're traveling away from home. Remember, the word "diet" comes from the Greek word "diaita," which means "way of life." A diet is something that should be a continuous way of living – and not a two-week starvation plan.

I have always had to watch my weight. I'm only 5'4", and I have short legs and a big bust. (I'm the same height as Britney Spears and Jessica Simpson, who, as the whole world knows, struggle with their weight. It's the same for me, and all of us short gals. Gain a mere two pounds and it easily looks like ten.) I can fit into size-two pants, but because of my bosom, I can easily look top-heavy. And my short legs don't help. Everything I do gives the appearance of being tall and thin – and that comes down to A-line skirts, turtlenecks, crew-neck sweaters, Empire waists, three-quarter sleeves, jumpers, and a lot more tricks. For me to maintain my weight and size, I have to under-eat by a little bit, and overexercise by a little bit. It's a serious commitment but I have to do it if I want to look my best. As I always joke, I watch my figure – to keep my husband Bill watching it too. (When he looks at me, sizes up my body and gives me a wink, he frequently says those three little words: "I love you," and also, "Ay-yay-yay.") I'm proud to say I still wear a two-piece bathing suit, and I still fit into – and frequently wear – a pair of white shorts that I bought in high school, in 1972. Ladies, let me put it this way – the only big, fat thing you should want in your life – are Big, Fat, Paychecks!

One of the smartest ways that I am able to maintain my minimum *avoirdupois* is that I always travel with carefully selected food – whether I'm driving to the gym, running errands – or jetting on a 747. I can't stand being hungry. I find hunger headaches and stomach aches so intolerable and downright painful. I try to never let myself get into a situation where I'm starving, and I'm going to get stuck eating something I don't want – and which is terrible for me (and my thighs). I found a few favorite snacks over the

3. **Almonds** –The Smokehouse variety are smokin' as are Cocoa Roast Almonds with no extra calories.

4. **String cheese** – if you want to fit in that string bikini.

5. **Skinny waters** – for all skinny Minnies.

6. **Puffed wheat and powdered milk with raisins** – the breakfast of gorgeous globetrotters.

7. **Vita-Tops** – to eliminate muffin tops.

8. **Fruitaceuticals dried cranberries** – berried treasures.

9. **Funky Monkey dried fruits** – fruits bursting with pizzazz. Tied with **Jungle Grub** for kids of all ages.

10. **Popcorn** – or anything – coated in Kernel Season's no-calorie seasonings.

years, and I've also done my research. Rely on these when you find yourself having a snack attack when you're away from home. So you don't have to "snack-rifice."

Here, I have to give a shout-out to Hungry Girl, for I read her fabulous newsletter every day and learn about all new kinds of snacks, some of which I've included here. I got inspiration from her newsletter, then did all of my own researching, interviewing, sampling, tasting, and yes, chewing – yum's the word! (www.hungry-girl.com)

Top 10 Snacks For Gorgeous Globetrotters

1). Powdered Peanut Butter. I am absolutely crazy about this product, and let me proclaim it THE BEST MIRACLE DIET FOOD EVER. Why? Because this powdered peanut butter really lets you have your peanut butter and eat it too.

Here's the 411 behind **PB2** – Say *sayonara* to Skippy. The folks at Bell Plantation in Georgia were asked by the FDA to come up with an easy, emergency meal replacement that could be shipped overseas, and while working on this project, they discovered peanut powder. You can't beat it – if you love PB, but don't eat it because of the high calories and fat, PB2 is for you. It will change your life – as it has mine! Two tablespoons have just 53.2 calories, and a mere 1.87 grams of fat. Debbie Layfield, Bell Plantation's COO, puts the powder in a plastic bag, then adds a sliced-up banana and shakes it all around to cover the fruit, for the perfect snack. ("Add two bananas and you're having lunch," she laughed.)

There's also a chocolate-peanut butter version – and if you're like me and you adore Nutella, be still my beating heart! (Pardon me, I'm drooling.) It has even LESS calories, just 52 for two tablespoons, and just 1.42 grams of fat. Coming soon: a peanut-based cracker "that's thinner than a Pringle," says Debbie. I still can't believe I'm having a peanut butter sandwich for lunch every day – and don't have to ever feel guilty. Guilt, be gone forever. And it's kosher too. *L'chaim*! (www.bellplantation.com)

Another brand to try is FitNutz powdered peanut butter, which is gluten-free with no trans fats and no added hydrogenated oils. Use it as a topping, in shakes, as a flavoring or just by the spoonful. The regular flavor has just 50 calories in two tablespoons, and 1.5 grams of fat. There's also a chunky version, with 60 calories and 2.5 grams of fat in 2 tablespoons. Either way, it's a shame-free snack that's easy to transport in a Ziploc bag – just add a few teaspoons of water and it's incredible and spreadable! (www.fitnutzbutter.com)

Say sayonara to Skippy and use fat-free powdered peanut butter instead.

2). **Sunsweet Prunes**. Just about every day, before I head to the gym, I eat five **Cherry-Essence Sunsweet Prunes** – for about 100 calories. I get the feeling that I am eating mountains of (highly caloric) dried cherries – but I'm not. That's the beauty of these little babies – they'll put a tiger in your tank. I love Sunsweet prunes, and the folks there would like you to make the "Sunsweet Swap." For example, instead of having microwave popcorn, the prunes will slash your calories almost in half and save you 14 grams of fat. Prunes also have almost five times the amount of potassium, and double the Required Daily Amount of copper. They also will give you an alluring antioxidant blast – all that potassium gives me the energy boost that I crave. The company even makes the prunes in 60-calorie packs, along with apricots in 70-calorie packs. Eat them, and you can feel proud of yourself!

I could also devour a box of raisins easily. And when they're covered in chocolate – my pulse races. That's why I also can't say enough about Sunsweet's dee-lish chocolate-covered mini prunes – I adore chocolate-covered raisins, but they're usually coated in horrible waxy chocolate. Instead, **Sunsweet's Plum Sweets** are bits of dried plum covered in an incredibly delicious dark chocolate, and there are only 120 calories in 14 pieces – that's about a mere EIGHT calories apiece. They're creamy on the outside, chewy on the inside and a divine temptation that provides a double shot of health-boosting antioxidants – because of the dried plums and chocolate. That's a smart snack – and one you'll want to take on the road – and even to the movies with you. Two thumbs up! (www.sunsweet.com)

Try It, You'll Diet!

Nuts About Almond Breeze

Next time you're in a chichi coffee shop, opt for some **Blue Diamond Almond Breeze** – the luscious-tasting dairy alternative has a low, low, low 40 calories in a huge 8-oz. glass of the Vanilla variety – which means you can really cut down on calories. That's exactly half the calories of an 8-oz. glass of good 'ol skim milk. The Original flavor clocks in at only 60 calories for a glass. Almond Breeze is also low on the Glycemic Index (GI), which means a smaller rise in blood-sugar levels after meals. Definitely better than the udders. Blue Diamond also makes Nut Thins, great snacks that contain no wheat or gluten, trans fat, saturated fat, and are also kosher. Try 'em in cheddar cheese, country ranch, pecan, hazelnut, nut and rice and smokehouse. Just 130 calories per serving (www.bluediamond.com).

If you crave chocolate, you'll also love **Figamajigs** – fine little fig bits coated in chocolate goodness. The Original Bites, for example are coated in cocoa and dark chocolate, and you get 17 pieces in a bag for only 150 calories. Sweet! Candy-coated bites have a crunchy candy exterior (like an M&M) and have about 150 calories per bag. Also available are mint bites and candy-coated mint bites, if you prefer a little peppermint. The best snacks, bar none, are the dark-chocolate-covered fig bars – in original, raspberry, mint, and almond, for 130-150 calories per bar. They're the greatest snack – and a wonderful way to prep your body for a workout, without any guilt (www.figamajigs.com).

3). **Almonds.** Yes, I know I should eat unsalted raw almonds – but please – have you ever tried **Blue Diamond Smokehouse Almonds**? They're addictive – I have to control myself to eat just 14 nuts – adding up to 85 calories and a paltry 8 grams of fat. Ounce for ounce, almonds have more calcium than milk, more protein than eggs and more fiber than any other nut. They're practically sinful, but a really smart snack that fills you up – especially when the treadmill is beckoning and you're depleted of energy. I can promise you this – eat your share of these protein-packed powerhouses, and you'll get so svelte you won't have to pray to Saint Cellulita anymore, to rid your thighs of their thunder. (Saint Cellulita is the Patron Saint of Thin Thighs.) (www.bluediamond.com) Another *nuttastic* choice are **Diamond Foods' Cocoa Roast Almonds** – the sweet snacks are roasted with a baked-on cocoa flavor, for a mess-free dark chocolate taste without added guilt. They also come in 100-calorie packs. If you compare the label with plain almonds, they're the same. (One ounce, about 24 almonds, has 150 calories.) Imagine! Cocoa added in for no extra calories! Says Andrew Burke, spokesperson for Diamond Foods: "Consumers told us they wanted the rich taste of chocolate with no added calories. We were happy to give it to them. The way we do that is a special dry roasting process (patent pending) that bakes the dark cocoa flavor into the almond." They're pure almond joy (www. diamondfoods.com).

4). String Cheese. And the cheese stands alone – because it's outstanding! Sargento, for example, makes strings of cheese that weighs in at 50 calories each, with 2.5 grams of fat, and 6 grams of protein. Have two for a mere 100 calories and you're sure to feel full. Also great to pack in your carry-on (www.sargento.com).

5). Skinny Waters. Here's the scoop. I never recommend getting your calories from liquids, because the whole idea is just too darn fattening. Drink too many calorie-laden liquids, and you'll just wind up on a detour on The Road To Sveltesville. I gave up alcohol when I was 21 years old, purely for that reason. I'd much rather eat lunch, do brunch, or have something to munch, than drink liquid calories. Sure, have a coffee made with calorie-free Torani syrup and a little milk (there's nothing better, in fact), but wasting your calories on vitamin water filled with calories is just plain dumb. (125 empty calories later, and there's only more junk in the trunk to work off – you know, more of what's loose in the caboose. Do you really want more

Try It, You'll Diet!

Chocolate And Other Flavors – Without The Guilt!

I adore **Torani sugar-free no-cal syrups** for your coffee (www.torani.com). Order them whenever you can, when you visit a coffee shop. Torani syrups come in 30 – count 'em, 30 – sugar-free flavors including chocolate-macadamia-nut, raspberry, almond Roca and white-chocolate. I love the hazelnut, chocolate and almond in my coffee, and lime in my sugar-free iced tea. (My newest obsession is hazelnut-flavored coffee, to which I add sugar-free Chocolate Torani, to get my Nutella fix!) But I've also just discovered **HerbaSway's Crème de Chocolat**, a completely calorie-free liquid that you can also add to your coffee – and it's equally delicious. (The slim bottle will also easily fit into your purse.)

The ingredients include cocoa extract, white tea extract, a proprietary fruit extract, Stevia, and cocoa powder. Just add a dropper-full to your coffee, to juice up your Joe without the excess calories of, say, a frappuccino. I usually mix my Crème de Chocolat with coffee and even some Torani sugar-free coconut syrup, to create a confection that I'm crazy about. Try it! Herbasway has no sugar, fat, preservatives, caffeine, alcohol or artificial sweeteners – but plenty of antioxidants. Your thin thighs will thank you (www.herbasway.com).

shakin' bacon?) That's why I'm crazy about **Skinny Water**, with ZERO calories, sugar and guilt. Each bottle contains a dash of Splenda, along with calcium, potassium and a green-tea extract. The Raspberry-Pomegranate, for example, contains purple sweet-potato juice as well, while the Goji Fruit Punch contains carrot juice and red-cabbage juice. It's delicious, and totally guilt-free. No wonder Kristen Bell and Nicollette Sheridan are huge fans. Other flavors include Acai Grape Blueberry; Passionfruit Lemonade; and Peach Mango Mandarin. Sip, Sip, Hooray! (www.skinnywater.com) You also can't beat something that gets you to drink more water. That's why I like **Crystal Light On The Go**. Just add the packet to your bottle of water (once you get through airport security) and you've got a taste treat. Available in flavors that include raspberry, peach tea, sunrise orange, strawberry, cherry pomegranate and lemonade. Newly introduced, making a total of 28 flavors

offered, are Focus Citrus Splash (with caffeine), Metabolism + Peach Mango Green Tea (with caffeine), and Red Tea Mandarin (without caffeine). All for just five calories. The experts say that quaffing water fills you up and quells hunger pangs – so drink up! (www.brands.kraftfoods.com) Another showstopper you'll want to swig: Minute Maid Light Lemonade. For just 15 calories in an 8-oz. glass, this tastes just like the Real Deal, and is amazingly lemony, sweet, tart, and delicious. It's like a lemon ice that has melted – and that's dee-lish! And there's even a luscious light cherry limeade in a can. Be still, my beating heart! (www.minutemaid.com)

Just say NO –
to calorie-laden drinks
and cocktails.

6). Puffed Wheat, Raisins and Powdered Milk. This is one of my all-time favorite go-to travel snacks. The beauty breakfast of champions. I eat this all the time – for breakfast, as a snack when I'm on the road and readying for the gym, and even for dinner when I'm in a hotel room. (I always travel with my own spoon.) What I love about it is

that all you need to do is add water – you could even eat it on the plane. Just bring all the ingredients in a Ziploc bag and you're all set. **Two** cups of **puffed wheat** are just 120 calories; a quarter-cup of raisins is 130 calories; and one-third of a cup of powdered milk is 80 calories. For 330 calories, you have a mini-meal with no fat and lots of fiber and energy. (I also love Kashi Go Lean; a cup has 140 calories and lots of protein, www.kashi.com.) If you're still hungry afterwards, have a small banana and you've devoured a full, low-calorie meal for 430 calories that makes taste – not waist.

7). Vita Tops. If you want to get rid of your stomach's "muffin top" – eat a genuine muffin top. Really! But not just any muffin top. You want a **Vita Top**, the most delicious indulgence that gives every flavor-craver something special. Kosher certified, with no artificial preservatives, Vita Tops come in numerous flavors. Try these on for size: The blue bran, deep chocolate, chocolate fig, double chocolate dream and the cran bran all weigh in at just 100 calories, with 15 vitamins and minerals. There are even 2-oz. Vitalicious muffins that have only 100 calories, such as the multibran and deep chocolate varieties, and there's even a 90-calorie sugar-free low-carb banana nut. They take the cake but don't leave you with weight (www.vitalicious.com).

8). Fruitaceuticals Supercharged Superfruits. Who doesn't love a Craisin? Now Fruitaceuticals goes them one better, with **PomaCrans** – antioxidant rich cranberries plus pure pomegranate concentrate – two of nature's top fruits. PomaCrans pack a one-two punch in your palate, offering the antioxidant power of one eight-ounce glass of cranberry juice cocktail plus two fresh pomegran-

Try It, You'll Diet!

Have A Bar For Near And Far

I want more-a, more-a of **Bora Bora**. Here's a "tasty-monial": Bora Bora organic snack bars come in five delicious flavors, but my vote goes to the 140-calorie cinnamon oatmeal snack bar that's made with fruits and nuts, and is totally gluten-free with no preservatives. These Bora Bora bars are simply made with rolled oats, raisins, peanuts, almonds, cinnamon and agave syrup (www.wellements.com). Another favorite in the Battle of the Bars: **Kelloggs Fiber Plus Dark Chocolate Almond Chewy Bars**, with 130 calories. They contain 35% of your daily fiber requirement and are a great way to tame a chocolate craving. Don't leave home without 'em! Kelloggs also makes Special K protein bars weighing in at a mere 110 calories, in chocolate peanut and chocolate delight, with 4 grams of protein each. It's yet another smart choice with serious snack appeal (www.kelloggs.com).

ates. That's upping the "anti" just the way we like it, with 100 calories in a quarter-cup (www. fruitaceuticals.com).

9). Funky Monkey Organic Freeze-Dried Snacks. Sometimes you want a piece of fruit – but a piece of fruit that's more fun-to-eat than your ordinary apple or banana. You know, a piece of fruit with *pizzazz*. That's where **Funky Monkey** snacks come in – made with 100% real fruit, with no added sugar, preservatives, colors or flavors. Using an original and proprietary freeze-drying process, 97% of the moisture content of the fruit is removed, producing a crisp, crunchy, go-anywhere snack that contains three of the four daily recommended servings of fruit. Funky Monkey snacks are gluten-, wheat- and dairy-free, and certified Kosher-Parve. Flavors? Bananamon (banana and cinnamon); Carnaval Mix (banana, pineapple, apple, papaya and raisins), Jivealime (pineapple and lime juice) and Purple Funk (banana and acai). They are scrumptious and a proud addition to my gym bag and carry-on (www.funkymonkeysnacks. com). I also must give an Honorable Mention to gluten-free **Jungle Grub** snack bars for kids – because we adults love to eat them too. Each bar has twice the protein of a granola bar and less sugar than a glass of milk. And for only 100 calories per bar! There's Chocolate Chip Cookie Dough (my favorite), plus Peanut Butter Groove and Berry Bamboozle. These little organic wonders also register just 2 points on the Weight Watchers diet program. Nutrition bars disguised as a snack bar? You bet! (www.organicnutrition. com)

10). Kernel Season's Seasoning for Popcorn and more. I just ate a big bag of broccoli that tasted like Nacho Cheese Doritos – all for a mere 40 calories. How did I do that? I dressed up my dinner and covered my bare broccoli with **Kernel Season's** dee-lish Nacho Cheese popcorn seasoning, and I devoured every bite. I'm in love with Kernel Season's. They're seasonings designed to coat popcorn – and any woman who loves SmartFood (but hates their high calories) or chocolate-covered popcorn, or caramel corn will love these singular sensations. There are just 2 to 4 calories in a quarter-teaspoon of seasoning, and the options are endless. Certainly try the sweet sensations (Apple/Cinnamon, Chocolate Marshmallow, Kettle Corn and Caramel) on popcorn – but also in coffee and on pancakes, oatmeal, toast, cereal, ice cream, you name it.

Try It, You'll Diet!

It's Just A Little Crush

I've got a crush – big time – on the **Berrie Crush** plus Vitamin C made by To Go Foods. Low-calorie and low-sodium, each packet, which you add to your bottled water, contains real fruits and vegetables – in fact, it's a juice bar in every packet. The Berrie Crush tastes like a cherry lollipop and contains a cornucopia of fruits – including – are you ready? – pomegranate, lemon and cranberry juice powders, grapeseed extract, organic honey, black currant,

Use the savory versions (Nacho Cheese, White Cheddar, Barbecue, Parmesan/Garlic, Cajun, Jalapeno, Ranch, Sour Cream/Onion) on any variety of vegetable, but also on chicken, hamburgers, nuts, seafood, eggs, pasta, you name it. Everything's kosher. The company also makes a signature super-premium popcorn that has just 120 calories in five cups. Ladies, start your engines – this is the super snackfood treat you've been waiting for and the 3-oz. seasoning bottles will easily fit into all your travels. As the Beatles would sing, Shake-it-a-baby now! (www.nomorenakedpopcorn.com)

Indulge in one – and only one – special, satisfying, superlative treat during your trip.

pumpkin, carrot, apple, raspberry, tart cherry – and that's just the tip of the organic iceberg. Just 23 calories too – which I like, because I hate drinking calories. I'm now planning a l-o-n-g flight from Boston to Dubai, and I believe the Berrie Crush will not only keep me hydrated, but provide the perfect antioxidant blast. There's also an Acai energy boost powder (24 calories), and a Go Greens (green apple, 32 calories) flavor that, I swear, is a salad bar in every packet. It has so many fruits and vegetables and offers 2100 International Units of Vitamin A and 28mg of Vitamin C, plus calcium and iron. If you need a little extra boost to get you to the gym – or to just get you to the airport – try these little cuties (www.togobrands.com).

A Lame Excuse

Ladies, I'm begging you to walk around when you sightsee. Please don't ever use the ridiculous, abominable contraption that rhymes with "Begway" to tour around in cities. Boston and Paris, for example, now promote these "Begway" tours, and with the obesity crisis what it is, I am appalled that tour operators offer these devices that don't even require you to move your two feet. Please, please get out there and put one foot in front of the other – and get some exercise at your destination.

Here are some more healthful additions to pack in your bag.

Everything But The Ants

I'm crazy about Picnics to go – with GoPicnic! These wonderful, ready-to-eat boxed meals make eating on-the-go enormously easy, whether you're in a plane, train, car or anywhere far from home and want to eat something delicious. All the foods in GoPicnic have no trans fats, no high fructose corn syrup and no added MSG. The brands you'll find in the adorable little brown picnic box are from companies who take pride in using minimally processed high-quality ingredients, to ensure that their food is the best it can be. There are GoPicnic meals for all appetites, including gluten-free, vegetarian, kosher and halal, to include more than 25 different meal options in all. Calorie counts and fat grams are listed on the back of the box. Prices start at just $3.99 per box. Take a look:

GoSavory (with 16 grams of protein and 380 calories) features turkey pepperoni, baked snap pea crisps, parmesan peppercorn cheese spread and organic crackers.

GoPrimo offers a croissant pastry, Nutella, strawberry preserves, Mediterranean apricots, a Lara bar and is certified vegetarian. One box has 540 calories.

GoPower, at 460 calories, contains baked bagel chips, creamy garden vegetable cheese spread, dried cranberries, a fruit and nut bar and a pastry cookie.

Just open, eat and enjoy. These meals don't require heating or refrigeration and have a long shelf life. (www.gopicnic.com)

Sensible Snacking

Chef Jay, better known as Jay Littmann, is a manufacturer and distributor of Tri-O-Plex protein bars and many protein-packed products. After spending a few years cooking around the city of Las Vegas, Chef Jay combined his longtime interest in business with his passion for cooking. He bought a little 700-square-foot muffin shop on the outskirts of Las Vegas and unknowingly created a hit. One of his products was a health bar that he made with honey and raisins, which he delivered to workout facilities in the area. He himself lost 200 pounds in eight months, and has kept it off by incorporating his eponymous products into a well-balanced diet and exercise program. And now, when you travel, so can you.

Try It, You'll Diet!

Add Some *Ooo La La* To Your Travels

Do I expect you to visit France without having at least one chocolate croissant, some French bread, or at least one Nutella crepe served on the street? Or would I visit Venice without munching on *gianduia* (chocolate-hazelnut) gelato, which makes my life worth living? Or Greece without baklava? *Mais non.* Here's what I do. Before I leave for my trip abroad, I make a deal with myself that I will have just **one** sweet treat – that is, one chocolate croissant (about 300 calories). Or one Nutella crepe. Or one ice cream cone. (Make it Lappert's Hawaiian "Kauai Pie" ice cream – Kona coffee ice cream, laced with fudge, coconut, and macadamia nuts. Oh, the thrill!). But that's it. **Just one**. And I make a big deal out of the day that I indulge. I usually like to treat myself halfway during my trip so that I'm continually looking forward to it. Then, when it seems like the right time, I indulge. In one. And focus intently on every bite. Not distracted by anything. Many times, I close my eyes and say over and over in my head exactly what I am eating so I can remember this lovely experience. I do it **consciously.** And I never feel guilty. So can you, *mon ami*! This way, you can have your *gateau* and eat it too.

He makes a wealth of goodies – but if you're watching your weight, stick with the Lite Bites. (Yes you can have one of his Gourmet Brownies with white-chocolate mousse, but it's 175 calories for half a brownie, with 63 calories from fat). The best options:

- Lite Bites Oatmeal Raisin cookies, which are only 78 calories per cookie with 14 grams of protein

- Lite Bites Chocolate Chip cookies that are only 80 calories per cookie, with 12 grams of protein

- Lowfat Protein Puffs, in Cool Ranch and Nacho Cheese, which are just 99 calories for half a bag (25 grams) (www. chefjays.com).

Dressed To Thrill

Passport to Pretty

I've had two dinners in my lifetime which I'll never forget. The first was at Ferraro's, an alfresco Italian restaurant at the luxurious Four Seasons Resort Maui – the height of Hawaiian ultraluxury. You sit outside, under the stars, serenaded by violinists, while you listen to the waves crashing below you – and you indulge in some of the most divine cuisine man – or God – ever created. But here's what I never forget: all the tables are set with white napkins. But if you go there wearing a gorgeous little black dress, the staff will immediately get you a *black* napkin. That way you don't get *white-napkin lint* on your LBD. Now that's the kind of five-star service we could use a little more of in this world!

Another time, years ago, my husband Bill and I had a scrumptious dinner in Arizona at The Phoenician Resort. Their signature restaurant (which has since closed) was called Mary Elaine's, and we are *still* talking about the scallops we had for dinner there. They were the most plump, moist, buttery little bivalves we had ever eaten. But here's the kicker – next to my chair was an attractive little wooden stool. Its purpose? Simply to hold my designer purse, so its delicate feet wouldn't touch the ground. To this day I remember that superb touch of elegance. If only all of life were this delightful!

Dig That Crazy Camel

We all know – and love – hummus. Especially the garlic variety. But imagine the satisfying chick-pea product made into a dessert – now you've really got my attention. Crazy Camel Dessert Hummus, made in New Hampshire, is a whole new twist on chickpeas. It was created by an executive chef, whose daughter disliked regular hummus, and blurted out, "Yuck – Can't you add some peanut butter to this?" And so he did – and a star dessert was born. If you want a healthy dessert that's actually good for you, you're in for a taste sensation. Crazy Camel comes in six great flavors, but the hands-down, ultimate, to-die-for delicious offering is the chocolate mousse – I swear, it's like eating genuine chocolate mousse cake – without the calories and fat. The other delectable flavors are pumpkin pie, toasted almond, caramel apple, maple walnut and peanut butter and they are all devastatingly *scrumptious*. Best of all, get this – all are gluten free, have only 60-70 calories per serving, and are also dairy free and vegan friendly. It's the treat your tastebuds have been waiting for (www.desserthummus.com).

The Cookie Diet

I sure as heck hate being hungry. Dr. Sanford Siegal could tell you all about it – back in 1975, the physician, who had been treating obese patients since 1957, engineered a food that's a hunger suppressant. After all, what was his patients' biggest complaint? "They're hungry," he told me, in a phone interview. That's when

Try It, You'll Diet!

Food Tips On The Fly

Cheryl Burke of *Dancing With The Stars* has several stay-slim strategies when she's traveling. First, she says to stock up on healthy staples at the local supermarket. "When I'm on the tour bus, I'll make a grocery list that includes salad, nonfat vanilla yogurt, lowfat granola and organic microwaveable soups." On the road Cheryl munches on Triscuits, peanut butter and cut-up vegetables, adding, "I always have a South Beach Living protein bar, fruit or almonds in my bag. At airports I depend on Subway or Quiznos, where you can have a sandwich made exactly to your specifications. They also display calorie counts, which is helpful."

"My Top 10 Tips For Eating Healthy On The Go," Shape Magazine, March 2010

Skirting The Issue

During a training run in late 2003, triathlete Nicole DeBoom glanced at her reflection in a store window and realized something was amiss. Her clothes had no sass or femininity. Instead of continuing on, Nicole ran home and started scribbling notes for a line of fun, edgy, sexy women's fitness apparel. The result? The world's first-ever women's running skirt. She founded Skirt Sports, her women's fitness apparel brand designed for runners, exercise enthusiasts, tennis players, swimmers, walkers and everyday fashionistas who need extra inspiration for their daily workouts. I'll tell you something – these adorable outfits give me the motivation to work out – and keep on working out. I own a "pink crush" ultra skirt (with shorts underneath), which is like a tennis skirt and will make you feel sexy and snazzy. I also own the black bike-girl mini workout skirt (also with shorts underneath), the short-sleeved "sweetest tee," and the long-sleeved Runner's Dream. When I go to any gym wearing these fashionable fitness outfits, I have extra spring – and spunk – in my step. And don't you want that when you're doing cardio and weights? (www.skirtsports.com)

Dr. Siegal created an ultra-secret mix of amino acids, made from milk, meat and egg proteins. His formula could have taken many forms, but he thought, "Why not create a cookie you can carry around with you?" He's in his Miami bakery once a week making them, and no one knows the secret formula except for him and his wife.

Dr. Siegal's cookies achieved immediate success back in 1975, and the rest is history. His prescription is to eat six cookies a day (amounting to 500 calories) and only when you're hungry (and not necessarily when the clock says it's time for breakfast or lunch). Dinner? A sensible meal of only 300 calories – "In our medical practice, patients are put on an 800-calorie-a-day diet."

The cookies come in five flavors – oatmeal raisin (the most popular), chocolate, banana, coconut and blueberry. If you're looking to snack on something that will control your hunger, this is the real deal. The cookies are available online, and the cost is about $60 a week for 42 cookies (www.cookiediet.com).

I'm Flat Out Delighted

Next time you're making a sandwich to take with you on the road, opt for some Flatout flatbread. I've tried it and the Earl of Sandwich would be jealous. A huge portion of the artisan five-grain flax bread has a mere 100 calories and is a whole grain – which I embrace wholeheartedly! You can rip it and dip it; make pizza with it; grill it; toast it; or just wrap it up with your favorite fillings. With these delicious breads, you don't have to feel guilty about eating bread – these have Bob Greene's "Best Life Diet" seal of approval. There's also a lite version for about 90 calories. Your chickie hot dog or turkey wrap will never taste better (www.flatoutbread.com).

Time-Tested Well-Being Tips

Some of the best diet/nutrition information I ever discovered was at Canyon Ranch in Lenox, Mass., one of the world's best destination spas. (I titled my article about the resort, for Community Newspapers, "Girl Gone Mild," as the trip was so relaxing and wonderful.) One of the great things about it is its "Lunch and

11 Rules to Solve Diet Dilemmas – Anywhere In The World

1. Order salad dressing on the side.

2. Hold the butter – and cheese – on vegetables, rolls and sandwich bread.

3. Request a double-order of veggies instead of a veggie and a starch. More filling food!

4. Ask for mustard instead of high-fat mayo on sandwiches.

5. Order fish entrees steamed, broiled or grilled dry – and not fried.

6. Eat a baked potato – instead of French fries and fattening potatoes such as au gratin or Delmonico.

7. Order hummus on a whole-wheat pita.

8. Drink water instead of fattening sodas. In France, order a *citron presse*, and add your own Splenda (packed in your purse.) It'll taste just like a lemonade but without any calories.

9. Order pizza with veggies, extra sauce, and less cheese. Stop eating when you hit the buttery crust. Eat two slices with salad and it's a complete meal.

10. Eat protein instead of carbs between meals.

11. Call your hotel and order a healthy room-service meal while you're still on the road – your delicious dinner will be ready and waiting for you when you arrive.

And for more info on eating right on the road, visit
www.healthydiningfinder.com.

Learn" program, where you eat a healthy, low-calorie and lowfat lunch – while you learn how to prepare it as well. I'll tell you one thing – I'm addicted to the 85-calorie chocolate-chip cookies made with Callebaut Belgian chocolate.

During a "Tools for Living" workshop, I learned some of these lifestyle and diet principles, which I heartily recommend to all travelers. Here goes:

1. Relax for at least 15 minutes per day.

2. Smile and say "I love to exercise," which tells your brain that it is happy. (Very good when ambition goes AWOL.)

3. Sleep in exercise clothes – to be already dressed for exercise success in the AM.

> ## Try It, You'll Diet!
>
> ### BYOB – Of Salad Dressing
>
> Bring your own salad dressing with you to restaurants – there's no reason to indulge in their fattening varieties of Italian, French or Raspberry Vinaigrette. You can eat without guilt with a spritz from your favorite. Your thighs will thank you. I got this tip years ago from a svelte staff member on a cruise ship, when I asked her about her stay-thin tips.

4. Forget about eating white foods, with the exception of oatmeal and cauliflower (and I would recommend, nonfat cottage cheese. I make lunch every day of one cup of nonfat cottage cheese, a half-cup of canned pumpkin, some water, Splenda, and pumpkin-pie spice whirled in the blender – it's the ultimate smoothie and it's packed with protein. For only 200 calories!)

5. Eat organic berries.

6. Make your own lunch – and make your kids' lunch. That way you're sure to eat something healthy and nourishing.

7. Take folic acid (which controls levels of homocysteine, which is closely linked to Alzheimer's disease, a debilitating mind-robbing disease).

8. Eat flaxseed, which contains the highest levels of essential oils in the plant kingdom.

Minimus.biz – Where Little Things Mean A Lot

Have you ever eaten in a restaurant, only to realize that you wish you had a small package of fat-free salad dressing with you, so you could still watch your weight? Dieters, have I got news for you. Minimus.biz is the world leader in all-things-travel-sized, so they have the answer – individual packets of fat-free salad dressing that sell for about 49 cents per pouch, including flavors such as raspberry vinaigrette, Thousand Island, Italian and French. "We have a huge following among dieters for our fat-free salad dressing packets," explains Paul Shrater, co-founder of the company. "It's hugely popular."

And that's not all. You name it – Minimus.biz has got it – foods, beverages, pharmacy and personal care items, so you can travel away from home and have everything you need. Paul got the idea for his company about five years ago, when he rented a cabin in New Hampshire, bought full-size bottles of barbecue sauce and ketchup for a cook-out – and left everything there afterwards, to go to waste. His mission thereafter? To focus on "everything small," he says.

Minimus.biz stocks a wealth of goodies you didn't know you needed – such as small sizes of, of all things, *duct tape* – a travel staple in my household – but now that I know I can get it in a small size – what's not to love? "It sells pretty well, especially among the military," says Paul. In fact, all kinds of travelers love the items from Minimus.biz – including people attending destination weddings, golfers, professional sports teams, and even private jet companies, who like to supply their flying customers with things such as travel sizes of Evian spritz and maple syrup.

Other petite packages you can get? Packets of organic peanut and almond butter. Natural fruit bars. Even kosher foods. Organic personal-care items. Toothpaste. Shaving cream. Charmin-To-Go toilet seat covers. There are also "kits" selling breakfast items, spa items, and goodies for the business traveler. In all, the company stocks more than 2,000 products and more than 100 pre-packaged gift sets and all can be shipped directly to your hotel. There's even a "hospital overnight" bag, and another for all the little things a bride might need on her wedding day, from antacid and hairspray to Altoids and Static Guard. All this small stuff is sure to hit a big note with you (www.minimus.biz).

9. Eat cholesterol-reducing walnuts.

10. The pastry chef's secret weapon? Use lowfat pureed prunes as substitutes for fat in cookies and cakes (www.canyonranch.com).

Tell yourself, "I love to exercise," and send your brain – and body – a positive message.

bites of chocolate dessert. And that was it. This is sensible advice that we can all adhere to. It's not easy – but do you want to wear your skinny jeans or not? The next morning, I was so grateful I didn't indulge. Remember this example – next time you're at a wedding, a business dinner, or Aunt Zelda's – where you can't control the menu.

More Than Fare

"Travel with healthy snacks. Brown-rice crackers and a packet of dry miso soup make for a really delicious energy boost that you can eat anywhere – all you need is a cup of hot water. I always take two or three servings with me on international flights. Plane food is never, ever a good idea."

Claudia Schiffer, "Ten Things I Learned As A Supermodel," *InStyle*, **Makeover 2009 issue**

Deb's Top 10 Diet Tips For Travelers

Here is my tried-and-true advice to be trim when traveling.

1. **Always wear shorts when you work out** – even if it means putting a pair of sweat pants over your shorts while you walk to the gym. Seeing your thighs in plain sight every day reminds you of why you go to the gym in the first place. This way, you won't be shellshocked on the first day of spring, when you put on shorts. You won't see some jiggle and wonder where it came from.

2. **Walk at the airport** – There's no better thing to do while you're waiting for your plane. Sounds like a no-brainer, but too many travelers plunk themselves down and *sit, sit, sit,* when there will be plenty of time to do that on the plane.

3. If you must have airport food or fast food, **opt for a turkey sandwich** (hold the mayo and cheese) with tomato, lettuce, and mustard, on whole-wheat bread. I personally love Subway sandwiches, and always eat exactly one-half of my open-faced sandwich (ordered with extra turkey) and save the rest for another day (www.subway.com). My second-favorite option? Pizza,

Hope Springs Eternal At Esperanza

One a recent trip to Cabo San Lucas, I tore myself away from Silversea Cruises **Silver Shadow** cruise ship (www.Silversea.com) to visit the luxurious Esperanza, a boutique resort that's spread across 17 lush acres on the Sea of Cortez. My mission? To visit its sexy spa, which I call the Salma Hayek of Mexican spas – it's gorgeous, intelligent, and deserving to be embraced. Everyone raves about the "Aguas Frescas," 11 delicious beverages made with indigenous vegetables, fruits and plants – there's orange/cantaloupe to cleanse the liver, a fat-burning grapefruit, aloe vera and prickly pear and even a purple bougainvillea/lime drink to heal sore throats and act as aphrodisiac. (The drinks are also frozen and served as popsicles at the pool.) In an open-air treatment room, Mirna, my English-speaking therapist, kneaded my muscles with the spa's signature lime body lotion. *Si*, I was in Mexico – but my head was transported to another part of the planet. The *piece de resistance*, however, was the grated coconut she softly applied to exfoliate my travel-weary body; it felt like a feather-duster caress, and the familiar fragrance reminded me of an Almond Joy candy bar. It took all my effort just to turn over. "You smell like a cookie with this treatment," Mirna told me. How sweet it is! (www.esperanzaresort.com)

but get a thin-crust pizza topped with vegetables (ask for extra sauce, for an extra hit of lycopene) – and blot out all the oil with your napkin. Doing otherwise will only force you to spend more time on the treadmill, "undoing the chewing."

4. **Do 50 sit-ups a day,** no matter where you are in the world. Just stick your feet under a piece of furniture in your hotel room, to let your abs know you mean business.

5. If your hotel room doesn't have a gym – **jumprope in your room – without the rope.** You can mimic what a rope would do, in very small and tight surroundings. But by all means, if you have a jump-rope (and a big enough room), skip rope with it. I've done this everywhere from Bermuda to Bora Bora when there's no gym, no place to walk, and I feel stuck.

Try It, You'll Diet!

10 Snacks Under 100 Calories

1. 1 ¾ cups raspberries

2. 90-calorie English muffin with spritz of faux butter or some preserves

3. Half-cup nonfat cottage cheese with Equal and cinnamon

4. 28 grapes

5. 13 animal crackers

6. One small orange, apple or banana

7. 1 ¾ cups whole strawberries

8. One ounce of lowfat cheddar cheese (such as Cabot)

9. 1 ¾ cups popcorn

10. 2 Tablespoons nuts

6. Want to practice waist management? **Bring your breakfast with you.** As I said, I always travel with puffed wheat, raisins, and powdered skin milk, which I take everywhere in a Ziploc – for breakfast or a healthy snack between meals. Maybe you simply pack instant oatmeal or a protein bar. You should also bring a lunch or dinner, depending on how long your flight is. My husband Bill makes us fresh chicken salad from cooked skinless breasts, flavored with diet mayo, kosher salt, chopped celery, and a drop of basil oil. It's delicious, lowfat and loaded with protein.

7. **Eat vicariously.** Let's face it – much of the fun of a "food" experience, is, for example, going to the ice cream shop, discovering the flavors, seeing the array, smelling the aromas. I enjoy everything about the experience – *and only sometimes, the actual eating.* I like to watch their faces, as my husband or friends dive into something scrumptious. You'll lose calories – and you'll lose guilt! I'm overwhelmingly interested in food and sweets, and I love to indulge my sweet tooth – but I don't want to die of shame when I put on my stretch gym pants. Another option: watch ***The Best Thing I Ever Ate*** on the Food Network. It's guilt-free snack TV!

8. **Limit yourself to just three bites of something scrumptious.** It's true – the first two or three bites of anything are always the best. *After that, it's all redundant.* If and when mocha chip calls out to me, I get my licks in with a kid-sized cone, a sample taste, or a demitasse-cup portion. (BTW, Herrell's Chocolate Pudding ice cream has my name on it.)

9. **Read lingerie and clothing catalogs on the treadmill.** Even if I'm feeling pooped, nothing says "incentive" more than seeing Heidi Klum wearing practically nothing. It also furthers my desire to wear beautiful clothes and feel confident wearing them. Translation: I better get moving and show my body who's the boss.

10. **Take the stairs**. That means you eschew the elevator or escalator wherever you are – at a hotel or even on a cruise ship. And if the fitness center's closed at your hotel, you can always climb the back stairs, over and over again. This is a quick, easy, sneaky way to fit more exercise into your life.

When All Else Fails, Get A Good Haircut

"You look thinner and younger when your hair is proportioned correctly," says Betty Ann Mighell, inventor of Facial Symmetry Analysis for men and women, also called "Visage." Betty Ann does Visage herself at her salon in Naples, Fla., Studio 37 Xtreme Lashes and Hair (www.studio37xtremelashesandhair.com). This is one spot you'll definitely want to travel to. You'll receive a consultation and haircut that includes a step-by-step analysis of your face, with before and after photos. She and her staff will create an ideal hairstyle that balances the right and left sides of the face, and equalizes each visage from top to bottom, focusing on everyone's best feature: their eyes. Betty Ann also recommends eyeglass shapes and makeup colors, and brings attention to the "good" side of everyone's face. "For some people, just changing their hair's part is major," says Betty Ann. "It can have a dramatic difference." She's even got the photos to make her point, many times over. She says that the wrong haircut only emphasizes the jowls, or other unflattering parts of the face. "And," she quips, "Would you really design a hairstyle around *your nose*?"

If you're in a cramped hotel room, you can jumprope — without the rope.

Now that you've figured out how to eat around the globe, you're ready to discover some of the world's best beauty secrets, given by flight attendants, travel agents, and professionals in the travel industry. Consider Chapter Two, The Plane Truth, your boarding pass to all things beautiful.

The Plane Truth

I really admire flight attendants. They work long hours in cramped places (with stale air) while they are essentially food-and-drink-providers-in-the-sky. And like you and me, they want to eat healthfully, watch their weight, and nourish their skin – in working situations where it's practically impossible to do so. Yet they manage to do it with a pleasant attitude and a smile on their face. (Make sure to thank them – and the pilot – next time you get off a plane. And give one of the female flight attendants the magazines that you've read on the plane – sometimes they have plane time to fill too!)

That's why I interviewed as many flight attendants as I could find – to ask them what specifically they did on airplanes, and while traveling in general, to maintain their beauty and well-being. Here's what they said.

Jeannette Simon, American Airlines Flight Attendant, www.aa.com

Jeannette has been a flight attendant on American Airlines for 19 years.

Her biggest beauty secret? Jeannette discovered it on a city street in Paris, at one of the outdoor fruit-and-vegetable markets that the City of Light is famous for. She noticed numerous French women lined up to buy something, and curiosity prompted Jeannette to go over and find out what it was. What was it? A bottled combination of argan oil from Morocco, and shea butter from Madagascar. "It's called DermaRescue," says Jeannette, and she loves it so much that now she sells it herself, on her own website, www.gypsyglobalchic.com. (Her website also sells jewelry in the Byzantine-era lost-wax method, and was featured in the movie *The Other Boleyn Girl.*) Jeannette swears by this special concoction. "I put it on over my makeup, and also use it on my hair, feet and body. It's the best thing for cracked feet and it's non-greasy and amazing. After three minutes it just sinks in; you get a healthy glow from it." She especially uses the oil when she's working on 777s. "The crew bunk room on the Triple-7 just sucks the moisture out of your body," she laments.

When Jeannette isn't working – she is shopping, in every city she travels to. "In Paris, I go to the grocery store at Monoprix, and buy rocket (arugula), beets, clementines and soups, and bring them on board to eat on the way home." She also stocks up on Monoprix's chocolate-covered pear cookies, which she loves to eat and give as housegifts. And when she arrives in Paris, when her colleagues hit the hay, she has a cup of coffee and hits the Rue D'Alesia, where there are great outlet stores.

Her other find? The Hotel Costes "for the very best candles and perfumes." (A mango-frangipani candle sells for 45 Euros at this chic hotel, where the models stay during Fashion Week.) Jeannette also constantly travels with her favorite French perfumes, Fracas, and Fleurs de Rocaille. And she does it all in a pair of Pedro Garcia shoes, which she laughs, she paid $520 for. "And they come scuffed in the heel and toe."

Jeannette also has a wealth of insider tips for every fashion-ista and every *beauty-ista*. She only uses a Baggallini tote (www.baggallini.com), which interestingly enough, is a brand that was started in 1995 by two veteran flight attendants who wanted luggage that better served their purposes. "I fold my clothes and put them in my Baggallini – then it fits right under my seat and I use it as a footrest – a stool. It makes all the difference for my short legs." She also recommends replacing your luggage wheels with those meant for Rollerblades. "Your luggage will practically wheel itself!"

"When traveling one of my best beauty and jet lag secrets is to visit a local hammam for several hours," adds Jeannette. "I like to go the first day of arrival if possible. In Paris my favorite is the Hammam Medina Center on rue Petite (www.hamman-medina.com) in the 20th arrondissement. After stretching and relaxing on a heated stone floor, then a steam sauna or a dried mud body treatment, you are scrubbed clean with a "kese" (a coarse soapy mitt). Then you sit in a hot pool or swim in a cold pool before you are given a full body massage, and the jet lag will be minimal. They finish with a glass of piping-hot mint tea to finish the pampering session. In Istanbul my favorite is the Cemberlitas Hamami, a Turkish bath that dates back to 1584. Turkish baths are similar to the baths of ancient Rome except there is no pool of cold water to plunge into at the end. Before changing your clothes you are given a "pestemal" (a cloth) to wrap around yourself and a pair of slippers to wear on the hot wet floor. In between steaming you will be scrubbed briskly with the kese and then rinsed. There is no time limit for your steaming and relaxing but I like to allow one-and-a-half to two hours, with a 30-minute massage at the end. You truly feel as though you have brand new skin after a Turkish bath."

Jeannette continued, "While in the United States one of the best hammams is at the five-star Intercontinental Hotel Montelucia in Paradise Valley, Ariz. The Joya Spa has 30,000 square feet of exquisite services that make you feel as though you are in Morocco without the jet lag!"

Jeannette also has her own brand of private-label beauty products, which she sells at spas around the States, and on her website. "From my travels I began collaborating with a doctor of Chinese medicine to recreate some of the beauty secrets I have come across. One is called Gypsy's Repose, which helps hydrate your face and body while on the airplane or any time. It consists of palmerosa

Special Subterfuge

Maybe you should follow the example of Marilyn Monroe, who had a special secret when she traveled by plane. Rumor has it, she not only wore a pretty dress on her flights – but she brought a second, exact copy of the outfit with her. After her dress got wrinkled during the flight, she would put on the second frock right before landing, so she could look picture-perfect! Another celebrity who did that was President Ronald Reagan. He donned sweats aboard Air Force One, and changed into a crisp suit right before disembarking, to be camera-ready for the throngs of media.

(a grass from Ethiopia), jasmine and frankincense. Another product is Gypsy's Luminous Night, which is applicable for day and night. It is based on the ancient wisdom of Chinese herbs blended with the finest resources from Africa."

Angela Greener, Flight Service Manager, Virgin Atlantic Airways, www.virgin-atlantic.com

"I find it very important to stay in shape and keep fit, especially when traveling," says Angela. "Most hotels I stay in have a gym or swimming pool, so I utilize these when they are available. However if there isn't one, or I don't have much time – if it's a short stopover – I do a few simple exercises in my room. I try and do 50 abdominal crunches every morning, with my feet tucked under the foot of the bed for support. I work on my biceps/triceps/shoulders, so I use two water bottles as dumbbells, and this works really well. Using a chair, I do dips, and the bathtub is a useful prop for doing press-ups against – excellent for the chest and arms. I pack a jumprope and resistance band in my suitcase. They're lightweight, don't take up much room, and with these, you can always do a workout in your room."

Replace your luggage wheels with Rollerblade wheels – your luggage will practically roll itself.

Come Aboard With Samantha Brown of The Travel Channel

Samantha Brown, Anchor/Host of numerous Travel Channel TV shows, including *Samantha Brown's Great Weekends*, www.travelchannel.com

Samantha is the beautiful blonde TV personality whose travel experiences and ability to convey the feeling of a destination instills trust in her enthusiastic audience. There are two things she never travels without. One is a jar of peanut butter. "I always travel with peanut butter, especially in Europe…in desperate times you can just stick your finger in the jar. It has frequently come to my rescue." The other thing Samantha can't be without are "Pinkie" rubber balls that you can purchase at a toy store: "You can lie on them and roll over them. It's a fast, easy way to get a quick massage after 10, 20 or 25 hours of travel."

Samantha, who travels about 230 days per year, also gave me one of the best travel tips I've ever heard – if you love to bag bargains. "I check out Goodwill and Salvation Army stores in wealthy destinations such as Palm Beach and Nantucket. You'll always find cashmere, where sweaters are $20 compared to $150. I also do this in destinations where I might need some warm clothing. In Dallas I wanted a pair of cowboy boots, and I found them for just $25. I also found Anna Lowe in Paris, (www.annalowe.com). (Anna Lowe was an American who founded the first discount clothing store in Paris in 1938.) It was wonderful."

When traveling by plane, Samantha always brings her own food – say, a cheese-and-turkey sandwich. "You should pack like you're going on a long car trip," she explained. "I also take almonds, energy bars and string cheese. I have to be self-reliant when it comes to my next meal."

Her beauty routine onboard the aircraft? "I always have some spray mist, eye cream, moisturizer for my hands and neck, and lip balm. Whenever I'm in a department store, I always ask for sample sizes of beauty products – that is a great way to get small-sized products that will be TSA-approved. I'm not married to one product line….One thing I do is that I've stopped using refillable toiletries. I like taking full bottles and my own hair dryer. I hate generic plastic bottles. I like seeing labels and colors in my bathroom….I check my luggage, and 95% of it is liquids – mousses, eye creams and moisturizers," she said with a laugh.

Samantha also exercises a great deal, not just for health benefits, but for the endurance and stamina that it gives her, for her job. "I go for a jog just as soon as I arrive at a destination, and also to sightsee. I also might work out in the gym or in my room. Luggage is great to use for doing bicep curls and chest presses."

When dining out at her destination, she also has some great secrets. "I always order soup first, if it's broth-based and not cream-based. It slows down my eating, so I don't overindulge. Entrees are usually grilled fish or chicken, with a salad. And I don't get jet lag. I've tried everything, but here's what works for me. Two days before I leave I abstain from caffeine. Then, at my destination, I do a double-shot of espresso. My body absorbs it like gangbusters."

Angela knows – even more than most of us – how dehydrating the air on a plane can be. "Whenever I fly, I always take pre-moistened makeup remover cloths – Neutrogena and Simple are good brands (www.neutrogena.com, www.simple.co.uk) – so that I can quickly remove any makeup before resting on a flight. Using an atomizer for your face and neck is good for rehydrating the skin – Evian is my personal choice." (www.evian.com)

And here's a bit of her advice I *didn't* expect – "I always carry a mini hot-water bottle with me, as it can sometimes be chilly on flights, and this helps me sleep better," Angela adds.

Bring a small hot-water bottle, which you can fill up on the plane, to keep warm.

We should all follow her dining advice: "I always pack snacks in my hand luggage – my favorites are muesli bars (Natural is my favorite brand); unsalted popcorn; dried fruit such as apricots (Crazy Jack's does a great organic selection); celery, carrot sticks, grapes and bananas. If I have a meal on the flight, I always have the salad option. Instead of drinking tea/coffee, try hot water with lemon, or green tea.

She also needs her sleep – "I find that sleep deprivation is the worst thing to experience. I always pack either a small bottle of lavender oil (Neals Yard of Covent Garden does travel-sizes, www.nealsyardremedies.com) or a lavender sachet in my suitcase, to use on my pillow in the hotel room. It really helps me to drift off to sleep and has a wonderful aroma."

"There are a few beauty creams I can't live without, when I am traveling," Angela says. "Elizabeth Arden 8-Hour Cream, which I use on my lips, eyelids, and any dry patches I have on my body (www.elizabetharden.com). My YSL Radiant Touch – Dior also does a similar product, called Skin Flash Radiance Booster pen – which is great for disguising any gray shadows under my eyes (www.ysl.com, www.dior.com). Thirdly, I love Clarins Beauty Flash Balm, which I put on underneath my makeup. It helps my makeup stay put and is very rehydrating (www.clarins.com). I always suffer from dry hands on a flight, so I always put my handcream into a travel-sized bottle. Cowshed (www.cowshedonline.com) does a lovely one, called Cow Pat moisturizing cream. For a more luxurious hand treatment, I sometimes take solid cocoa butter, and cotton gloves in my suitcase, and use them as an overnight treatment. By morning, my hands are velvety soft. As I stay in hotels so often, I take some comforts from home in my beauty case. Among my favorites are my Jo Malone bath oils – they come in a handy 30 ml.-size bottle, so are perfect for travel – I love their lime, basil and mandarin body lotion, which smells divine." (www.jomalone.com)

"When I'm in India I get my eyebrows threaded, as they are simply the best at this, and it gives fantastic and long-lasting results. India is also a great destination for booking head massages, which they do with oils, and they are wonderful."

Jet lag? "It's a constant problem," Angela says, but she takes small catnaps of one to two hours, and always has her eye mask and earplugs with her. She says to try to get eight hours of sleep per night, and drink 1.5 liters of water per day.

And she loves a good bargain – just like the rest of us. "My favorite destination for cosmetics bargains has to be Hong Kong. It's fabulous for cosmetics and

You've Gotta Be Taut

Seeking that perfect dream cream? You just might find it at Sasa, whose website lists a dazzling array of beauty brands, from Aizim to Zino. Listed on the stock exchange of Hong Kong, Sasa offers round-the-clock access to the best beauty and health products – and ships worldwide. You'll find the usual suspects, as well as others to tickle your fancy, including Fairy Drops' bestselling mascara; Jelly Pong Pong's soap Popsicle; and the Dr. G. line of skincare, which is wildly popular in Seoul, and which is used in the first-class amenity kits on Asiana Air (www.sasa.com).

fashion. They have little beauty shops called Sasa on every street corner, which sell all the famous beauty brands, such as Clarins and Lancome, but at a much reduced cost."

Patti (who asked to remain anonymous), Delta Flight Attendant, www.delta.com

Patti has great skin – and it's no wonder. "I've used Retin-A for years," she told me. "And I am told I look younger than my years. I also drink tons of water." She also told me her beauty secret: safflower oil, "which I've used for years to remove my makeup!" (It's even the secret ingredient in some Erno Laszlo products too, such as Special Skin Soap.) Patti also likes to use Clinique's Dramatically Different moisturizer. Her other beauty tricks? "Sleep and a B-complex vitamin."

For snacks, Patti eats almonds, apples and popcorn – "No salt – it causes bloating and water retention. No soda. We bring food

J'adore Dior

Who doesn't love Dior cosmetics? My life has been transformed by using DiorSkin AirFlash – a mistake-proof foundation that is dispensed in an elegant can, through micro-diffusion, for an airbrush finish. You won't believe how velvety it makes your skin look – as though it was airbrushed for a glamour magazine. I save it for all my special occasions and TV appearances. Then there's the Skin Flash Radiance Booster Pen, a beloved beauty product that, with just one stroke, diminishes shadows, fine lines and imperfections. Wear it under or over makeup. And let's not forget Diorshow Mascara – the iconic instrument of gorgeousness that models swear by, creating dramatic lashes. Eye, eye!(www.dior.com)

Just Don't Follow Her Example

Pauline Frommer, author, Pauline Frommer's Travel Guide Series, www.frommers.com/pauline

I had the pleasure of interviewing Pauline Frommer, daughter of the legendary travel professional Arthur Frommer. Pauline is the author of **Pauline Frommer's Travel Guide Series,** which has won, from 2006-2009, the title of "Best Guidebook" from the North American Travel Journalists Association. Pauline writes a series of budget books known as the "Spend Less, See More" guides, and is constantly on the go. "And I am the poster child for what NOT to do in terms of diet and beauty," she told me with a laugh.

In other words, you may want to avoid her approach to being a gorgeous globetrotter.

"I don't want people to know who I am, when I travel. I need to be incognito," Pauline explains. "So when I travel I don't wear much makeup."

"At home, Weight Watchers has worked for me," Pauline explains. "I'll lift weights. And I get my hair professionally blow-dried – it costs me $20." (Her secret is Astor Barber in New York City.)

"At the market in Union Square, I found a favorite moisturizer – it's called NIO. I tend to be pretty simple. When I'm on CNN they do my makeup for me."

And Pauline wouldn't even *think* of flying First Class – after all, she writes about value for her readers. "I always travel economy class and I like Jet Blue. I bring my own food – sushi or a sandwich like turkey on whole wheat. I'm always on a roller-coaster. I'm 5'3" but have never weighed more than 135 but I like to be closer to 115."

Her luggage is the Frommer's brand (of course!) made by Delsey (www.delsey-usa.com).

"I *only* own carry-on luggage, so I have to edit myself when I'm packing. Besides, now the airlines charge you for your luggage, so it angers me. I wear jeans and khakis, and bring a little black dress for nightclub forays for my books."

Pauline's best beauty find is in New York: Ray's Beauty Supply. "It's where all the Broadway showgirls go. It's beauty nirvana, and it's inexpensive." (www.raybeauty.com, which has more than 10,000 items in stock.)

Do It Like Dorothy

Think back to your childhood and you'll discover the very first female traveler, who loved a good spa treatment: Dorothy in *The Wizard of Oz*. And so did the Tin Man, Cowardly Lion and the Scarecrow. Remember how they stopped to get spa treatments before meeting the Wizard? The movie shows them at the "Wash & Brush Up Co.," where Dorothy gets a bow in her hair; the Scarecrow gets new straw; the Tin Man has a rubdown; and the Cowardly Lion gets ribbons in his fur and his nails clipped. Little did Dorothy know back then that she was a trendsetter!

from home and I love peanut-butter-and-jelly on whole wheat." Her other tip? Emergen-C, the fizzy low-calorie vitamin drink that many celebrities swear by (www.alacer.com).

Suzanne Schneider, US Airways Flight Attendant, www.usairways.com

Suzanne says that the way she stays in shape is that "I always have my laptop with me so I can do my Pilates DVD. A lot of flight attendants also run the staircases in hotels for exercise." She adds: "It's important to move around during a long flight, so make sure you get up once in awhile and take a stroll somewhere – hopefully not while the flight attendants are doing their service. (That's just smart "jetiquette!") And drink water – not alcoholic beverages."

Diet tips? Suzanne usually brings trail mixes from Trader Joe's. "And I always bring a Dunkin' Donuts or Starbucks coffee on board, possibly some yogurt and granola mixed together and a meal to go that I usually purchase at the airport." She doesn't recommend drinking out of the glasses in the hotel: "I never drink out of hotel glasses or mugs because I saw a TV program about how they are usually just cleaned with Windex spray."

As far as her beauty routine goes, "Moisturizer is key and Crème de la Mer is definitely the best moisturizer out there (www.cremedelamer.com). I also use Lancome tinted moisturizer as my foundation, (www.lancome-USA.com) then a Sonya Dakar Omega 3 Repair complex because it's a light serum that really helps moisturize (www.sonyadakar.com). I only use Biolage shampoo (www.matrix.com) because it's the only shampoo that works for me consistently, with all the different iron contents in water. If my eyes are puffy, I use Tracie Martyn's lotus sculpt eye pads (www.traciemartyn.com). They work amazingly well."

Massage, Munch, And More In Munich

Munich Airport offers a surprising oasis of good health in a world of takeoffs and landings. The **AirportClinic M** is sought out by travelers for orthopedic surgery. **Napcabs** entice road warriors with the comforts of fluffy comforters, Internet access, flat screen TV and coveted privacy – just minutes from their gate. The **Cosmetic Institute** is an elegant beauty lounge with a genuine spa-like décor and a long list of available treatments. One traveler opting for a day pass to **Kempinski's executive health club** and spa, **"Fit & Fly Spa,"** located between Terminals 1 and 2, described the experience as an "interlude of pure indulgence." Personal grooming at the distinguished **Brants Barber & Shop** is a regular stop for business travelers enroute. And those with minutes to spare can snap up **a relaxing massage – offered right at the gate**-- or perhaps a quick and nutritious meal at the **Bistro Organic**, one of 40 restaurants and bars at the airport. Yum's the word! (www.munich-airport.com)

Oprah Winfrey Checks In

"Anyone who tells you that having your own private jet isn't great is lying to you."

Oprah Winfrey, in her advice to Duke graduates, as reported in *Us Weekly*, June 8, 2009. Oprah spent $42 Million on her bombardier Aerospace Global Express XRS Jet, a custom-built private plane that she uses to visit her $50 Million home in Montecito, Calif., and her $13 Million vacation pad in Maui. *Us Weekly*, July 19, 2010.

Beth Blair, former Southwest Airlines Flight Attendant and Founder of TheVacationGals.com, www.southwest.com

"I pack my yoga mat for the hotel room," says Beth. "If the weather is nice at my destination I open my sliding door (assuming there is one) and go through my yoga routine with fresh air. There's nothing like stretching after a day on the plane."

"I started a habit when I was a flight attendant, to do 100 jumping jacks as soon as I get to my room. If the hotel has a poor gym, I turn my hotel room into my own fitness center, by using chairs or the bed for biceps dips, doorknobs to hold bands (for band exercises) and designate a towel for floor exercises. I have also carried leg weights so I can do leg exercises in the evening while I'm working on the computer or just watching TV."

"If the hotel offers bikes to guests, I'm all over it. Riding a bike is a great way to get a little exercise and see the town from a local's perspective."

"When my girlfriend and I travel together we do lunges up and down the long hotel hallways – we'll also hit the stairwell, but always get permission from the hotel first, to make sure we don't get locked in (I refuse to hit the stairwell alone)."

Here's a tip that Beth learned from the "senior mamas" – the flight attendants who had been flying for decades: a lemon-sugar scrub that exfoliates dry hands, and can be done right on the plane or in your hotel room. "Squeeze one slice of lemon in both hands, then pour one packet of white sugar in one hand. Using the combination, rub your hands together and use your fingers to massage around the nails. Finish by rinsing off with a half a can of club soda. Have a paper towel ready for drying."

"I'm a big Weight Watchers fan – and while some people say it's hard to follow while traveling, I disagree. Staying within my points allowance (or at least trying to) helps me remained focused and reminds me that mixed berries for dessert is a better option that the sugar-laden chocolate dessert that will also keep me from getting a good night's sleep."

Beth flies with her own oatmeal packets, soup cups and also Luna bars. She also brings her own travel pillow and blanket in her carry-on – she uses the ones from Plane Comfort (www.planecomfort.net).

An old pro at traveling, Beth also brings sanitizing wipes for hotel phones, remote controls and doorknobs. "I never use dresser drawers in hotels because I have no idea whose dirty laundry was in there an hour ago. Instead, I only use the closet and request more hangers if needed, and use the Rojeti Travel Laundry Bag that hangs up (www.rojeti.com/products.asp). I never ever use the bedspread in hotels – I know this one is cliché but it disgusts me."

She also never flys without Clinique's Moisture Surge Extended Thirst Relief (www.clinique.com). To avoid jet lag, she is a fan of FlyRight Jet Lag Formula – "It's worked great. I feel fantastic when I get to my destination." (www.jetlagformula.com)

Gwen Tanguy, Flight Attendant, Air France, www.airfrance.com

Gwen says that exercise comes with traveling and her job – but when she's on a stopover, she avoids the elevators and uses the steps whenever possible. "I also try to go swimming. Personally, I never go anywhere without my Pilates book, which helps and motivates me to do exercises in my room."

For meals, Gwen snacks on fruit and suggests to other travelers that they eat "just a little bit of everything, but avoid anything with too much sauce, and fizzy drinks that bloat you." She adds: "If you have trouble relaxing onboard the plane, a few drops of lavender essential oil does the trick on a tissue."

She prefers Clarins, especially the hand cream (www.clarins.com). "My hands get in an awful state on board. She also uses a tinted moistur-

> **Angelina Jolie Checks In**
>
> The superstar companion of Brad Pitt got her pilot's license in 2004, and uses it to navigate her own private plane, a Cirrus SR22. *US Weekly*, July 19, 2010

izer instead of foundation, and if her face gets oily on the plane, she uses The Body Shop Chamomile Facial Blotting Tissues (www.thebodyshop-USA.com).

"Onboard I also wear my uniform shoes, but once I am at my destination it depends on where I am. For beach destinations I always have my Havaianas flip-flops."

How does she find beauty bargains when she travels? "Shop where the locals shop – just ask them!"

Angelika Schwaff, Director of International Public Relations, Germanwings Airlines, www.germanwings.com

Angelika travels a great deal for her job with Germanwings, a discount European carrier. When she arrives at her destination, she checks www.runtheplanet.com for routes to run, compiled by locals. "If the weather is bad I am a sissy and use the gym or do some gymnastics in my room." On flights, she orders veggie or vegan meals, along with fruits and salad bought at the airport. Her preferred beauty brands include Biotherm, Clarins, Clinique and Kiehls, with Yves Saint Laurent's iconic Touche Eclat concealer her all-time favorite (www.ysl.com). "It's the reason why people think I slept 10 hours, when I only spent five hours in bed." When puffy eyes are her problem after a long flight, she orders a cold yogurt from room service and applies it to her face. And when she seeks a fabulous find such as the name of a good local hairdresser, she simply asks a good-looking local woman at her destination. "Tell her how you like her looks, and she will tell you where to find it!"

Karin (who asked to remain anonymous), Flight Attendant on Lufthansa, www.lufthansa.com

"I carry two 8-ounce/500 ml. plastic bottles with me. I fill them up with water and use them as weights when I wish to exercise in my hotel room. Yoga is also a favorite of mine. As a snack, I enjoy nuts and dried fruit, and there's always chocolate in my purse."

Karin also travels with a hot-water bottle – "for when I'm in a country where my feet get cold…I also have a tennis ball in my suitcase, for shoulder tension. Put the tennis ball between your shoulder blades and the wall, and slowly move side to side, up and down, giving yourself the pressure you need."

Cortney Williams, Flight Attendant, Jet Blue, www.jetblue.com

Cortney, who hails from London, has one of the best tips I've heard. When she's in a new town, "I go and get massages from students at a massage school. It's less expensive," she says. (The American Massage Therapy Association lists institutions on its site, searchable by state, including Alaska and Hawaii, at www.amtamassage.org/amta-cos. Steiner Education also has a nationwide chain of 17 accredited massage schools in nine states and offers massages by students, www.steinered.com.)

What does she do to stay fit and trim? "I eat fruit, nuts and drink a lot of water, and coffee and tea to stay awake. I try not to eat bread or salt. I might have some turkey and cheese. I find a grocery store when we land, and buy my own stuff – a ton of produce, veggies, and hummus. I also usually bike and walk a lot, or run on the treadmill." Cortney's beauty routine includes Cetaphil moisturizer as a base (www.cetaphil.com) and a tinted moisturizer on top of that. "I love lip gloss but my lips are sensitive – I love Rosebud Salve, (www.smithsrosebudsalve.net). I take antibacterial wipes to use in the hotel to wipe everything down. The other things I take are speakers that plug into my iPod so I can dance in my hotel room. I like that a lot better than watching TV. On layovers, I sleep a lot – I don't shop, otherwise I'd be shopping every day. I use eBags luggage. I also need a thick-heeled shoe. It can't be a stiletto – it was in the beginning, but that quickly changed," she laughed.

Heidi Barclay, American Airlines Flight Attendant, www.aa.com

Blonde, bubbly Heidi "worked the room" on one of my flights to Los Angeles, and has been a flight attendant for 21 years. The first thing she told me is how the TV remote is always "the dirtiest thing in your hotel room." She said that the best thing to do is to cover the remote with a sealed plastic bag, or just use a clear hotel shower cap placed over it, or even the plastic liner found in the ice bucket. "Also put a 'towel trail' from bed to bathroom – do not walk barefoot on the hotel carpet. Hang towels on the bathroom doorknobs, and open the doors with the towels over the knob." (Another flight attendant in the galley told me that she sprays Lysol disinfectant over everything in her hotel room.) For meals, Heidi and her colleagues usually bring their own thermal lunchbox, filled with dry ice on the bottom, to keep food cold. "I also bring lots of Trader Joe's items such as trail mix, yogurt and hummus. Because London and Paris layovers can be expensive, flight crews will all usually purchase one item each, and then we all have a picnic and share."

She continued: "Being German, I was brought up on Nivea cream (www.nivea.com) although I also love Kiss My Face cream that I find at Trader Joe's." (www.kissmyface.com)

She says that all flight attendants are big users of vitamins and supplements, "and we also love Airborne. We swear by it." (www.airbornehealth.com) Her biggest beauty tip? "Sleep, sleep, sleep."

A View From Below: Tips & Tricks from Travel Professionals and Traveling Executives

Lori Ansaldi, Executive Producer and Travel Journalist, The Travel Channel, www.travelchannel.com

Lori travels 20 weeks a year. We could all learn from her insider's tips – as she told me, not only is she expected to be a professional reporter, she is also expected to look good on camera, and even more, "to try the cuisine in all of the destinations. I'm always at events, eating soup to nuts."

She adds, "I hate the dreaded 'big ass' syndrome. It's hard to say no to food in a five-star resort or restaurant, because food is the biggest part of travel. What do I do? I made a deal with myself, even though I rethink it every year. I *must* exercise every day that I am on the road. I use the gym at the hotel. If there's no gym, I take a walk outside. I "bank" myself – if I earn calories, I can spend calories." She continued: "I always try to order lean proteins and be very aware of my alcohol intake. Every restaurant wants you to try their food with a great glass of wine. It is up to me to limit my portions."

Lori added, "I also seek activities that are indicative to the spot where I've traveled. In Santa Monica, where there are yoga classes 24/7, I bike on the beach, then work out in one or two yoga classes. It's easy because the weather is always great, and you can rent bikes right on the beach. I want to take tai chi classes in New York City. My rule in New York is to always walk or take the subway. I am on a mission to never take a cab unless I have to."

"My biggest secret? I always order the vegetarian meal on the plane. It's a better meal than the other types, because it's fresher and hotter because it has to be made special. I don't drink alcohol or caffeine on an airplane – it dehydrates you more – and I always have a Pria or Fiber One bar with me, when they're shelling out the pretzels. But hydration is the biggest thing."

"My 98-year-grandmother swears by Oil of Olay (www.olay.com). I use Oil of Olay as a facial moisturizer and I use a heavier cream at night, L'Oreal Regenerist (www.lorealusa.com). As soon as I exit the plane, the first thing I do is visit the airport bathroom, wash my face, and apply Oil of Olay and Burt's Bees lip balm." (www.burtsbees.com)

"You know what's awesome? I found a travel yoga mat that folds flat, and I use it, and put it over my mat when I'm in a class, so I don't have to use a public mat. I also use it for yoga in my hotel room."

Luggage? Lori has two Samsonites, an Eddie Bauer bag, and a Tumi (www.tumi.com) – "I love her." She also has a Tumi toiletry case "that's like a thick notebook." In every piece of luggage? Her Havaianas flip-flops.

Lori also has a wealth of gorgeous-globetrotter shopping secrets at her destinations. "Century 21 in New York City. Loehmann's on La Cienega Boulevard in Los Angeles – it's the best one in the country, as they have to compete with all of the boutiques in LA.

Samantha (Brown, also a Travel Channel broadcaster) and I discovered Anna Lowe in Paris, for discount shopping. Sam and I both bought Chanel pieces there. It's funny – the French simply do not believe in sale items – they would rather buy their clothing at full price! In Miami I visit Lincoln Road on South Beach, where there are hundreds of vintage boutiques where you can find everything from Hermes scarves to Louboutin shoes."

The perennial traveler also has her favorite escapes when she's not working. "Telluride, Colorado, because it feels like a small town, and Mill Valley in Marin County, Calif., which is a small chunk of Heaven."

When Lori gets away, because she loves to buy fresh produce at farmer's markets, she always visits www.VRBO.com – Vacation Rentals By Owner – so she can rent accommodations with a kitchen. "It keeps you healthy," she says. "When I travel with my family, we would rather rent a home or an apartment than stay at a hotel. This is great because I can visit the local farmer's markets and bring in our own fruits and veggies and we can cook instead of always going out."

Diane Sukiennek, Food and Wine Writer, www.foodandwineaccess.com

Diane and her longtime partner Michael do something in their travels that I had never before heard of – they take a pool thermometer with them on all trips. Says Diane: "Yes, we always choose hotels with pools but have often been disappointed because even when they say it is heated – there is no consistency in 'swimmable temperature.' So we get there and we can't swim.....bummer! Now, as soon as we arrive, Michael checks the temperature, and if it's not our definition of 'swimmable' (81–84 degrees) we immediately request a temperature adjustment and they are usually very responsive. It takes several hours to heat up a pool so that's why we 'check in and check it' even before we unpack! That's one of our secrets to staying slim as we eat and drink our way around the world!" She adds: "If the fitness center hours do not meet our schedule we request that they open it for us…We exercise every day – some combo of walking, stationary biking, light weights, stretches, core strengthening exercises and swimming depending on what's practical. We have done stretches in un-crowded sections of airports and even in the aisles of airplanes."

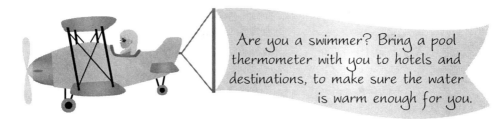

Are you a swimmer? Bring a pool thermometer with you to hotels and destinations, to make sure the water is warm enough for you.

Lori Rackl, Travel Editor, *Chicago Sun-Times,* www.suntimes.com

"I actually work out *more* when I travel than when I stay at home," says Lori. "It's usually very easy to pop down to the hotel's gym and ride the recumbent bike while reading a copy of the local newspaper – gotta love multi-tasking! I've noticed a lot of hotel gyms are charging guests to use the facilities – a concept I think is pretty ridiculous, given how much these hotels charge per night. Anyway, if that's the case I'll often opt to go on a run instead. It's a great way to get accustomed to your surroundings, and it's a way to feel like more of a local than a visitor." On planes, "My snack of choice is always nuts. Full of protein, tasty with cocktails, and they keep you full – not like empty carbs that leave you hungry an hour after you've eaten them."

In Lori's suitcase are "as little as possible. But Bliss beauty products are good, especially their Body Butter (www.blissworld.com). I also love Shiseido's face moisturizer (www.shiseido.com). It's under two ounces so I can carry it on and it leaves a nice, clean finish. And it has SPF 15."

Jet lag? It's not in her plans: "It's rough, to be sure, but I try to live by the local time as soon as the plane lands. The kiss of death is taking a nap as soon as you arrive, no matter how tempting that might be. The first day is always rough, but it's the quickest way to adjust to a new time zone."

You Snooze, You Win

Travel with your own satin pillowcase, and put it over the cotton case in the hotel. Or put it over the pillow you use on the plane. You'll sleep better – knowing it's yours – and it won't wrinkle your face, or bend your hair, which cotton can do. Satin is much more s-o-f-t and forgiving.

Heather Mikesell, Executive Editor, *American Spa Magazine*, www.questex.com

Heather's always traveling to some sybaritic spa location – it's a job that all of us envy!

"In flight, I'm a germaphobe, so I sanitize everything around me," says Heather. "That includes the tray table and the remote. I bring my own pashmina and a satin eye mask."

In terms of dining options, "I'm a big sandwich person, and I always carry food with me. I'll have a peanut-butter-and-jelly sandwich, or turkey. On morning flights, I take cereal with me, and fresh blueberries, and I get milk on the plane. For snacks, I eat almonds and dried apricots."

Heather also takes everything in a carry-on. "I never check luggage. Even on a three-week trip, I take a carry-on. I have it down to a science."

"I use Sonya Dakar's jet-set kits – I use her omega oil on my face, for dehydration and as sunscreen, (www.sonyadakar.com). But I downsize to the bare necessities; I'm low maintenance when I travel. The best beauty bargain I ever found was slathering myself with Dead Sea mud while staying at a resort near the Dead Sea in Jordan. It's certainly less expensive than paying someone else – a spa attendant – to slather on that same mud in a treatment room. You can often find great products for treating hyperpigmentation in Asia, as Asian skin is much more susceptible to the condition. And there are always fashion finds to be found in Thailand. Last time I was there, I snagged a pair of designer jeans for about $30 and had them hemmed for free in about five minutes."

Exercise is also key to her travel regime. "I'm a big runner. I love to explore new cities. I check in with the concierge, get a map, and I'm there. I also take advantage of complimentary classes at the resort or spa I'm staying at. Many times I'm the only one there for the class, so I get a private session. I go straight to the spa after I arrive, to get a massage."

Marianne Braly, Travel Agency Owner, Now Voyager Travel, and featured "Top Travel Agent" in *Travel + Leisure Magazine,* www.nowvoyagertravel.com

Marianne travels with a blow-up ball. "I flatten it to pack it, and put air in it when I get to my hotel. You know, the super large rubber balls that you can stretch on? I tend to have back problems, so the ball really stretches my back and keeps it in shape. I also do my stomach crunches on the ball."

Marianne has allergies, so she also travels with a plastic travel Neti-pot – a nasal wash with non-iodized salt, which you insert into your nostrils, one at a time, to clear out your sinuses.

Snacks? Marianne usually eats nuts such as pistachios and dried fruits such as Craisins. "I eat the airplane food if I'm in First Class, but if I'm in coach, I don't touch it."

"I also only travel with Paula's Choice products (from Paula Begoun, 'The Cosmetics Cop,' www.paulaschoice.com). All her lotions and cleansers come in small, plastic containers and are perfect to travel with. I use her products at home also."

"When I arrive at my destination, I enjoy the destination, because before leaving on my trip, I've already had my facial; my hair is cut and colored; legs are waxed; eyebrows shaped; and eyelashes and eyebrows are dyed."

The Tan Commandments

Will you be sitting in a window seat on the plane? Trust me on this one – you don't want to get a tan – or a burned red face – from your seat. Make sure to shield your skin with sunscreen. The rays can penetrate through the window – and who needs that? One to try: Coppertone's NutraShield Faces SPF 70+, which provides UVA/UVB sun protection plus antioxidants to promote natural skin repair. Waterproof, non-greasy and moisturizing, it also won't clog pores. Says Dr. Elizabeth Hale, Clinical Associate Professor of Dermatology at the New York University School of Medicine: "Choosing a broad-spectrum sunscreen with a high SPF can help protect against skin burning, signs of aging as well as some types of skin cancer." Beautiful! *Soleil* a little lotion on me (www.schering-plough.com).

Marybeth Bond, Travel Author, Women's Travel Expert, *Oprah* guest and Creator of www.gutsytraveler.com

Marybeth is the award-winning author-editor of 11 books, including the best sellers *50 Best Girlfriend Getaways in North America, A Woman's World* and *Gutsy Women.*

Marybeth has hiked, cycled, climbed, dived and kayaked her way through more than 70 countries around the world, from the depths of the Flores Sea to the summit of Mount Kilimanjaro. She studied in Paris for four years, earned two degrees, and had a business career in high-tech marketing.

Marybeth has traveled – along, with her gal pals, daughters, sisters and mother and husband – researching travel books and articles, and for adventure. She reminds us that gal-pal time and getaways are good for women's health.

Believe or not, this road warrior who takes two trips a month told me, "I start thinking about my trip the day before," Marybeth said. That's when she thinks about all of the leftovers in her refrigerator, and what she can bring on the plane. "I've taken rack of lamb, salad, Egyptian mint sauce – I have the best food on the plane. I take fresh tomatoes and basil, and some protein. Then idea is to have a variety, and a piece of chocolate. It makes me feel like a million bucks when I'm squeezed in like a sardine." She has also been known to take an extra portion, so she can share her largesse with a passenger sitting next to her – isn't that smart? – and generous? "I eat Total cereal (www.totalcereal.com) and scrambled eggs for breakfast the day I travel, and try to eat the same thing every morning that I travel. I like to load up on vitamins and minerals at breakfast."

Marybeth has a firm comfort ritual on the plane – and believe me, she definitely sends out a message to her seatmates, alerting them that "I mean business – please don't wake me up!" "I keep one bag always at the ready," she says. "As soon as I get on the plane, I take an Airborne (www.airbornehealth.com). And I carry my own water bottle. Plus I have 12-hour nasal decongestant spray, ChapStick (www.chapstick.com) – that's really important – liquid tears, and an inflatable pillow with a cotton cover that you can wash." After going onboard, she puts on her Mini Mate Ionic Air air purifier ("I wear it around my neck, it takes 95% of the bacteria out of the air," www.weinproducts.com), along with her Sennheiser nose-muter travel headphones (www.sennheiserusa.com). Then she plugs silicone earplugs into her ears. She also can't survive the flight without her eye shades. Now that's a smart, seasoned traveler whom we can all learn from! "The message I give to folks around me is, 'I'm gonna be quiet on this flight,'" she told me with a laugh.

Marybeth also never flies without hairspray to shape hair that goes flat after flying; a tiny deodorant; and No Jet Lag tablets (www.nojetlag.com) as well as five granola bars, a banana and an apple. "They're all great snacks." Marybeth also carries her own bags of mint and herbal tea, to enjoy in her hotel room, as well as instant oatmeal. "It prevents me from ordering a hamburger from room service," she told me.

She also has a boatload of travel tips for her comfort. "I take a hot bath when I get into my hotel room, and use a good all-over body cream. My first breakfast is a locally made yogurt. For example, I did this in Cambodia, and I had no stomach problems. I also carry a Ziploc with sliced cashews and almonds. I even take my own soap, because the soap in some hotels can be so harsh. I take lavender soap made by Mistral in France (www.mistralsoap.com) because it smells so good and makes me feel good. Plus, I take a pumice stone. They don't weigh anything, and I actually have more time to spend on myself when I travel."

In her hotel room, she does yoga; puts all the hotel information in drawers, to get rid of the clutter; and displays flowers she buys for herself, to make herself feel more at home. "Also make sure to check that the alarm clock isn't set to go off in the middle of the night," she advised, in case it was set for the previous person who booked the same hotel room. (That's a great tip – because it has happened to me more than once!)

Another tip? "Make sure to get a good haircut and style before you go, and take your favorite makeup and costume jewelry," she adds. "If you're rested, hydrated, and your hair and nails look good when you travel – you'll feel beautiful."

Marybeth's luggage is the Samsonite Spinner. "I am a fanatic when it comes to tiny little bottles of everything. I never do checked luggage. Even when I went to the Galapagos and carried a wetsuit and a mask. With this Samsonite, you

Spice Up Your Travel-Sized Samples

It's smart to constantly keep your beauty case stocked with your favorite travel sizes, as I do. That way you're always ready to go – and look First Class fabulous. But if you still have plenty of extras to store (or you've just come from Sephora, which offers a slew of samples) here's what to do. Go out and purchase a revolving spice rack, which you can paint the color of your bathroom cabinets or walls. Its tiny clear-plastic or glass jars are ideal for storing small, travel-sized objects like lipsticks and glosses, creams, elastics, barrettes, opened pencils, you name it. And you can twirl the device around, to get to what you need. Variety *is* the spice of life.

can push, not pull it. It's light, has solid sides, and the handle has different heights." (www.samsonite.com)

At her destination, she's sure to eat "a little something" all during the day. "That's the secret of losing weight when you travel," she told me. She also loves to walk. "I try to walk in nature. In Paris, on the Left Bank, I took a walk in the Luxembourg Gardens. It doesn't ruin my hair, and it puts me in a great frame of mind."

Her idea of a good time? Renting a bike to pedal along the Chicago waterfront or San Francisco Bay. Or shopping, especially going to thrift and consignment stores. "Like the Trashy Diva in New Orleans."

Carole Terwilliger Meyers, Author, *Weekend Adventures in San Francisco & Northern California* (Carousel Press), www.caroletmeyers.com

When flying, "I discreetly fortify myself with a Q-tip of Neosporin up my nostrils," says this professional travel writer. "When I do this, I don't pick up the usual airplane cold/cough. I enhance the effectiveness by wearing an air ionizer. Not beautiful in flight, but it keeps you beautiful and healthy after the flight."

"I always take a Kashi brand TLC granola bar (I like the roasted almond crunch) and sometimes a favorite chocolate bar (such as Kit Kat) or snack food. I NEVER buy the meals on the plane, even when I'm starving. And I don't order water unless I can see that it is bottled. I also have a pre-packed cosmetic bag that allows me to just grab it and go."

To stay at the top of her game, "I use No Jet Lag, (www.nojetlag.com). It is a homeopathic remedy and really works for me. I land on my feet, running. I only use it for international flights that go through four or more time zones."

Keep your travel and sample-sized cosmetics in a revolving spice rack with clear bottles.

Naomi Serviss, Freelance Spa and Entertainment Writer, www.spatrekking.com

How does Naomi stay in shape on the road? It all starts with a cup of coffee. "I bring my own coffee from home, along with filters. Plus I ask for a little Half-and-Half from the kitchen the night before, to store in the refrigerator." Then she does her yoga poses while the coffee brews.

Naomi uses an orange-grapefruit dry shampoo from Pretty Fly (www.pretty-fly.com), as well as their moisturizer, when flying. She also likes to use her newest favorite brand, Sia Botanicals (www.siabotanics.com), which makes a range of skincare products in travel sizes. Her other swear-by item? Her yoga socks, called ExerSocks, which are made of bamboo and have a grip bottom. She wears these in-flight. And inside her checked bag is an empty backpack, "because you always end up with unexpected items."

Fix Yourself Up – As You're Going Down

As the plane descends, and you want to freshen up, you want Pretty Fly, an adorable collection of orange blossom soap, lemon zest lotion, grapefruit dry shampoo and lime lip balm, all available in a single-serving and all natural. It's a lot of good things – in a small blue envelope, sealed in plastic. Very cute! The invigorating orange blossom soap, for example, contains organic coconut, olive and jojoba oils, and organic orange oil, while the dry shampoo contains cornstarch, cornsilk powder and grapefruit and tangerine essential oils. Sweet! Sold for $7 per package (www.pretty-fly.com).

Naomi's beauty secret when traveling? "If there is time, I go to a good neighborhood and find an upscale thrift store. Not a 'boutique/vintage' place but the nitty-gritty. I have found some incredible names and labels at such places."

Jennifer Stein, Editor-In-Chief, *Destination I Do Magazine,* www.destinationidomag.com

"When I'm traveling I take every opportunity to get moving," says Jennifer, the Editor-in-Chief of one of the country's top destination-wedding magazines, whom I met in Hawaii on a press trip. Jennifer says: "I always use the stairs, and even at the airport. At my destination, I stick to my workout regimen, typically in a gym or on the treadmill, or running on the beach. If I'm on a press visit and there's a physical excursion, I always do it. I find that when I'm out of town, I'm even more active."

"If I have a sedentary day – say I'm at the beach drinking Margaritas – I will do lunges, sit-ups and push-ups while watching TV at night, during the commercials."

"On the plane I always have fruit – apples are my Number One, but so are grapes and bananas, plus dried fruit. Special K protein bars are a staple – they are always in my purse. I adhere to Weight Watchers. In the mornings I eat a good breakfast like oatmeal before I get on the plane. For lunch I bring sushi from Trader Joe's. Plus salads with just a lemon wedge and vinegar."

Jennifer also has a swear-by secret, which her at-home aesthetician told her about: using ice on her face. "I have combination skin, adult acne, and anti-aging issues," says Jennifer. "So I ice my face morning and night, after using a glycolic face wash."

"I fill a Dixie cup with ice, and apply it to my face. The ice expands and contracts your pores, and pulls the medication/serum into your skin deeper. My fine lines have decreased, and the puffiness has reduced. I do this technique when I travel, for 90 seconds. It's free, accessible (just about every hotel has an ice machine) and everyone can do it. I noticed a difference in my skin in just two weeks. My aesthetician's name is Kristen Doutsas and her business is Clear Impact Skincare in Scottsdale - her icing trick is kind of her signature (www.clearimpactskincare.com). She is also the one who got me addicted to Jan Marini Vitamin C Serum." (www.janmarini.com)

When you get to your hotel room, ice your face. It pulls medication/serum/lotion into your skin deeper. Instant improvement!

For nausea or motion sickness, Jennifer uses peppermint oil. "I keep it in my purse at all times. I used it with success in Thailand on a ferry, while everyone else got sick."

Crease-Release Your Wrinkles!

Dr. Fredric Brandt, with two practices in New York City and Miami, is world-renowned for making his patients look younger and healthier. Dr. Brandt's love of skincare started at Sloan-Kettering where he specialized in the research and treatment of leukemia. There he dedicated his studies to using natural elements to fight against the growth of cancer. Green tea, Vitamin A and Vitamin C became studied treatments under Dr. Brandt's expert eye, and would be the basis of his future skincare line. Dr. Brandt skincare is the combination of science with eastern botanicals; its custom formulations are created to achieve and maintain radiant, glowing skin regardless of age or condition. His Crease-Release contains GABA – Gamma Amino Butyric Acid – which he claims will relax stress and tension in the skin's muscles, to visibly smooth the appearance of fine lines and wrinkles. Put it on and you can feel it working! Wait just two minutes and then follow with your moisturizer. Says Dr. Brandt: "The results are similar to a Botox treatment but are achieved in the comfort of your own home." Or hotel room (www.drbrandtskincare.com).

She has a slew of beauty products she swears by: Jan Marini Vitamin C Serum and Bioglycolic face cleanser, (www.janmarini.com) and Exuviance Rejuvenating Treatment Masque (www.exuviance.com). "It's like a giant Biore pore cleanser."

"And on days when you need a little extra help around the eyes and are planning to be in natural light, or taking pictures, I get incredible results by using Dr. Brandt's Crease Release (www.drbrandtskincare.com). It reduces fine lines immediately."

Jennifer is also a big fan of using hotel hair conditioner – on her legs, before shaving. "I put it on right when I get in the shower, and allow it to soak in – it moisturizes the skin and hair so that it is easier to shave – and reduces the irritation."

Jennifer also says she "loves, loves, loves" her Diane Von Furstenberg "Hearts" collection luggage – "It's pretty and easy to identify."

Kirsten Gum, TV Host of *The Treasure Hunter* on The Travel Channel, www.travelchannel.com

Adventure traveler Kirsten Gum travels the world to dig up undiscovered gems on the Travel Channel's *Treasure Hunter: Kirsten Gum.* The show, Kirsten and her guests will inspire the adventure traveler and treasure hunter in you. "I trade travel tips with Samantha Brown (host of another Travel Channel TV show), all the time. We always travel with peanut butter."

Travel is like air for Kirsten – she's got to have it in order to survive. She started her career as a local newscaster, covering NASCAR, then the Tour de France. "In a span of 15 years I've traveled more than 95% of the people I know, in quite harsh conditions. I'm a true Sagittarius – filled with wanderlust. I get up and go at any chance – I absolutely love it."

And she loves to exercise – so much so that she sold her car and uses her bike to get around at home. "Exercise is a necessity for me – I run a ton on the road – *Treasure Hunter* takes me to desolate locations. I also take a jumprope with me, and stretch bands – those are excellent to travel with. I set a goal on every trip – say, 100 sit-ups per day. I *have* to keep in shape for my show. I'm swimming with the sharks and rappelling down mountains. I also take my yoga mat as a carry-on, on the plane – I do stretches (in public) when I'm waiting for a plane in the airport. I get strange looks at the airport. I also do it when waiting for my bags in baggage claim. My big tip? Visit www.yogichocolate.com and www.yogaglo.com to get downloads of all types of yoga classes, for a donation. They offer fantastic classes! (She had just used both websites, for three weeks, while in Ecuador.) Just hop online and you have a yoga class at your fingertips."

Another tip? "Spas at the airport! You can get massages, pedicures and facials. I don't have the luxury to do it at home, so I'm a big fan. Once I had a six-hour layover at the Detroit Airport. I had a manicure, pedicure, massage, and ear candling. I felt like a million bucks. I travel with a clean, moisturized face, and I put moisturizer on my feet and travel in Uggs or flip-flops." One brand of product she loves? Apivita products from Greece, (www.apivita.us). "I like the skin renewal night mask with carrot. I also love coconut oil – to eat, and it's great for your skin, or in your hair, as a pre-wash conditioner. Coconut oil is not just for eating on toast, it's my makeup remover, lotion and hair conditioner!"

"I travel with Dakine luggage (www.dakine.com). I have two fantastic suitcases – you can snap them together to make one suitcase, or you can check it as two suitcases if it's more than

Ah, Spa! At The Airport

What to do when you deplane, after being scrunched up in coach for several hours? Head to the airport spa! XpresSpa is the only "Premium Class" upscale, international airport spa company in existence. The company transformed a first-class, upscale Fifth Avenue Spa concept into a successful airport spa wonderland, where you can enjoy The Full Monty of pampering pleasures, from massages to manicures. Their spas, which are designed to encourage tranquility and well-being, feature warm earth tones of beige, leathers, wooden floors, gentle indirect lighting, bamboo trees, rippling waterfalls and soothing background music to create a relaxing environment that attracts both men and women. Visit the website to discover if there's an XpresSpa location in your travels. It can make a bon voyage – even better (www.xpresspa.com).

Sole-Mates

I once met a naïve young gal who was going on her first cruise, for two weeks. What was she packing? A different pair of shoes for every day of the week and every outfit – that's 14 pairs of shoes! *No one should ever do such a thing.* You need a pair of flip-flops for the beach, workout/running shoes, a pair of heels, and a good pair of walking shoes. And *please* – do not go sightseeing wearing ugly workout sneakers or Crocs (clown shoes) – they scream "ugly." Why would you want to traipse through the streets of Paris – or Piccadilly – when you look like Queen of Slobbovia? Try my preferred pair of walking shoes: mahogany Bass Weejuns. Mine even have tassels and a kiltie. They look fabulous with jeans and shorts, have a comfy rubber sole that make walking a breeze, and are a preppy classic. Another choice? Tod's driving shoes (love them in hot pink), a pair of simple ballet flats, Tory Burch flats – and if you can afford a pair boasting two interlocking C's (for Chanel), well, lucky you!

50 pounds. She's also into traveling 'green': "I carry chopsticks, bandana and wrap. The chopsticks are so much more streamlined than forks. The bandana can be used as a napkin, hairband or scarf. And the wrap/sarong is a skirt, towel, dress, swimsuit cover-up, beach blanket, pillow, or wrap for cold planes."

Susan Foster, Author, *Smart Packing for Today's Traveler*, (Smart Travel Press), www.smartpacking.com

When I spoke to Susan she was leaving for a trip to Paris and setting things aside to put in her Magellan's brand carry-on (www.magellans.com). "I'm flying in Chico's stretch jersey pants – which will become my dressy pants for dinner," she told me. "I'm taking black, black and more black. I add color in tops and accessories. To go from daytime to nighttime, I simply change my earrings and add a dressy scarf or shawl."

Her beauty routine? "For me, it's all about the lotions and potions. Oh honey, I have to have the beauty products…when I travel for business I take my own hair dryer."

"I travel with Kiehl's Eye Alert, to combat puffiness and dark circles. Kiehl's sells a lot of sample sizes plus they give a lot of samples (www.kiehls.com). For jet lag, I use a product called No Jet Lag (www.nojetlag.com). It makes me feel better when I get to my destination. Plus my Bose noise-cancelling headphones – they are worth every penny I spent on them. It cancels out the drone (www.bose.com). I also swear by Air Supply – a portable, tiny thing (www.weinproducts.com). You wear it around your neck. It's a tiny air filter – I used it traveling to Vietnam and Singapore. Everyone else on the plane was hacking and coughing and I emerged unscathed."

Her diet routine? "I love Lara bars and they don't melt in your purse."

Phyllis Ellerman, Fitness Director, Boar's Head Resort and Sports Club Fitness Director, www.boarsheadinn.com

Phyllis, in her travels, does something I had also never heard of: she takes a rolling pin. That's right – the same rolling pin you would use to make pastry. "I use the rolling pin for tight IT bands and quads. It can also be used under your foot, on your hamstrings, and calves too."

OK – but what's an IT band? "Your IT band is your iliotibial band," she explains. "This connective tissue originates from the outside of your hip, runs down the side of your thigh and past your knee cap (visualize the Adidas stripes on the side of pants). Any knots or shortness in this fascial tissue may have implications such as pain or inflammation at either your hip or knee. For some people (especially active ones) their knees may bother them on the outside edges after or during exercise. Mine don't, but I know that I am tight there (you shouldn't feel tender or have bumps...I do). I travel with the rolling pin (I use a large foam roller when I am not traveling) to roll tight musculature (for me this includes my quadriceps or front of the thighs). Rolling is a form of self myofascial release and is basically massage. It is great for when muscles are tight. Typically, tenderness or bumps felt along the IT band benefit from myofascial release. Initially, the rolling process can take a little time and be uncomfortable."

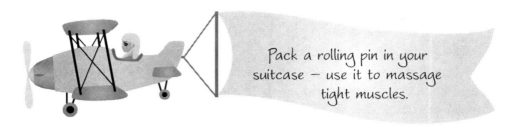

Pack a rolling pin in your suitcase — use it to massage tight muscles.

Phyllis also travels with a theraband – which she uses for back exercises – and a fitball. "It's great for soreness anywhere I feel tight."

For meals on airplanes, she prefers cherry pomegranate Nectar bars by Clif – "They are organic, have just four ingredients, have seven grams of fiber, and count as two fruit servings." She also brings baby powder, packed in a Ziploc bag – "On the mornings I don't wash my hair, I use baby powder on the roots. It works fabulous!"

When Money Is No Object...

Tempur-Pedic sleep mask $35
Cashmere Blanket $450
First-class, one-way air ticket $6,500
Sleeping as you sail
through the skies   Priceless

Tone (Pronounced "Tona") Moller, Owner, Avila Hotel, Curacao, www.avilahotel.com

Tone is the owner and Director of Commerce of the Avila Hotel in Curacao, where we stayed on a press trip. The hotel is lovely, and had just opened a terrific new spa on the day we were leaving, where I had an excellent massage. "I always travel with five-pound ankle weights and running shoes," says Tone. "I have done leg lifts in every country I have ever visited and jogged five miles in most cities." After she arrives, she does everything to make her hotel room as comfortable as possible – "Sometimes I even move the bed!" she says. And as far as beauty treatments go, her favorite products, since she was 18, are Elizabeth Arden beauty creams (www.elizabetharden.com).

Ruthanne Terrero, Editorial Director, *Luxury Travel Advisor Magazine,* www.questex.com

Based in New York City, Ruthanne travels one week a month for her job, to conferences, trade shows, "and I go to hotels to check them out." Her travels lead her throughout the United States and Europe. "Some days I eat whatever the airlines give me – which is a big mistake, because everything's too salty. But I might also take snack bars or Atkins bars, or a turkey-and-Swiss sandwich, or cans of nuts. I really like those almonds coated in cocoa. I tend to do the Atkins diet." At her destination, "I walk a lot. I have no time for anything else. Maybe the treadmill. And I lift hand weights."

The only beauty products she brings with her and swears by are Clinique's Dramatically Different moisturizer (www.clinique.com), Shiseido suntan lotions (www.shiseido.com), and her Omega-3 vitamins. And when she feels jet lagged, "I get a jet-lag massage," she said enthusiastically. "They're magical. I had one at the Hotel Arts in Barcelona, and it was fantastic. I found myself in their time zone. But I usually go to a destination and go right to sleep."

"In London, I visit the Spitalfields Market in Liverpool, in the East End, near the area for fabulous Indian restaurants. It's like a giant flea market, with used clothing and new stuff. I have bought unusual jackets and dresses there."

Rochelle Lieberman, Travel Agent, Gateway Travel, www.gatewaytrvl.com

"I travel a great deal over the world," says Rochelle, whose business is located in Farmington Hills, Mich. "And the less you eat on the plane, the better. Drink a lot of water. I always carry an apple in my purse, and I take trail mix for snack food." And you'd never find this frequent-flier with more than one suitcase. "I only pack one suitcase, no matter how long I go," she explains. "It's just too cumbersome." Her best tip is to take a travel wallet: "Leave your grocery cards and other cards at home. Take a travel wallet, and take a medium-sized purse that can hold the wallet and a small camera. And take Le Sportsac to hold great items you've found shopping, to pack them in on the way home."

Heather Clancy, Professional Singer On Cruise Ships and Land Venues

I first met Heather onboard the Regent Seven Seas *Voyager,* and then on other Regent Cruises (www.rssc.com). Today, when she's not cruising with her husband, an executive chef, Heather sings professionally on a variety of cruise lines. She's got a stunning voice – and a figure to match – so I wondered what her particular secrets are.

"A few years ago I discovered personal trainer Grace Lazenby and iTrain (www. ITrain.com)," she confided to me. "Every month I can choose three new downloadable workouts for my iPod. The workouts can be varied depending on how much time I have and what, if any, equipment is on hand when I'm on the road. The variety keeps me motivated, and Grace's boundless energy make working out fun. She's my own personal cheerleader!"

Heather's other secret? "Water, water, water…drink it, spritz it, breathe it. On long transatlantic flights my skin feels like the Sahara. A spritz of Avene Thermal Water does the trick. I'm a singer and that re-circulated air kills my voice. The Ionic Breeze Personal Air Purifier and Humidifier saves my chords and creates my own personal space – something the airlines have in short supply."

Wear a personal air purifier on the plane, to create your own environment of breathable air.

"If I can avoid it, I don't eat in-flight meals. They are loaded with preservatives and salt," she adds. After a performance, when Heather's legs get quite a workout, she swears by Dr. Hauschka's Birch-Arnica Body Oil (www.drhauschka. com). "Pre-show or pre-workout his Rosemary Leg and Arm toner also warms up the skin and starts my circulation."

And with the airlines' regulations regarding liquids, flying has become more difficult. "Flying these days is tough," says Heather. "All of the rules and regulations have made us safer, but not quite as pretty. Not being able to pack your favorite cosmetics in your carry-on bag can make a girl feel apoplectic. I've made the switch to Bare Minerals Cosmetics and couldn't be happier (www.bareminerals.com). Lush cosmetics lotion bars are solid and travel especially well (www.lush.com). GHD's Indulgence Treatment Weekly Conditioning Mask (www.ghdhair.com) are single-use capsules that also travel well."

Laura Hughes, former Editorial Director, *Elite Traveler Magazine* (a private-jet luxury lifestyle magazine), www.elitetraveler.com

"At the most I travel two weeks per month," says Laura. "More than half is international – to speak at a conference, inspect a new hotel or spa, or meet luxury industry leaders. On an overnight trip I don't eat the meal on the plane, and I try to be asleep when the meal is served. I drink a lot of water. I'll eat breakfast and lunch if it's time to be awake." Laura's exercise routine when she travels is her own home workout, with weights every other day and running in between. She will also do P90X (www.beachbody.com) when she has to do a workout in her room, and she uses resistance bands. She also downloads yoga podcasts from Nike's website. "On my last overseas trip I stayed in an apartment in Basel, Switzerland, and it had a full-service gym. I paid for it on a daily basis. I recommend finding a local gym when you travel."

Laura's moisturizer? The *crème de la crème* of skin creams: La Prairie (www.laprairie.com). "They have nice, small pots of moisturizer and

The Great French Hair Disaster

Whatever you do, **don't** do what I did on one of my trips to France. Feeling carefree and seeking that certain *je ne sais quoi*, I visited a top French hairdresser and proclaimed, "Do whatever you want with my hair." I just felt like it. The result? A disaster. I have wavy hair with a bend, which I don't just blow-dry – I beat it into submission. He took my crowning glory and cut some of my bangs so short that they were *barely* 1/8-inch long. I'm not exaggerating. Then he insisted on having it air-dry. I had to *beg* him for a blow-dry, so I could have some resemblance of my former self. When I flew home, my husband Bill barely recognized me at the airport, when he came to pick me up. It was *that* bad. "Don't ever give a hairdresser carte blanche," says my hairdresser in Boston, Alex Safar, owner of the French salon, Acote, on famed Newbury Street (www.salonacote.com). "It just gives him too much free reign."

Beauty at 35,000 Feet

If you don't care what the other travelers think – you may be the perfect candidate for the SheerinO'kho of Paris' First Class Flight Mask. Try it, even if you're in coach. Just spread a thin layer on your face and enjoy the flight. It contains 100% natural ingredients to detoxify and replenish your skin, including hibiscus, jojoba, Indian senna, vitamin E, bentonite clay, apple, raspberry, peach leaf and orange neroli. Don't worry – it will sink into your skin, so you don't look like The Masked Wonder onboard. Once you've landed, your dermis will be dazzling – moisturized, plumped and radiant. You should also use it after any long trip, when your pretty little face is parched – $100 for six .25 fluid ounce packages. It's amazing how it sinks into your skin, and immediately puts life back into your face. Consider it an injection of perfection. SheerinO'kho also makes a First Class Flight Cream that smells divine and is chock full of fine ingredients including neroli, rosewood, chamomile, acerola, horse chestnut and linden. It's great before, after and of course, during any flight. It weighs a little over one ounce (perfect for carry-on) and even comes with its own felt carry-on case. Available exclusively at Space NK. (www.spaceNK.com, www.sheerinokho.com) So wonderful, it's "to-fly-for!"

eye gel. For fragrance, I wear Aqua di Parma, and it comes in a nice tiny bottle." And here's a great tip she gave me: "If you know you'll be in Europe a lot, do what I did and buy a hairdryer and flat iron with the *local* plugs. That way you'll know that it will work on your trip abroad…I also take a heart-rate monitor."

Her tote bag is Louis Vuitton; her carry-on is Tumi; her checked luggage is Samsonite Black Label; and her handbag is Valextra (www.louisvuitton.com, www.tumi.com, www.samsonite.com, www.valextra.it).

"Today I went to the new Guerlain spa at the Waldorf-Astoria. It is vast, and I would definitely go back there. I also love the Hotel Arabelle in Vail (www.arabelle.rockresorts.com). They have excellent services for skiers, such as warmed boots. You can even tell them what you want in your mini-bar."

Irene Ann Aroner, Manager, Tropical Villa Vacations luxury villa rentals, and former Chief Concierge at Four Seasons Resorts in Seattle and Beverly Hills, www.tropicalvillavacations.com

Irene, who used to be a member of the prestigious "Clefs d'Or USA" (golden key organization) while a concierge, is a savvy, sophisticated world traveler who now heads a villa rental and management service in Maui. She travels with a pink travel blanket, pillow, and Bose noise-reducing headphones (www.bose.com). And when she's at the airport, she doesn't waste time sitting around. Instead, "I walk laps in airports," she says. "Sometimes I think security has their eye on me – wondering why I'm going in circles. But I love to burn off nervous energy, while enjoying the special buzz and pace that can only be found in an airport. I'll walk and walk and walk until I am the last person to board. I stay on my feet until they almost have to tackle me and strap me in!" Her walking shoes of choice? Donald J. Pliner zip-up stretch shoes that she can wear with socks, and easily remove when going through security. Her luggage is strictly Louis Vuitton, as well as a brown rolling case made by Brighton. "That bag still looks new, even after 10-plus years as a road warrior." (www.louisvuitton.com, www.brighton.com)

Into her bags goes Dermalogica antioxidant hydramist with licorice, white tea and vitamin E, plus Epicuren rose enzyme moisturizer (www.dermalogica.com, www.epicuren.com).

And here's some great shopping advice: "I take my favorite shirt to Hong Kong and have it duplicated a dozen times over, using gorgeous Chinese silks in different colors and patterns. I can find fabrics there, never seen in even the best designer boutiques."

Irene's favorite airline is Hawaiian Airlines. "Hawaiian Airlines is without equal for service to the US West Coast. The moment you step on board, the 'Aloha' mood is evident. I feel as though I am home again. They do the best job of setting the right frame of mind for someone heading over to Hawaii to rest and relax. Their planes, service, staff and food are just the best."

Maralyn Hill, Writer and Photographer, President of the International Food, Wine and Travelwriters Association, www.Ifwtwa.org

"I take at least 20 trips a year," says this former flight attendant, who started traveling at two weeks old, when her parents took her aboard a train. "I was born to travel. I love different cultures," she says.

Maralyn has a host of insider tips for the well-traveled. "I try not to eat on the plane," she says. "I always take granola bars. Quaker True Delights are exceptional. They're delicious and 140 calories. I like the raspberry ones. If I'm going overseas, I'll eat the airline food but not the bread. It's a different quality of food when you fly internationally. I'll eat the airline food if I'm upgraded to First Class."

"I swear by Jan Marini products (www.janmarini.com). They're the best. My daughter is an aesthetician and she used to give it to me. It's super fantastic. I'm spoiled, especially with their small travel kit. I just placed an order for Jan Marini products this week. It lasts a long, long time. I use her facial cleanser, antioxidant protectant, C-esta serum, and bioglycolic cream. I order it all from Skinstore.com, because you get free postage and free samples."

For exercise, Maralyn totes an exercise band or a long tube with handles. "If there's not an exercise facility, the bands work great. I also take a pedometer, and take at least 5,000 steps daily. But I try for 10,000 steps daily. If the weather's bad or the treadmills are filled, I walk the hallways of the hotel. If I do 18,000, I'm ecstatic – and exhausted. My luggage is Travelpro (www.travelpro.com). It's paid for itself. It has great warranties. If you have any problems, just ship it back and they'll replace it or fix it."

"I shop when I travel. For bargains, I love Thailand and the Thai silks. Buying custom suits there is the best investment. I have a suit or two made every time I go." (I agree – on my trip to Thailand, I had four fittings in three days and bought a wealth of gorgeous custommade silk outfits. I highly recommend it.)

Janice Nieder, Food, Wine and Travel Writer, S.F. Girlfriend Getaways Examiner, www.examiner.com, The Dining Diva for www.tangodiva.com, and The Token Redhead for www.vagablond.com

Janice Nieder could be the love child of Indiana Jones and Julia Child. After being bitten by the travel bug, her culinary adventures took her to over 65 countries, where she shared a smoked monkey dinner with a generous Shuar Indian family deep in the Amazon Jungle; helped Ethiopian tribal woman bake injera bread on hot stones in 108-degree heat; and crashed a wedding feast in Pakistan, where she was wined and dined by over 200 men — and no women.

Here's how she stays trim in hotels: "I do a complete mini-workout in my hotel room starting by turning on the radio to some peppy station and warming up with five minutes of shadow-boxing moves while dancing around," says Janice. She also does push-ups, triceps dips from the chair, and on alternate days, "I duplicate my free-weight routine using rubber tubing for resistance. 'Spri' has an excellent selection of rubber tubing and flat rubber bands that also work great for stretching and pack into nothing." (www.spri.com)

On the plane, "I bring 100 calorie fat-free microwave popcorn that nicer flight attendants will usually pop for me to nibble on during the movie," she says. "I know I shouldn't drink while flying (supposedly it increases bloating, puffiness, and jet lag) but I always order a Bloody Mary or a glass or three of champagne. But I do counter each drink with two glasses of mineral water."

Another beauty tip Janice recommends on flights: "Since you'll certainly have the time, although it might cause a few stares, wash your hands in warm water, slather on gobs of thick baby oil gel, cover your hands with two old socks (you can throw them away afterwards) and relax for a few hours. Your hands emerge as soft as a new-born baby's behind."

Her fave beauty secret? "I always stock up on Retin-A skin cream available at about 90% off in a good Mexican pharmacy, (no prescription needed). My tube says "Tocoderm Acido Retinoico."

Say *Ola* To Tretinoin

Traveling to Mexico? If you want gorgeous skin – without a prescription needed – visit any pharmacy south of the border and get a tube of generic Retin-A, called Tretinoin. It will cost you about $5! I have personally done this tons of times in Puerto Vallarta while on shore break from a fabulous cruise ship. It will add just enough vitamin A to your repertoire, for a dazzling dermis.

Dining at 35,000 feet? Here's what Janice does. "I bring my own stash of healthy snacks such as a bag of mini-carrots, apple slices, fat-free popcorn, and licorice-spice tea by Stash," says Janice. "If I'm driving to the airport, I stop at my fave *bahn-mi* store and pick up a BBQ chicken bahn-mi for the plane (it's a healthy delish Vietnamese sandwich stuffed with shredded carrots and herbs). Or if I remember in time, the day before my flight I special-order the Hindu or Muslim meal, which is usually some healthy, tasty version of a veggie curry with legumes and spicy seasoning. I always pack Peppermint Sugarless Bubble-Yum, which blows the world's biggest bubbles and I always bring enough to give to kids I meet on the road. I always bring a few ampoules of Go Smile's tooth whiteners to brighten up my smile since I'm usually sampling a lot of red wines on the road (www.gosmile.com). I've stopped bringing my arsenal of electric converters, and usually just buy an inexpensive hair-dryer *in-country*, which is always the right wattage."

Buy a cheap hair dryer, locally, in the country of your destination, to get the correct voltage.

"Due to changes in water and temperature, my skin tends to break out more when I travel, particularly if I'm in a hot climate where I have to use more sunscreen. So I was thrilled when I discovered Colorescience SPF 30 water-resistant sun protection powder (www.colorescience.com.) I no longer have breakouts, it really protects and it is a non-liquid."

"My all-time best product is a big vial of plain ol' baking soda. It makes an excellent calming facial scrub. I have used it as an antacid after many a rich meal (1 teaspoon in ½ glass of water), and it even pinch-hits for toothpaste and mouthwash when necessary."

A fave offbeat item? The "vibrating" Infinite Powermascara by Lancome (www. lancome-usa.com). "Although I scoffed when I first read about it, after one try I became a convert. It really zeros in on all those little end lashes, which usually go completely unnoticed, and plumps up every last fella."

"One unbelievable bargain I've found is the two-hour stone massage with a fragrant rose petal soak at Bali Healing Spa in Ubud (a remarkable town in the middle of Bali), which will leave you with change from a $20. I just returned from a local fave (again both the spa and hotel get three thumbs up) – The Ojai Valley Inn and Spa (www.ojairesort.com)."

"Many unique workshops are offered in their artist's cottage such as a fantastic aromatherapy class where you'll custom blend your own fragrance."

Valerie Wilson, Chairman and CEO Owner of her eponymous high-end travel agency specializing in luxury travel, www.vwti.com

"I eat sparingly on planes – half the pasta, salad, and a piece of chicken," says Valerie. "If I had my way, my sandwich would be smoked salmon or simply caviar. When I used to commute to London, I would make my own smoked salmon sandwiches. Frankly, I wish airline meals were simpler, with no garlic and no sauces. I tell them that all the time. I'm a big fan of Coca-Cola. If they don't have it, after security I buy one and I carry it on the plane."

Valerie has a very specific routine on the plane. "Most people think I'm nuts. I carry flat shoes in my carry-on, a down travel-size pillow in a pillowcase, and a pashmina, travel blanket and book. Plus my Hermes scarf that I'm wearing (which I collect). I'm in comfortable slacks. I'm often asleep before the plane takes off. It's very important to have your own 'little space.' I put the scarf right over my face, in order to sleep."

"At my destination, my first choice is to have a Swedish massage, especially after a long flight. I'd rather get a massage any day, than exercise."

"Red is my signature color, and I carry red luggage by Victorinox." (www.victorinox.com). She might also take her lightweight Rimowa luggage. In her garment bag she has placed all of her clothes, which are separately packed in individual plastic bags. "It helps tremendously with avoiding wrinkling."

Valerie also can't resist a good hotel gift shop. "I always check them out. I've purchased scarves, handbags, silk tops, books and gift items that represent the specific destination or property."

Amy Skudlarczyk, Owner of a Travel Agency, Trilogy Travel, www.trilogy-travel.com

Amy says that she runs every day and does cardio no matter where she is in the world. However, there have been times when it wasn't possible to run, due to safety issues. "So I have come up with creative ways to do cardio. In Costa Rica one time, I ran the stairs at the Four Seasons that's built up over a mountain, to the other side of the beach. I did this four times to get an hour of cardio."

In her Louis Vuitton backpack (which she loves) (www.louisvuitton.com) she packs a vanilla or crisp-linen travel candle, plus workout bands, Burt's Bees products (www.burtsbees.com) – "They make a great travel bag" – and Clean and Clear oil-absorbing sheets (www.cleanandclear.com). She adds, "I've had my Louis Vuitton backpack for 10 years, and it's held up great!"

Betty Jo Currie, Co-owner of Currie & Co. Travels Unlimited, a boutique travel agency specializing in adventure and exotic travel, www.curriecotravels.com

"I generally fly Business Class like my clients, though not always," says Betty Jo. "Domestically I tend to get upgraded, and we know the consolidators who can find the discount business fares. At that price, it is nearly always worth the cost. Two things most people don't realize is that there's significantly better food and much, much more water in Business Class, as well as cleaner bathrooms – and of course, the seats are infinitely more comfortable. You'll stay much more hydrated – they even stick a bottle of water in your lap while you are sleeping."

Betty Jo washes her hair the night before a flight, and typically wears Saint Grace black knit pants (she now has them made locally for her). "They look like yoga pants with flowing wide legs. I generally have on clogs and dark socks – they're really comfortable – and a Hanro undershirt, blouse, cashmere sweater and pashmina scarf."

Betty Jo also has an offbeat item that she swears by: an eye mask that contains magnets. "I've been doing this for 16 years and I swear by them," she told me. "They are twice the size of a regular eye mask, and they make my eyes feel more rested and less puffy. When those go on, I'm ready for sleep." (Find them at www.therionresearch.com.) "I also nibble on the edge of an Ambien instead of taking a whole one. Another great tip: I take a small bottle of lavender oil if in coach, where odors can be an issue. I put it on the fabric of the airplane seat or pillow. I must sound like a precious priss – but I'm not."

She also has her exercise regimen down pat. "I'm over 50, so I have a lot of experience doing strenuous exercise to Pilates. I might go to the gym for 30 minutes, or I'll do 25 push-ups and then use a rope or rubber band for stretching. Exercise is built into my day, because strength is a requirement for adventure travel."

Her luggage? "I am married to the Hartmann 22-inch grommeted suitcase; with the grommet zipped, it will fit in the overhead compartment (www.Hartmann.com). You pack to carry on this bag when you leave home, and on your return, you unzip for extra room (for the purchases and books!) and check it locked (with a TSA lock). I have the black one and I just bought it in tweed. Its size and flexibility can't be beat." She says she's also a big fan of duffel bags made by Red Oxx (www.redoxx.com). "My name is monogrammed onto them, with an extra nametag tucked away."

 She always buys tea tree oil at South African pharmacies, and "I always buy bug repellent in the country I'm in at the time – it works better," she advises. And Betty Jo acknowledges what we all know: "It's a challenge to travel attractively and look good, without being a slave to clothing, hair and makeup." Best advice of all? "Glance, don't stare, at the mirror much, and decide you look wonderful. When you travel like this, you do!"

Passport to Pretty

Catch A Whiff And Take A Sniff

I don't know about you, but when I've been trapped in a steel aircraft with stale air, I want to inhale something terrific! That's where **Herban Essentials** come in. These moist towelettes smell divine – they're made with real essential oils – and they will uplift your spirits and send your olfactory senses into overdrive. Pack 'em in your purse, suitcase, backpack, briefcase, car, wallet or gym bag. They come in lemon, orange, lavender, peppermint and eucalyptus. But don't just use them on the plane – they have TONS of uses. For example, use the lavender to tuck into your pillow at night, relieve itching from bug bites, and remove makeup. Use the lemon as an aftershave on your legs, or use it on your computer keyboard, or as a pick-me-up after exercising. Peppermint can relieve motion sickness, and combat mental fatigue (www.herbanessentials.com). Enjoy! And there's more where that came from. **Pocketaroma** was developed by international flight attendant Maria Kolins, who use to travel with a cotton-ball infused with lavender essential oil, tucked into her pocket. After another stressed-out flight attendant asked her for one, Maria decided to create the Pocketaroma so everyone could enjoy it. Just squeeze the sides, breathe deeply and relax (www.pocketaroma.com). Like the Pocketaroma, now there's **SniffnGo**, a personal aromapod and innovative inhaler that fits into your pocket or purse. It's available in six varieties, including Energize (rosemary and lemon oils) and Harmony (orange). You'll wonder how you ever traveled without these little guys (www.sniffngo.com). If you board with your own pillow, tuck in a **Sleep Scentsations** scented pillow liner that's available in 12 scents ranging from white tea and lily, to fresh-cut grass and even "My Boyfriend's Shirt." Sleeping has never been more sensual. (www.sleepscentsations.com). And here's something I've never heard of before – the **Poof** personal toilet deodorizer – but apparently this product was developed in Japan, where, according to the press release, "close quarters and strict social rules make toilet odors unthinkable." Poof is used – how can I put this delicately – when you don't want the restroom smelling stinky for the next person. A single drop in a toilet bowl, immediately before or after, will completely trap odors and perfume the potty. A quick flush and voila! The telltale smell disappears and the only aroma is that of Japanese mint. Wouldn't you love someone to do that for you, before you step in the tiny restroom, next time you're in coach? (www.poofdrops.com)

Buy bug repellent in the country you're in – it tends to work better.

Nancy Strong, Travel Agent, Owner of Strong Travel, www.strongtravel.com

"I've traveled the world – I'm very involved with many travel boards, and Virtuoso, our marketing organization," says Nancy. "Airline food is cardboard – it's never very exciting. I remember when Braniff Airlines served great food. If you want to feel good traveling on the back of the bus, just eat healthy and drink lots of water. I travel Business or First Class, where they might give you a pizza. I don't eat the crust and dig out the low-calorie tomatoes. I always order the fish dish and eat the salad. No wine. And on every flight it's a must to take your own pashmina or blanket."

Her beauty routine is quite simple: "My beauty secrets are the three S's: Sun, Sleep and Sex," she told me with a laugh. In flight she simply puts on some Kiehl's cream and lipgloss – and that's it (www.kiehls.com). Her "ace in the hole," she says, is the massage that she gets immediately after long flights, "to iron out the kinks right away." At her destination she's partial to Frederic Fekkai shampoo and conditioner (www.fekkai.com) and Living Proof – "It's new and I love that stuff," she says (www.livingproof.com). (They're the creators of the science behind breakthrough frizz-fighting technology.) She also swears by Trish McEvoy lipgloss and flawless concealer (www.trishmcevoy.com) and she always makes sure there are ice cubes in her hotel room, so she can ice her puffy eyes after a long flight.

"Over the years, I've also used every type and piece of luggage. Now I use a good Tumi and a Swiss Gear Lugano wheeled duffel bag I bought at Target." (www.tumi.com, www.swissgear.com)

Pallavi Shah, Travel Agent, Owner of Our Personal Guest Travel Agency, www.ourpersonalguest.com

"By and large I avoid eating meals on planes," says Pallavi. "I avoid 'heavy stuff.' On short flights I pick up a panini, and on long flights I hope for the best and eat lightly. But I do take my own blend of unsalted trail mix with dried cranberries, or a chewy granola bar, plus breath mints."

"I always carry a face spritzer – it's very refreshing. I use Evian – that's my staple (www.evian.com). I also use Lancome dual-finish makeup because of the nice coverage it gives me (www.lancome-usa.com). Lipgloss? I like Lancome Juicy tubes and a Stila pencil (www.stilacosmetics.com). I also try to have some sort of all-purpose lotion such as L'Occitane (www.loccitane.com) – I always buy the three-packs and they're everywhere."

Onboard a plane, she does her best to make herself comfortable. "I use my carry-on as a footrest. I take a shawl, and neck pillow and rubber-soled slip-on socks." She also stores her necessities in three or four mesh bags, which makes them easy to fish out of her purse. "You have to make yourself at home on a plane." Pallavi can't survive in the skies without her music on her BlackBerry, plus an iPhone that she's downloaded with 12 hours of TV shows.

Lena Katz, Travel Columnist for *Orbitz*; Author of *Travel Temptations* series for Globe Pequot Press

"I travel one-half of each month, if not the entire month," says Lena. "Plane food is a guilty pleasure, and it's hard to say no if it's right in front of you. I like to buy healthier snacks such as whole-grain crackers before I board."

Even when traveling to the Caribbean or Mexico, Lena wears socks and a sweatshirt, because "I tend to get really cold in flight. And I always travel with hand sanitizer and wet naps."

Lena aims to make exercise part of her travel experience. "In Thailand we'd do the treadmill for an hour, but it made more sense to kayak outside to an island, or take a beach walk or a yoga class. It's a good way to see your surroundings."

Passport to Pretty

The Singapore Girl – A Symbol of Elegance

Singapore Airlines, which is consistently named the top international carrier by readers of both **Conde Nast Traveler** and **Travel + Leisure** magazines, prides itself on uncompromising service that's delivered by a highly trained and motivated staff. So who's that gorgeous gal in the galley? Why, she's one of the flight stewardesses commonly referred to as a Singapore Girl. (But if you want to be hired as one, just make sure you can fit into a sarong.) In 1972, Singapore Airlines (SIA) hired French haute-couture designer Pierre Balmain to design a special version of the Malay *sarong kebaya* in batik material as the uniform, which later became one of the most recognized signatures of the airline, making the Singapore Girl one of the most successful corporate images ever. The creation of the "Singapore Girl" has turned out to be a very powerful symbol and has become an icon with an almost mythical status. In fact, the image of the Singapore Girl is so strong that in 1993 a waxwork of the Singapore Girl was unveiled at Madame Tussaud's Museum in London – the first commercial figure to ever be displayed at the museum. Madame Tussaud's said that the figure was chosen "to reflect the ever-growing popularity of international travel" and also in recognition of the 21st birthday of both SIA and the Singapore Girl.

About 90% of all Singapore girls are either Singaporean or Malaysian. She must meet strict rules regarding makeup and hair; for example, hair that is longer than the collar must be worn in an updo such as a French twist, and show no bobby pins. She also works under renewable five-year contracts, because it's assumed that at some point she's going to settle down. The Singapore Girl embodies Asian values: caring, warm, gentle, elegant and serene, to showcase SIA's commitment to astonishing service and quality.

Singapore Airlines also runs one of the most comprehensive and rigorous training programs for cabin and flight crew in the industry, to make sure the SIA brand experience is consistent. Training to be a Singapore Girl lasts about four months, which is among the longest of any airline in the industry, where she learns about customer care, safety, and self-development.

In other words, these reasons are why women who consistently work 10-hour flights, in a long tube, always look so good – and offer great service. (www.singaporeair.com).

Actor Patrick Stewart Checks In

"**I can tell you it got me an upgrade on British Airways.**" Patrick Stewart, on the announcement that he was to be knighted
As reported in *The Boston Globe* on Jan. 16, 2010

Lena has her eating down to a science at her destination. "I keep my morning meal light, and I get one piece of toast and one egg, coffee and juice. Then it's fine to eat a big lunch, especially if I've been moving before and will also do so afterwards. I like 'passed hors d'oeuvres events' in the evenings so you can graze and not have a sit-down plated dinner. It's a good way to control portions."

She loves shopping in Malaysia. "Kuala Lumpur is great for bags, shoes and clothes – it's great shopping. It's crazy. Like a videogame. It's an insane maze full of stuff. It's fast-paced. All the shoes are $5 American. It's like a videogame, it's so much fun, and you don't have to bargain like you have to do in Thailand."

Now that you've uncovered the beauty secrets of women from around the world, you need to make check-in easy and breezy. It's what singer Gwen Stefani might have meant by her "sweet escape." That's the subject of Chapter Three.

CHAPTER THREE

Check-In Strategies

Let's face it – you don't want to be left NOT holding the bag. In other words, you don't want to find yourself in Jamaica, with your luggage lost, and no bathing suit in your carry-on. That actually happened to me once, and I spent two whole days in a long-sleeved jumpsuit at an all-inclusive resort (Swept Away), feeling like an idiot, because I couldn't go to the beach, and I was just too darned hot.

Here's what I – and you – should take in your carry-on luggage, and I speak from experience.

Top 10 Items For Your Carry-on Luggage

1. Photocopies of your passport (Put your actual passport in your purse) and all prescriptions (including contact lenses) plus a copy of your itinerary

2. All medicines

3. Cameras

4. Bathing suit, shorts and top (if going to a sunny destination) and underwear

5. All cosmetics (no liquids or gels)

6. Contact lens solution (less than 3 oz.)

7. Travel pillow with satin pillowcase

8. Travel blanket/eye shades/earplugs

9. Reading materials, iPod, noise-reducing headphones

10. Snacks

Once you get that down, make sure you have all of your important medicines. Here are 10 that are my favorites, to tote in your carry-on bag.

Top 10 Items In Your Medicine Bag

1. **Oscillococcinum.** I swear by this homeopathic medicine, and I buy it in bulk when I'm in France for about $5 a package. (Just visit any French drugstore). In fact, in France, where Oscillo has been around for more than 65 years, it is the best-selling over-the-counter product in the cough/cold/flu category and a top-selling brand in pharmacies. Of course, you can also buy Oscillo in the

States. It won't interact with other medications and is not contraindicated with pre-existing conditions. As evidenced by four clinical studies, Oscillo helps to reduce the duration and severity of flu symptoms. "It is an industry secret found on many production sets in Hollywood," says Chris Gilbert, M.D., a general practitioner in Torrance, Calif. (www.boironusa.com).

2. **Emergen-C, Eboost and Life Shotz.** Beloved by celebrities who include Kristen Bell and Liv Tyler, the potent packets of Emergen-C pack a punch. For example, you can drink a Super Energy Booster with 1,000 mg. of Vitamin C in a super orange-flavored fizzy drink. Most have about 30 calories, but I like the Lite versions that only have 5 calories per serving. Who can beat that? Flavors include pink lemonade, acai berry, tangerine and raspberry. It's sure to put a spring in your step. Just introduced: Emergen-C O SERIES. It has all the benefits of the original blend including 1,000 mg. of vitamin C, plus seven B vitamins, antioxidants and electrolytes. The O SERIES is made with 70% organic ingredients (the box is even made from 100% recycled materials). Plus the flavors will send shivers of delight through you as well: Pomegranate Tea Blend and Island Fruit Breeze. Available exclusively at Whole Foods Markets nationwide (www.alacercorp.com). Another fabulous option you'll get juiced up about: Eboost, which makes five-calorie packets of pure goodness offering Energy, Immunity, Recovery and Focus. Eboost mixes with water to become an orange or pink lemonade effervescent drink. All contain a natural proprietary blend. For example, the orange contains 1,000 mg. of Vitamin C, 500 mg. of potassium, 200 mcg. of folate, and a whole lot more, including green-tea leaf extract. It's also sold on airlines including Virgin America and Hawaiian Airlines, and has a huge celebrity following including Madonna, Heidi Klum, Kelly Ripa, and Oprah (www.eboost.com). If you're seeking more energy, look into Life Shotz, quite possibly the most potent and talented drink to hit your lips. These 20-calorie powder sticks of vitamin sweetness contain 1,025 mg. of acai and goji berries, with NO added sugar, preservatives, artificial dyes or high-fructose corn syrup. Yes, it tastes a little vitamin-y, but you know you're getting a great dose of all

QueaseEASE Quells Nausea

Tired of getting motion sickness – and then getting drowsy from taking the medication? Try QueaseEASE, an all-natural product developed by a nurse. QueaseEASE is great for adults and children afflicted with motion sickness due to travel by car, boat, train or plane. It was originally developed for use in hospitals to quell post-operative nausea, and contains 100% pure and natural therapeutic grade essential oils of lavender, peppermint, ginger and spearmint. Just breathe in the aroma – the molecules from the oils travel the olfactory track to the central nervous system, where they interrupt the nausea cycle. And it doesn't cause drowsiness. In a hospital study at Miles Memorial Hospital in Maine, 67% of patients required no further anti-emetics when QueaseEASE was used. A motion sickness study in Hawaii found that 83% of all users believed it worked for their condition (www.soothing-scents.com).

the alphabets including B and D. Also includes Resveratrol, a cutting-edge anti-aging compound, as well as Extramel— a super antioxidant derived from a special type of melon. If you do a Google search you will see that Life Shotz has remarkable qualities to counteract stress, obesity, and disease. Plus, if you love it, you can get paid to take it, through multi-level marketing! (www.21Ten.com/ss)

3. Aspirin – Great for headaches and heart attacks

4. Antacid

5. Antihistamine (such as Benadryl, which treats bug bites and will also put you to sleep)

6. Alka-Seltzer

7. Pepto-Bismol tablets

8. Bandages and small packets of Neosporin

9. Motion-sickness pills or patches

10. A filled prescription, from your doctor, of a Z-pack of antibiotics, in case you're sick in a foreign country and can't get to a doctor. You don't want to pay

$100 out-of-pocket, do you? Bill and I never go anywhere without it. It's a "just-in-case" strategy.

Bring a FILLED prescription for antibiotics – just in case.

If you're confused about what you can or can't bring in your carry-on bag, follow this advice.

Here's The 411 On Using 3-1-1

The Transportation Security Administration (TSA) recommends that you follow the 3-1-1 rule for carry-ons. Use **3-oz. bottles** or less (by volume) to hold your liquids. Place them in a **1-quart-sized**, clear, plastic, zip-top bag. Put your **one bag** per passenger in the screening bin. One quart bag per person limits the total liquid volume each traveler can bring and the 3 oz. container size is a security measure.

Consolidate bottles into one bag and X-ray separately to speed screening.

Be prepared. Each time TSA searches a carry-on it slows down the line. Practicing 3-1-1 will ensure a faster and easier checkpoint experience. If in doubt, put your liquids in checked luggage.

Declare larger liquids. Medications, baby formula and food, and breast milk are allowed in reasonable quantities exceeding three ounces and are not required to be in the zip-top bag. Declare these items for inspection at the checkpoint.

Come early and be patient. Heavy travel volumes and the enhanced security process may mean longer lines at security checkpoints.

Other Easy Options

Travel Rite Accessories has created the complete, carry-on, Must-Have Travel Kit. It conforms to all international air transport security regulations and includes all travel essentials: three 2-oz. bottles, four 1-oz. bottles, two .25-oz. jars, one atomizer, one package of travel towelettes and one sheet of pre-printed labels (www.travelriteaccessories.com).

Want to achieve a comfortable sleeping position on the plane? Try the new SkyWinks SleepSeat, an exclusive sleep-in-your-seat pillow and blanket set. Three components comprise the set: a neck pillow that attaches to the seatback; a lightweight blanket that provides internal arm support; and a seatback panel that fits over the top of the seat and features a small pocket for easy packing and storage. Made of wick-away performance fabric, it also includes an eye mask and earplugs (www.lovetotravelproducts.com).

And for all you glamour girls out there – why put your beauty essentials in a sandwich pouch? Kiki C makes "Glam Bags" – quart-sized zippered carry-on bags with pink zippers and pink foliage artistically covering the clear plastic. Here's the stylish way to stow and organize cosmetics, toiletries, apparel, electric chargers and other essentials. You'll call them Wrapper's Delight (www.kikic.com). You should also upgrade to Trina's trendy 3-Piece Travel Pouch Set that features three travel-ready bags to help keep you organized. The outer clear PVC bag with stylish gold detailing houses your carry-on essentials and keeps you looking posh all the way through the security check. You can store other cosmetics in the medium-sized pouch, while the mini pouch holds your ID, change and other travel necessities (www.trinastyle.com).

If you want the sexiest smile ever, do not, I repeat, do not go anywhere without the adorable travel-sized dental pouch from Oxyfresh. In it you'll find fluoride toothpaste, a must-have tongue scraper to give you sweet-smelling breath, 3 oz. of alcohol-free mouthrinse, lemon-mint breath spray, toothpicks and a toothbrush. Now you'll pucker up with confidence! (www.OxyFresh.com/ss)

Now that you've gotten through security, make sure to have these beauty items with you, in your **checked** bag. The following are some of my favorites, from snazzy potions with pizzazz, to a la mode makeup.

Passport to Pretty

Lock In Moisture With Youngblood Liquid Minerals

Here's one of my best beauty secrets. Before I put on any moisturizer, I make sure my face is moist. Either I have just washed it, and not completely dried it, or I spray on a toner. When I then use a moisturizer, it locks in and seals in the moisture – thus eliminating wrinkles. Usually I use a toner – and then I discovered **Youngblood Mineral Cosmetics**. What they offer, which is revolutionary, are liquid minerals that you can spray on your face – they're called Minerals in the Mist. They're fantastic for a wealth of reasons – but first off – the aroma. My nose just craves the fragrance of the Refresh, my favorite – it's a mix of citrus, tangerine and grapefruit – one whiff and you'll swear you're in an orange grove in Florida. Not only does this spray contain the oils of those fruits, it also contains Hematite, Malachite, Rhodolite and Zincite – to rejuvenate your skin cells, while antioxidants and Vitamins A and E protect your skin against environmental aggression. The two other scents are Restore – (citrus, grapefruit, lime and rosemary) and Recharge – (spearmint, peppermint, ginger and lime) which smells just like Doublemint gum. It's a wonder no one thought of these products before! Pauline Youngblood Soli started her career as a licensed medical esthetician, working with prominent dermatologists and plastic surgeons in the Beverly Hills area. Unsatisfied with the results she witnessed by patients using traditional cosmetic options for sensitive skin, she developed her first Natural Loose Mineral Foundation, which provided excellent coverage and a natural appearance, while still allowing skin to breathe. Her patients experienced such dramatic success with the formula that they continued using it long after their skin had healed. Before long, patients and friends convinced her to make the Natural Loose Mineral Foundation commercially available, and Pauline founded Youngblood Mineral Cosmetics in 1996. Today the company manufactures and supplies the highest-quality cosmetics to doctors, aestheticians, spas, medi-spas, and salons throughout the world. Other products in the repertoire include mineral primer, ultimate concealer, eyeshadows and the brow artiste for fully groomed eyebrows (www.ybskin.com).

Top 10 Beauty Items For Your Checked Luggage

1. **Toner.** I LOVE the blueberry-infused toner from the Cliff House Spa in Maine. It smells wonderfully sweet and is great for your skin. Spray first, then moisturize, to seal in the very-berry humectants. It's a joy (www.seacliffhouse.com).

   Another favorite: Youngblood Minerals in the Mist. "Refresh," for example, is a delicious blend of tangerine and grapefruit infused with minerals, nutrients and vitamins. Spray it on your face right before putting on moisturizer, and you'll wake up your skin to a wonderful scent (www.ybskin.com). Another scent-sational offering: Epicuren's Orange Blossom freshening mist (www.epicuren.com).

Yes, You Can Take It With You

When I was in graduate school, back in the Seventies, I walked into Henri Bendel in New York, and was entranced by the aroma. All I could smell was the enticing scent of oranges, cinnamon and cloves – and I instantly knew I had to own *whatever* that was. Now, I was a student living on a budget – but I didn't care what it cost – I **had** to have that smell and bought it I did! It was Agraria. (Today a box of the legendary potpourri goes for $50).

What got it there? Henri Bendel's legendary director, Geraldine Stutz, had smelled success when she got her first box of the bitter orange potpourri. She invited Agraria's founders, Stanford Stevenson and Maurice Gibson, to showcase Agraria at the front door of Bendel's "Scentiments" shop. It was so successful that **The New York Times** reported that "the woodsy blend from San Francisco called Agraria turned up in half the living rooms on Park Avenue."

Today, you can purchase Agraria in a "Tasselaire" – a perfumed tassel that you can pack in a suitcase and hang on a hotel doorknob, closet hook or armoire key. (How did I ever live without it?) The company also makes fragrance sheets in Agraria (as well as in lemon verbena, lavender and rosemary and balsam) which you pack in your Samsonite – or even put into your car – so you can enjoy the fragrance on your trip (www.agrariahome.com). Plus, it makes a travel kit in a plastic pouch, containing the exquisite bitter-orange aroma in shampoo, conditioner, shower gel and moisturizer. Happy travels!

2. **Wen Cleansing Conditioner by Chaz Dean**. Here's a terrific 2-in-1 product that's shampoo and conditioner in one, with no harsh sodium laurel sulfate. Especially important if you've had a Coppola Keratin straightening treatment, because the sodium laurel sulfate in most shampoos strips the keratin out of your hair. Wen Sweet Almond Mint Cleansing conditioner smells exactly like that, and also doesn't contain other harsh ingredients such as mineral oil and propylene glycol. Instead, it contains glycerin, cherry bark and rosemary extract (www.guthy-renker.com). Wen is a dynamic duo!

3. **Retin-A**. I can't live without this prescription product, which I slather all over my face, neck and décolletage. It's the gold standard of retinoids, which can make a dramatic difference in your appearance. A facelift in a tube. Make sure to buy some for only about $5 when you visit a Mexican pharmacy – a sweet price, versus the $150 it costs in the USA.

4. **Imported Toothpaste**. Why not add a little luxury to your travels  via your toothpaste? Try Marvis from Italy – minty goodness in very elegant packaging. Comes in exotic flavors such as Ginger Mint, Paradise Fruit Mint and Jasmine Mint. (For just $4.50 a tube). Or, try some from Weleda – their Calendula toothpaste tastes just like black licorice (it's full of fennel) and I swear, you'll want to eat it! $5 a tube. Also comes in unusual flavors such as plant gel (for sensitive teeth) and salt (yes, that's salt) for whitening (www.weleda.com).

Pamper your pearly whites with imported toothpaste in an exotic flavor.

5. **Lash Lengthener.** Many companies make these little marvels and I confess that they really do work. Look for lash lengtheners made by Jan Marini, Neulash and B. Kamins (www.janmarini.com, www. NeuLash.com, and www.bkamins.com). Neulash, for example, is a fast-acting formula made of potent bioengineered polypeptides containing amino and fatty acids. The company has received positive feedback from customers, who rave about having fuller, longer and darker eyelashes in just weeks.

6. **Room and Linen Sprays.** I LOVE to be in a hotel room or cruise-ship cabin that smells wonderful. That means that I take air fresheners with me to spray in the room and on my pillow and linens at night. Cuccio (www.cuccio.com) makes laboratory-strength elixirs that can be used on your towels, linens and in rooms, in luscious fragrances such as milk-and-honey, and Tuscan citrus herb with bergamot and clary sage. Originally meant for spa use, these are aromatic elixirs with a twist. Citrus Magic (www.citrusmagic. com) is 100% natural premium concentrate made from the purified, active oils taken from the peels of citrus fruit – you'll find cans of grapefruit, lemon, lime and orange, all ready to make your surroundings succulent. The time is ripe to use any and all of them. Diptyque (www.diptyque.com), the French company, also makes de-lovely room sprays, and I'm crazy about the Pomander (any time of the year) and also the Violette, which sweetens up any room space. Yankee Candle also makes a wide variety of products you can take in your travels. There are Car Gels in flavors such as lilac, Macintosh apple, pear and coconut – which make driving a dream. Or try their new Yankee Candle On-The-Go Travel sprays – use them in your car, closet, boat or any small space. They come in .15-oz. containers so you can even carry them on the plane. I love the vanilla lime scent, but there are also many others including coconut and Macintosh (www.yankeecandle.com).

Yankee Candle makes scented Car Gels and On-The-Go Travel Sprays – get a whiff!

7. **Go Smile Travel Tubes.** Green apple, fresh mint and watermelon – what a delicious way to whiten your teeth! In fact, maintaining a white smile has never tasted so good. Go Smile is the best way to wow the world with your award-winning smile. These adorable ampoules come in their own carrying case (14 count) and it's the best accessory to take on a two-week trip. Just flip-and-pop the ampoule, apply the serum with its soft applicator tip to your teeth, and you're good to go, with amazing results – no sink required. Also available: the Jet Set Kit containing tubes of AM (lemon, lime and orange) and PM (lavender and vanilla) luxury toothpaste and a travel toothbrush (www.gosmile.com).

8. **L'Oreal Elnett Satin hairspray.** For 50 years, beauty insiders were besotted with this legendary hair spray found in the elegant gold can – and it was only found in Europe (and typically smuggled back into the States). Since the Fall of 2008, however, this super little hair spray has been available at Target; it's great because you can spritz it all over your hair, and still comb it out later, with great "touchability." Elnett is the gold standard of hair sprays – so make sure to take the gilt trip (www.lorealusa.com).

9. **Vitamins.** Always make sure to have your daily vitamins with you – especially if you can find them in a gummy version (see Sidebar). I'm also a big believer in One A Day, which makes vitamins in the formulas of Women's, Women's 50+ Advantage (to support memory, concentration and bone strength), and Women's Active Mind and Body (to support mental alertness and physical energy). A little daily dose will do ya (www.oneaday.com).

10. **Sample sizes of cosmetics.** Ask your dermatologist or plastic surgeon for some of the many free samples they stock. Or make sure to get your three-free samples when you shop at Kiehl's, Ulta and Sephora, and load up at department stores when you bag the bigger sizes.

Passport To Pretty

Silk 'N Dreams makes creamy soft travel and lounging accessories that make every trip seem like First Class. You'll find downy soft contoured neck pillows, eye masks with silk-covered straps, and soft blankets, all designed to take the rough edges off travel (www.silkndreams.com).

First Class Is Oh-So-Fine

Who doesn't like flying First Class? Or Business Class? The amenities are wonderful; it's much more roomy and comfortable; the food tends to be better than that of coach; and the service is all with a smile. Here's a brief round-up and a small sample of what a few of the airlines offer in these two posh categories. Be prepared to be amazed.

British Airways – In 1996, British Airways was the first commercial airline to introduce a revolutionary flat bed. It featured individual cabins with electronically-controlled seats that convert to a six-foot, six-inch bed, allowing passengers to choose to sleep, work or relax at anytime during their journey in complete privacy. In November 2006, BA debuted "turndown service" (just like a hotel), offering slippers, blankets, cushions, crockery, cutlery and glassware that quite literally, elevate the First Class cabin. At Heathrow, Terminal 5 has six lounges within the BA terminal, collectively known as "Galleries," and can host up to 2,500 passengers. These lounges embrace a decadent new look with crystal chandeliers, fabrics by Osborne and Little, art installations and mood lighting. At Heathrow, and also at New York's JFK Airport, there's even an Elemis Travel Spa, with sleep and relaxation treatments for depart-

ing guests, and awaken and energize therapies for the arriving guest. Passengers can also request a face, foot, hand and scalp massage (www.ba.com).

Cathay Pacific Airlines – Stellar service starts in the two award-winning lounges, The Wing and The Pier, at Hong Kong International Airport. In the lounges, First Class passengers can relax in elegantly upholstered chairs, have a drink at the Long Bar, surf the Web, and enjoy a full meal at the upscale

Yummy Gummies For Adults

Finally – the world has answered my prayers. I discovered yummy gummy vitamins – for **adults.** At only 10 calories a pop. Why should Junior have all the fun? Hero Nutritionals offers delicious fruit-flavored gummy vitamins, in five versions: Multivitamin; Omega 3/6/9/ (fish-free omegas from a vegetarian source); Vitamin C and Pomegranate; CoQ10 (which promotes healthy heart and cardiovascular function); an Energy gummy that's a blend of natural vitamins and herbs for an energy boost; and lemony D3 that fosters calcium absorption. All are allergen- and gluten-free, and also don't contain any yeast, wheat, egg, soy, shellfish, or artificial colors and preservatives. The multivitamins, for example, contain natural cane juice, gelatin, and the natural flavors of orange, lemon, strawberry, cherry, pineapple and grape. They are a little joy to enjoy every day, while you also do your body a favor.

"Our customer care team reported that mom after mom would rave about how easy it was to get their kids to take vitamins thanks to our Yummi Bears. They would invariably end conversations by inquiring about a similar product for themselves," stated Jennifer Hodges, founder and CEO of Hero Nutritionals. "We continually strive to bring innovative products to market that address the nutritional needs of children, tweens and adults."

Hero Nutritionals also makes Healthy Indulgence creamy milk chocolate balls with calcium and vitamin D, to give women 100% of their recommended daily intake of calcium. This is one of the most delicious ways to prevent osteoporosis and have a daily taste treat. Ladies, all of these products are a great way to start your engines. (www.heronutritionals.com, www.sliceoflife.com).

The folks at One A Day also make delicious VitaCraves Gummies, which are complete adult multivitamin gummies formulated with ingredients to support energy and immunity. Also available as Sour Gummies too. No matter what flavor you savor, they are all delicious, and a great little present to yourself every day (www.oneaday.com).

And for more gummies galore – try Vitafusion gummy vitamins – which they claim were the very first gummies for adults on the market. The MultiVites, for example, contain 15 calories in just two, and come in three delicious flavors – berry, peach and orange – without any gluten, milk, eggs, peanuts or soy. The range of Vitafusion gummies also includes lines of Calcium, Vitamin D, Power C, Defense E, Boost B, Energy B12, and even Fiber Gummies. (The company makes the award-winning L'il Critters gummy vitamins for kids.) Who knew being a healthy adult could taste so good? (www.nwnaturalproducts.com/vitafusion)

Chew on these – and eschew all other traditional vitamins!

restaurant, The Haven, before departing on their flight. One of the unique features of The Wing are The Cabanas - five lavish spa rooms where passengers can refresh themselves before their flight and settle down for a soak in an enormous bathtub. There is also a shower, hand-basin, toilet, deck-chair, a mini-bar, and a view of the water feature. The Cabanas allow passengers to cocoon themselves in a private space.

First Class passengers also each receive a pair of Shanghai Tang pajamas and matching slippers. The First Class men's amenity kit is from Acca Kappa from Italy, while the women's is filled with products from Aesop of Australia. In Business Class, men and women receive amenity kits filled with either Dermalogica or Murad – including Dr. Murad's dee-lish, luscious pomegranate lip protector (www.murad.com). If your lips are rough or really chapped, this little miracle worker in a tube will help you, or for that matter, Stella, get your groove back (www.cathaypacific.com).

Emirates Air – Luxury starts in the lounge, which offers gourmet cuisine around the clock; an array of Arabic, Far Eastern, Western and vegetarian cuisine; and business centers with individual work stations and complimentary broadband and wireless LAN access. Complimentary airport transfers to and from the airport are available to First and Business Class passengers in many of the cities Emirates serves. Up in the air, since 2003, First Class suites costing $124,000 each were installed on Emirates' Airbus A340-500s and Boeing 777 fleet. The First Class suites, featuring privacy screens for maximum exclusivity, have massage-enabled leather seats that convert to flat beds, and offer fabric sleeping suits with slippers, down pillows and cotton-lined blankets. Other luxurious touches include a dining table, built-in vanity table and overnight amenity kit. Seven-course meals (and low-calorie meals) can be ordered from an extensive menu that might feature lobster on noodles with Thai chili, oven-roasted lamb, crème brulee and cappuccino. Award-winning wines selected by Emirates sommeliers are also served, as are champagne and Arabic coffee. The onboard entertainment system includes more than 600 channels (www.emirates.com).

Etihad Airways – The national airline of the United Arab Emirates offers private suites onboard, which include a personal wardrobe and mini-bar, 23-inch wide LCD screen featuring more than 600 hours of on-demand entertainment, 80.5-inch flatbed, in-seat massager with lumbar support, and designer amenity kits. In Abu Dhabi, Terminal 3, which is exclusively for the use of Etihad Airways, there's a full-service spa, marble showers, library, cigar bar, business center, 24-hour white-tablecloth dining, and concierge (www.etihadairways.com).

Qantas – The First Class Lounge at the Qantas Sydney terminal features a Payot Paris day spa, offering its First passengers a chance to wind down with a range of complimentary treatments, from a 30-minute express energizing facial to a 50-minute full-body massage. A selection of new treatments includes the Face Pick Me Up, a power-packed revitalizing cocktail mixed with cocoa, orange, mint and spices to make the face glow with radiance and luminosity. Body De-Stress encourages the skin's microcirculation with back exfoliation and cleansing, enhancing the skin by ridding it of dead cells and rough skin. Or prepare for the long haul ahead with Light Legs, a cooling and relaxing treatment that soothes tired limbs immediately, dispersing feelings of heaviness and discomfort; it's a relief from daily tensions using Hematite extract. Designed in tandem with the new Qantas A380 aircraft interiors, the lounge is the beginning of a seamless travel experience for premium customers – from airport to aircraft. A spectacular vertical garden – with 8,400 plants designed by internationally celebrated tropical botanist Patrick Blanc – welcomes guests at the entrance (www.qantas.com.au).

Astonishing Virgin Atlantic Services – At The Airport

Calling all jet-rosexuals! The Virgin Atlantic Clubhouse at Heathrow offers an amazing array of totally FREE treatments, specifically for Upper Class passengers (www.virgin-atlantic.com). They are based on the original Cowshed at Babington House, a distinctive 28-bedroom hotel and private members' club in the heart of Somerset, England. Named after its former occupants, Cowshed is a spa and gym offering a complete range of therapeutic treatments and products.

The treatments you can receive from Virgin Atlantic at the airport include:

COWGROOM: Express treatments designed to pamper and indulge you in the comfort of the Cowgroom chair. All treatments include Virgin Atlantic's signature shoulder massage and last 30 minutes.

SHAVE TREATMENT: A power cleanse, wet shave and massage that leaves you feeling completely refreshed for your flight. Includes:

- Shoulder Massage
- Power cleanse and invigorating scrub
- Wet shave with hot towel infusion

FACIAL: Facial pick-me-up offering a refreshing and energizing lift for dehydrated skin. Includes:

- Shoulder Massage
- Double cleanse and exfoliation
- Hot towel infusion
- Eyebrow grooming

COLLAGEN EYE TREATMENT: Concentrating on the delicate area of the eyes incorporating pressure-point massage and a collagen eye mask. Helps detoxify, reduce puffiness and combat fine lines. Includes:

- Shoulder Massage
- Double cleanse
- Pressure-point massage around eyes
- Collagen eye mask

MANICURE: A tidy-up of the hands and nails, this treatment nourishes and softens even the driest of hands. Includes:

- Filing
- Cuticle cleanup
- Hand and arm massage or polish

PEDICURE: Refreshes and revitalizes tired legs and feet as well as stimulates blood circulation. Includes:

- Cleansing and exfoliating foot soak
- Filing
- Cuticle clean-up
- Refreshing leg massage or polish

SHORTER TREATMENTS: When time is tight, consider quick 15-minute treatments such as a shoulder-and-neck massage and head massage, as well as:

EYEBROW GROOMING: Shaping and definition of your brows.

FILE AND PAINT: A quick tidy-up of your fingernails or toenails followed by a polish. This will only take 15 minutes.

ST. TROPEZ SPRAY TAN: Step into a state-of-the-art St. Tropez tanning booth for a flawless, allover tan. Choose the fully automated option or have it applied by a professional staffer.

Get a St. Tropez spray tan at the Virgin Atlantic Clubhouse at Heathrow. It's tan-fastic!

The Cowshed bath, body and face range is a collection of 100% vegetarian products made using hand-picked herbs from the walled garden at Babington House, Somerset, England. Each product is a delicate blend of herbal infusions and high-quality pure essential oils from around the world. The levels of essential oils bear a therapeutic value and can ease skin irritation, stimulate circulation and relieve stress. They contain no petrochemicals and are not tested on animals.

Holy cow! It all sounds amazing (www.cowshedproducts.com).

For more dazzling info, all you need to do is hear how the rich and famous travel. That's the next "Tour of Beauty" – in Chapter Four.

CHAPTER FOUR
Celebrity Secrets

The rich – and famous celebrities – are different from you and me. Sometimes. But not necessarily when they travel. They still suffer from dehydrating airplane and hotel air, germs and temptation from the mini-bar. (Of course when they book a suite at The Four Seasons, they get a private gym, which is certainly the case at the George V in Paris.) Read on to discover some of their insider secrets on how they make travel ever so tolerable, if not, terrific!

Joan Lunden, TV Broadcaster, www.joanlunden.com

Photo credit: Gus Butera

I grew up watching Joan Lunden as the co-host of *Good Morning America*. She left the show, but since then she's still made her mark in television. Joan's currently the host of Lifetime's Health Corner aired on Sunday mornings, and she works on about 10 media campaigns annually, for such diverse groups as Oral-B, the American Heart Association, the Colon Cancer Alliance, and Uncle Ben's – all of which are health-related.

Joan told me that she is bombarded with skincare products – "and then Dr. Murad came along and asked me to be the face of his Resurgence line of skincare." (www.murad.com)

"My makeup artist noticed the difference in my skin in just a month. 'Your skin is amazing,' she told me. 'I can't get over your skin.'" From that day forward, Joan has sworn by Resurgence – and loves the fact that Dr. Murad's products come in travel sizes. "I'm on the go all the time," Joan says.

"My secret potion is the Resurgence Age-Diffusing Serum – it's formulated for hormonal aging, which starts in every woman in her late twenties – it replenishes everything."

"Murad also offers a SPF-based Pomegranate line that's fantastic, especially the Energizing Pomegranate Lip Treatment." (It speaks in shine language – making your lips kissably soft and glossy.)

Joan is just as dedicated to her fitness regimen, especially when she travels. She has a gym in her home; a gym next door to her office; and she also has a personal trainer who comes to her home. "My trainer taught me a 10-minute routine for when I travel, so it's easy to stay on track. I take Dynabands, which I pack into my suitcase. I use them to do arms, leg lifts, obliques, abs. If you just get into the habit of exercising every day, you will be amazed at the results."

Other tips? "Water, water, water in the plane, or when getting ready to do a TV shoot. Never drink alcohol or carbonated drinks, or eat salty foods, on a plane or before a TV or photo shoot."

Another secret weapon she loves is rice blotting papers. "Keep them in your purse – put them against your skin, and instead of re-powdering your face, blot the oil on your face onto them. This is a great little secret weapon."

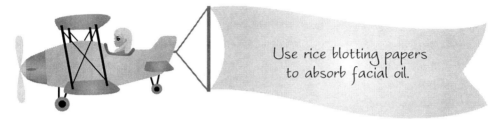

Use rice blotting papers to absorb facial oil.

Joan also re-sets her makeup throughout her travels with mineral or rose water.

She also packs a satin pillowcase "so you don't ruin your hair," ("It also prevents a wrinkled face," she says) and she always has a beauty travel case at the ready, filled with Resurgence products, L'Oreal Vitamino shampoo and conditioner, and Shu Uemura products. "I also bring food with me on the plane – a turkey sandwich, yogurt, and a banana. And I make my own trail mix."

Pack a satin pillowcase to prevent wrinkles in your hair – and on your skin.

Her other special secret weapon? Spray Hot Sets by Redken – spray it on your hair as you blow-dry, she advises, for great results. (It's a thermal setting mist that creates heat styles with staying power, www.redken.com).

Her luggage? "I only carry Tumi luggage (www.tumi.com), and almost always a carry-on only with wheels! I have really learned to pack wisely. I don't take six pairs of shoes in different colors. On a short trip I decide on a "bottom" color and that may mean black sandals, black flats or loafers that are comfortable for the trip (I NEVER travel in heels) and black heels for dressing up. A

Kim Kardashian, Reality TV Star, Checks In

"I always travel with a blanket and pillow. I have one carry-on bag with just that blanket and pillow inside…I love bargain shopping at H&M and Forever 21."

US Magazine, Feb. 23, 2009

pair of black pants for travel with tops packed to bring out color. When making appearances I take knits like St. John that won't ever wrinkle. Tissue paper helps prevent wrinkling when you pack. When I come home from a trip, I refill my "travel size" containers so they are ready to travel at a moment's notice. I travel with a purse with lots of compartments and not too heavy before being filled up – I've learned how bad it is to carry heavy bags on your shoulder."

"I am a fan of Ritz-Carlton – I just came back from the St. Thomas Ritz, and I always know if I am in a city with a Ritz I will be well cared for. I also love Cap Juluca in the Caribbean – does it get better than a pina colada on a white-sand beach? For winter I love skiing in Aspen (staying at Little Nell) and Deer Valley (staying at The Stein Ericksen Resort)."

"And finally when traveling with kids I take LOTS of things to do, books, coloring (nothing that makes noise) and also snacks and their favorite sandwiches. My kids have traveled the world with me – often while I worked – and I feel you MUST plan ahead so your kids are entertained and don't bother other people."

Today, committed to helping Americans live healthier lives, Joan is the visionary behind Camp Reveille, a women's weekend getaway on the shores of Long Lake in Naples, Maine. Camp Reveille offers busy women an opportunity to reconnect with their sense of play, jump-start their fitness, or relax and connect with other women. "In fact, I've chosen The Ritz-Carlton at Dove Mountain in Tucson, Arizona as the locale for my next session of Camp Reveille, my girl getaway wellness weekend." (www.campreveille.com)

Emme, Full-figured Supermodel, www.emmestyle.com

She's known by just her first name – Emme – probably the world's most famous full-figured supermodel. She gets paid to look good, and here's what she does when she's on the road.

"First, I find out beforehand if my hotel has a gym and a pool," says Emme. "Then I pack my bathing suit, cap, goggles and flip-flops, as well as my running shoes and gym clothes.....also be a tourist, and get out there and go for a walk," she advises.

In general, Emme advises road warriors "to always eat green every day, drink more water than usual when you're traveling, and have a treat once in a while (she was eating a piece of chocolate as we spoke).

In-flight, Emme uses a thick moisturizer such as Kiehl's Crème de Corps (www. kiehls.com) and Burt's Bees lip balm (www.burtsbees.com). "I also spritz water on my face regularly," she adds. "I also used to travel with a mini humidifier, and a white mask to protect myself from the poor air quality. I didn't care how I looked." She also takes carrots, celery and fruits to snack on, along with her own handmade GORP (good 'ole raisins and peanuts). And she's never without Trader Joe's individual packs of almonds – "They tide me over like no tomorrow," she adds.

"I travel with Louis Vuitton (www.louisvuitton.com) and Tumi (www.tumi. com) rolley bags." In her suitcase Emme swears by her essential oils in peppermint, lavender and lemon; olive oil for her rough elbows and knees; Jurlique jet lag oil (www.jurlique.com); and Laura Mercier tinted moisturizer (www.lauramercier.com).

"I really enjoy going to the Langham Hotel in Pasadena when on business in LA. I sleep well without the noise of Sunset Blvd. I can swim nice long laps and have a tremendous massage if I decide I need one. Also if I have the urge

Vanna White Checks In

I have to say, I owe much of my size-4 shape to Vanna White. That's because every day, even when I travel, I get on the treadmill while I watch her on **Wheel of Fortune.** That, followed by some **Jeopardy,** and before you know it, you've logged three e-a-s-y miles, and gotten your brain to work overtime too. I highly recommend it! Here are Vanna's time-tested travel tips.

What do you do to stay fit and in shape while you travel? I do push-ups and sit-ups and run in place while watching TV.

What do you snack on when traveling? How do you handle meals on airplanes? Nuts. I pick at the food on airplanes but try to eat before I get on the plane.

for cookies, the chef always whips some up for me...you can't get any better than that!"

Cheryl Tiegs, Iconic Supermodel, www.agelesswomanonline.com

Cheryl Tiegs has been modeling since she was 18 years old, and her beautiful face has graced practically every magazine cover imaginable, everything from *Glamour* to *Sports Illustrated's* swimsuit issue. And who can forget the stunning poster of her in that pink bikini? I had the pleasure of interviewing Cheryl, who told me that as part of her modeling career, "I've traveled all over the world – First Class, in canoes, by foot, and every which way."

Her beauty routine onboard the plane? "I don't change my habits from when I'm off the plane to when I'm on one," Cheryl said. "I eat protein and vegetables, with no bread or dessert. Or I might have some nuts. It's easy to have chicken with asparagus and salad – there you go. You can easily do it at a restaurant." The same simplicity goes for her beauty routine. "I put on my skincare before I leave the house for the airport," she told me. "I have a line of skincare, Ageless Woman – they have a great wrinkle relaxer and smoother." Then, before the plane touches down, "I put on some cosmetics before landing," Cheryl said.

To maintain her flawless figure, Cheryl exercises and wears a pedometer – every day! "The key is to walk 10,000 steps – Oh my God, I love my pedometer," Cheryl told me. She added: "I run around my property or jog in place watching *Larry King*. It really helps with the weight situation."

When traveling, Cheryl has been known to bring along a jumprope, to help her stay in shape. "I was just in Israel, jumping rope on the Tel Aviv boardwalk."

Another one of her traveling diet tricks is to request that her hotel put a scale in her room. "I'm hooked on weighing myself every morning," she says. She also spends one hour daily in quiet meditation. "I'm addicted to it," she explains.

Cheryl also never checks her luggage and has some great packing tips. "I'll go two weeks with carry-on. Beyond that I FedEx my luggage," she explained. "I can FedEx three days in advance and it turns out to be relatively inexpensive, especially now that airlines are charging you for bags. I even use FedEx Ground on the return home. I've gone as far as Africa this way, just with carry-on." That's amazing!

What do you bring on the plane with you for snacking and for your comfort?
Usually granola bars, raw almonds and herbal tea.

What do you pack in your suitcase, as it relates to travel/health/beauty/fitness?
I pack as little as I can. I always do carry-on so I leave the facial masks, etc., at home till I return. I do bring yarn for crocheting!

Do you have a beauty-grooming/health/fitness item/product that you swear by or can't live without?
I like washing the makeup off my face with Perfectly Clean by Estee Lauder (www.esteelauder. com). It lathers up nicely and seems to remove the makeup well. I use a washcloth when I do it.

How do you deal with jet lag?
I try and get on the time zone I'm traveling to (while I'm there and when I come home).

How do you stay in shape?
I exercise at least five days a week. I spin, run, lift light weights, do sit-ups and push-ups (www.Vannastyle.com).

Brian Williams, Anchor of "NBC Nightly News," Checks In

"I do try (to take care of myself), but I travel a lot, and it's hard to eat anything healthy in the back of a cab or on an airplane. It doesn't help that I am blissfully in love with mall food courts. My problem is limiting the choices. I will do a slice at Sbarro, or I'll go to A&W – their cheeseburgers are underrated, and need I say more about a cold mug of frosty root beer? Cinnabon exhaust fumes have a hold over me like crack cocaine would over an addict. And when I'm on the road and see that friendly Arby's, Cracker Barrel, or Waffle House sign, it might as well read, 'Brian, Welcome Home.'"

Parade Magazine, Nov. 16, 2008

OK – so how does Cheryl do it - with just **one bag**? Here's Cheryl's advice: "Get five or six T-shirts, and roll them up in a Ziploc bag. It's a small package. Then take five or six little Indian skirts, and squish and roll those into a Ziploc. And I always take pashminas or shawls – they add color and protect me from the sun. You roll those up too. Take one pair of day shoes, one pair of night shoes or sandals, and one athletic shoe. That's it." Cheryl only wears Nike slip-ons when traveling, because they make it easier to get through security checks. "And I always bring slippers," she explained. In addition, she usually carries a pillowcase, which she can stuff with shirts or blankets, so she has a soft pillow on the plane, now that most planes don't stock them anymore.

So where does this famous model, who has access to the world's best designers, shop? Cheryl's favorite places to shop around the world are the marketplaces. "I was in Venice and saw some amazing La Perla underwear, and I figured I would just buy some back home in Beverly Hills – but, as it turns out, they didn't stock it. That was a lesson learned," she explained.

Her favorite destination, by far, is the Seychelles. "I like to go to a place that's very, very quiet." Along with that, she said, "I might also rent a villa or chateau in the south of France or in Italy, so you feel a part of the community, as opposed to checking into a hotel."

FedEx your luggage to your destination, to make your journey all-the-easier.

Nancy O'Dell, Broadcast Journalist, and Author of *Full of Life: Mom-to-Mom Tips I Wish Someone Told Me When I Was Pregnant* (Simon Spotlight), and Founder of Bettysbattle.org, a website created in memory of her mother who died of ALS, www.nancyodell.com

It would be hard to keep up with Nancy O'Dell, the stunning blonde who, for 13 years, was the on-air anchor of *Access Hollywood*, the long-running hit TV show. Today, Nancy is an entrepreneur and business woman, who is launching her own line of furniture, as well as a jewelry collection. In 2009, she was awarded the inaugural Beautiful Humanitarian Award by the Professional Beauty Association, given to a public figure who exemplifies beauty inside and out.

Today, Nancy is the spokesperson for Rusk Hair Products – which is natural for her, since she fell in love with the entire brand years ago. "I have been a huge Rusk fan, forever," she says. "All of the TV stylists used Rusk on me, and they're super. I loaded up on them. I even have an extra set of them just for travel." (www.rusk1.com)

She swears by Rusk W8less Hairspray, in a small can that she can pack into her luggage. "It's the best product on the market," she says. "I put it on at 8AM and it's still good at 6PM. It's one of my favorite travel items." Her other favorite Rusk go-to items include Deepshine oil – "My hair is styled nonstop and this makes it soft and silky" – plus Deepshine Phyto-Marine Lusterizer. "It's a great pick-me-up after a flight, to prevent frizz and even enhance your highlights."

"I'm a big traveler – I'm on the road twice a month," adds Nancy. "My baby girl Ashby is even accustomed to going with me. As soon as she sees security at the airport, she knows to take her shoes off – and she's only 2 1/2 years old!"

Nancy typically flies First Class, and brings her own food. One product that she can't live without is her Isagenix Cleanse. "I love it – it's amazing," she told me. "It makes you lose weight easily. I tend to do it for 9-11 days, and then eat normally. It just makes you feel better." On the plane, she'll bring her Isagenix Cleanse, as well as organic fruit, celery and carrots, and maybe even a small salad, plus almonds (www.isagenix.com).

For her comfort and well-being on the plane, Nancy brings Clinique's Dramatically Different Moisturizer (www.clinique.com) plus Thymes Filigree hand cream (www.thymes.com). "It's the best smell ever," says Nancy. "My husband loves it too – he gives me massages with it." Another item she can't live without is her Cle de Peau foundation. "Oh my God, it's expensive – but worth it," she admits. "I need things that last all day long, and this goes on so smoothly. I don't even use powder. I just put blush on top of it. I couldn't live without it (www.cledepeau-beaute.com). But the best thing, which is great for travel, is the BaByliss U-Styler Iron that straightens and curls my hair – it does both (www.babylisspro.co.uk). It's fabulous for travel because it eliminates bringing two hair tools."

This blonde beauty also has other products that keep her looking glamorous. OPI nail polish (www.opi.com). Diorshow mascara (www.dior.com). Guerlain face bronzer (www.guerlain.com). And Sally Hansen spray-on tanner (www.sallyhansen.com). "You get Barbie legs from it," she said with a laugh. "It smoothes out your legs – I love it."

Her luggage is Samsonite (www.samsonite.com). "I just got a new set, and it's not too expensive, but it acts like it is. All four wheels go every which way." When traveling, she wears flats, Puma shoes, or little boots, with which she can wear socks, to keep her toes warm.

Nancy always watches her weight, especially when traveling. "I'm more careful about what I eat on the road," she explains. For exercise, she might visit the gym, or run at her destination. And she always makes sure to leave enough time for shopping. "I love the Nine West shoe store in New York – they are always stockpiled with incredible shoes that are very affordable. And I love the pashminas that you can buy on the streets of New York for next-to-nothing."

When it comes to favorite spas, there's only one destination for her: Bacara Spa in Santa Barbara, Calif. "My husband Keith and I got married there, and it's filled with great memories, as well as an amazing spa and restaurants, beautiful rooms and gorgeous grounds." (www.bacararesort.com)

Opera Soprano Deborah Voigt, one of the world's leading dramatic sopranos, internationally revered in the operas of Richard Wagner and Richard Strauss, www.deborahvoigt.com

When you're on the road nine months of the year, like Deborah is, you need to find ways to make your life happy and comfortable. For Deborah, the secret is her little Yorkshire terrier, named Steinway (like the piano). "He travels much better than me," says Deborah. "He is just five pounds and sits under the seat in front of me on a plane. He is the key to keeping me happy on the road, because traveling is exhausting and depressing. I never anticipated I'd spend this much time on the road." And that's not all Deborah does. "I put flowers and candles in whatever residence I'm in, to create some semblance of home. The dog helps in that respect too. I like my hotel to be quiet, with a lot of light, and not a walk-up. With a grocery store nearby, 24/7 room service and with a spa attached, all the better." She also brings a personal humidifier with her – "I put it next to the bed. The rooms are so bloody dry – that's deadly for singers." Deborah also takes a tennis ball with her: "I have horrible arthritis in my feet, and I use the tennis ball to roll my foot on the plane. It's kind of silly, but it works."

Set out flowers and candles in the room at your destination, to make the surroundings serene and pretty.

To avoid jet lag, says Deborah, "I switch my watch to whatever time zone I'm in. And it hits me on Day Three more than anything else. It's the worst. On that third day I have to be slapped around at rehearsals, when we start at the ungodly hour of 10AM."

Cindy Crawford Checks In

Supermodel Cindy Crawford travels with superlative sleepwear. "I always take a pretty nightgown when I travel so I feel a little bit at home."

"Welcome To My Life," InStyle, October 2009

On the plane, "I tend not to eat, as the food is really bad. I take nuts, trail mix, a little protein (along with a music score, packed in her bag). I might pick at salad or soup. If I'm on a diet, I order a special meal. Or I'll eat when I'm on the ground. I'm a turkey-on-white-kind-of-girl." She also carries Evian mist bottles. "Dehydration is the worst for singers," Deborah says. "I slather on moisturizer I get from the duty-free shop. I love Guerlain's Super Aqua Serum. It smells really nice and has a nice sheen. (www.guerlain.com). I use Aveda Hand-Relief Cream (www.aveda.com). I really love that product, and its homeopathic smell. I swear by Burt's Bees cuticle rub. It's really helpful. I have terrible nails and they do better when I smear that on (www.burtsbees.com). I do most of my shopping at the duty-free shop, and I love Yves Saint Laurent's Touche Eclat (www.yslbeautyus.com). I have a serious problem with dark circles, due to dehydration."

Deborah also just discovered what she says is a "really great" mascara: Blinc (www.blincinc.com). "It's like cement. I always find myself pulling at my lashes, and with this, I don't. It's really waterproof and yet it doesn't smear."

For exercise, "I try to take a walk immediately after landing. I have a lifetime of struggling with my weight and exercise. Swimming at a hotel pool is usually good for me. I also do stretching with a stretch band."

Lisa Lillien, aka "Hungry Girl," www.hungry-girl.com

Lisa is the "foodologist" and creator of the wildly popular Hungry Girl website and cookbooks that have made *The New York Times* bestseller lists. Over a million people devour her daily email blast, filled with diet "tips and tricks for hungry chicks." I'm definitely one of them – I love to read her daily newsletter, and you should too.

"I'm a protein maniac," says Lisa. "I always carry emergency snacks with me. I take 100-calorie almond packs, beef or turkey jerky, or even soy jerky and an apple."

"I eat the meals on the plane – I special-order the low-calorie meal, which is usually the best option."

Dolly Parton Checks In

"My husband and I travel a lot by RV. I guess that's because I grew up on tour buses.....We like staying in cheap hotels – heck, if I can sneak into a Day's Inn, I'm there…You don't need to be fancy to travel well. You just need to be curious and willing."

"One on One," **National** *Geographic Traveler,* **July/ August 2009**

In restaurants, "I'm good at navigating menus. I have my own method of dining out or ordering out: entrees that are baked, broiled or grilled, with a double order of veggies instead of a starch. And I love appetizers – I always get a salad or shrimp or a broth soup."

To stay in shape, Lisa stays in hotels that have 24/7 gyms. "I work out at night," she says.

In her Tumi luggage she brings "Everything I use at home – I bring a GIANT bag of cosmetics – I use a lot of Kiehl's and MAC, as well as Paula Dorf eye pencil in Baby Eyes. And Smashbox PhotoFinish. I love that." (www.kiehls.com, www.maccosmetics.com, www.pauladorf.com, www.smashbox.com)

If she has an hour to kill when traveling, Lisa shops. "I love to shop. And I love Loehmann's – the more obscure the location, the better stuff they have."

Ivana Trump Checks In

I've always been a big fan of Ivana Trump. I met her in person years ago, in her stunning New York townhouse, when she launched a magazine called ***Ivana's Living in Style***. She was warm, gracious, and beautiful – with killer legs. She graciously granted me this interview about her travel regimen.

What do you do to stay fit and in shape while you travel?
I spend so much of my time flying to my various business meetings, so I've perfected the 100-meter-dash to airport gates. And I walk hotel stairs and don't use the elevator! They're quick, free, and get the heart rate going.

What are some of your in-flight beauty-grooming/health tips and tricks?
Moisturizers – lipgloss, anything to keep skin and hair sleek and supple. And sleep; long flights are a great way to indulge in beauty sleep.

Do you have any beauty-grooming/health/fitness tactics that you use at your destination?
Sit in the sun for one hour – it really helps with jet lag. I find the sun very restorative, and after a long soak in a shower or tub, I'm on local time.

What do you snack on when traveling? How do you handle meals on airplanes?
I bring my own yogurt, or a health drink in a thermos. It all helps beat jet lag and calories.

What do you bring on the plane with you for snacking and for your comfort?
Cashmere blanket or a huge wraparound cashmere cape (depending on the weather). I'm not the world's biggest eater, nor its pickiest, so fresh fruit as well as a veggie plate are just fine by me.

What do you pack in your suitcase, as it relates to travel/health/beauty/fitness?
Makeup – it's an indulgence, but I love to use brands I feel secure with. Of course, if I'm visiting one of my homes around the world, I keep full set-ups of everything I love and need on hand. Making life easy is what it's all about.

What are your favorite beauty-grooming brands and products that you use in your travels?

Crème de la Mer creams and products – they are very expensive, but when you see the wonderful results all the time, then they're worth the extra money (www. cremedelamer.com).

When you arrive at your destination, where do you go and what are some of your favorite spas/beauty treatments/fitness plans?

It begins with the sun, then a relaxing spa treatment (or two)… a wonderful, relaxing swim, and a short visit to the gym. Then I'm ready for action.

Do you have a beauty-grooming/health/fitness item/product that you swear by or can't live without?

Maybelline Mascara – I've tried everything but always come back to that standard pink-and-green wand! Three coats with Maybelline, and you don't need false lashes. It never runs, but responds quickly to a good remover (www.maybelline.com).

Do you have an offbeat beauty/grooming/fitness tip?

I find that some healthy local water and some freshly sliced lemon slices really revive me. And, the lemon slices are also good to place on the eyes to make them calm and clear.

How do you deal with jet lag?

Ignore it! There's just no time for it really. As I said, a little relaxation, a jolt to the system, and I'm ready to go. It doesn't matter what time I arrive where, I am always ready to go… to a fashion show, business meeting, or event. And, I catch my sleep on local time.

What luggage do you use in your travels?

Many Louis Vuitton bags – some almost vintage at this point I've had them so long (www.louisvuitton.com).

What purse do you travel with?

Domenico Vacca – crocodile – it holds everything, and makes me feel secure and elegant (www.domenicovacca.com).

Soprano Renee Fleming Checks In

"Since so much of my adult life has been spent 'en route,' I have discovered that it's in my best interest to pack efficiently and as quickly as possibly...I hang out all potential clothing on the canopy of my bed and then cull...Adding the shoes, makeup, jewelry and hair products for a concert can easily take up half of one large suitcase...Ziploc bags are invaluable for packing lingerie....I prefer the best-quality Travelpro luggage, since it is light and relatively inexpensive."

"The Soprano and Her Suitcase," *Four Seasons Magazine*, Issue One 2010

What about shoes?

Manolo Blahnik lower heel or Chanel flats (www.manoloblahnik.com, www.chanel.com). I used to wear my super-high heels. But I find that running through airports, dodging people, getting through security, it's easier to do it in "running" shoes. So, flats it is.

What's your favorite destination or resort/hotel/spa, and why?

My homes – I have them in the Czech Republic, London, St. Tropez, Palm Beach, Miami, and of course, New York. They are heaven for me, my safe haven.

Socialite Ivana Trump swears by Hall-of-Fame Beauty product Maybelline Great Lash mascara.

Wendie Malick, Actress

I used to admire Wendie's long, lean, lithe body, when she played Martin Crane's girlfriend on the hit TV show *Frasier*. How does she get those good looks? "My trainer, Patty Winter," she says. "I work out with a fabulous group of women in a little dojo. Some of us have been together almost 18 years. Patty's class is very Pilates/core based. I attribute this work to helping keep me toned and flexible and I know it's improved my posture. I can take it 'on the road' with me and do it virtually anywhere without equipment." Wendie also walks at her destination, "and I also travel with those little core reformer bands and can do my own form of Pilates if there isn't a gym." She also eats right, especially on the plane. "I always travel with baggies of raw almonds and cashews, and either order the vegetarian meal or just eat the salad and veggies. I'm a 'pesca-tarian' (wild caught fish only). Sometimes I carry on a sandwich or salad. No dessert. And LOTS of water."

Her swear-by items include those by Liz Earle (www.uk.lizearle.com). "I love Liz Earle's line of cleansers and moisturizers. I'm also a big fan of Mychelle's line, particularly their firming serum, pumpkin moisturizer and fruit enzyme cleanser." (www.Mychelle.com)

Wendie hates to check her luggage – that's why she only takes carry-on and packs clothing that she can mix and match. She prefers to travel in Lululemon attire, and always takes a small spray vial of her favorite scent, such as "Beach" by Norma Kamali. And when Wendie arrives at her destination, she sprays the lightbulbs in her hotel room, so the fragrance gracefully wafts through the air!

Carmindy, Makeup Artist on *What Not to Wear* on TLC, and Author of three beauty books, *The 5-Minute Face* (Harpers Studios), *Get Positively Beautiful* (Center Street Publishing), and *Crazy Busy Beautiful* (Harpers Studios), www.Carmindy.com

Carmindy has painted faces in the studios of Paris, on the beaches of Brazil, and on the streets of Havana. She's lived in Los Angeles, Milan, Miami, and now makes her home in New York, where she has established herself as a top fashion makeup artist. "Every week I'm on a plane," Carmindy told me. "I travel throughout the US and Canada, and I'm working on my third book. I make in-store appearances at drugstores, I have a house in Miami, and I'm in London a lot too. Any free weekend I'm jumping on a plane with my girlfriends." And when she's traveling there, she says "I'm never without my Greens Protein Bar – they're covered in dark chocolate and they're my favorite. I can't be on a plane without them." (The peanut butter variety has 260 calories in one bar, www.greensplus.com.) Carmindy also takes raw almonds, fruit, and powdered green matcha tea. "It makes green-tea cocoa. Sometimes I take tuna jerky, if I need a little piece of protein. And I drink tons of water."

Carmindy, who recently launched her line of Natural Beauty cosmetics by Sally Hansen (www.sallyhansennaturalbeauty.com) has, not surprisingly, a very specific beauty routine. "I slather on moisturizer when I get on a plane. I wear no makeup. And midflight, I reapply moisturizer. Then I whip out my 'five-minute face' before landing." She explained that to achieve the five-minute face, you must do the following: Apply foundation; tap on concealer; add cream highlighter to your cheekbones, inner corner of your eyes and under the browbone; dust your skin's T-Zone with powder; smudge eyeliner in chocolate at the lash line; tap cream blush onto the apples of your cheeks; sweep on mascara; add some lipgloss – "and you're good to go." Carmindy swears by Skinceuticals sunscreen (www.skinceuticals.com) saying, "I never go anywhere without it," and also loves Crème de la Mer moisturizer (www.cremedelamer) and her Sally Hansen foundation and cream blush. She's also crazy about Blinc mascara (www.blincinc.com) – "I love it, it's nice and light – it's a polymer – and it doesn't smudge or budge, yet it comes off with water."

Carmindy travels with Tumi (www.tumi.com) – "I have the whole line, all black leather, and it's the best. They'll also fix it at any Tumi store at the airport." When it comes to purses, "I have a different one every month." In Paris recently, she bought a Zadig & Voltaire purse at their eponymous store (www.zadig-et-voltaire.com). "It has tons of pockets for your passport and iPod, and I can put in a cashmere throw. I like to get funky bohemian purses."

And of all the places in the world, Carmindy loves to shop for beauty products in Bora Bora. "I bought all the oils, in frangipani and coconut, which I mixed with moisturizers. I bought honey perfume. I went to different spas and also to roadside stands." Carmindy is also crazy about 100% argan oil. "I stumbled on it in London at my favorite market, the Borough Market. I got it really cheap.

You can even eat it. I mix it with moisturizer and essential oils for my body, or I put it on my hands and then put on cotton gloves."

One thing that travel has taught her: " I love to see the universal beauty that all women possess, everything from Masai women to Greek women – you can appreciate unique beauty, and when you travel you see beauty everywhere. Travel opens up your mind."

Leeza Gibbons, Broadcaster, www.leezagibbons.com

She has been called a social entrepreneur, but if you ask Leeza Gibbons what she does, she'll simply answer, "I'm a story-teller." From television news journalist and host, to radio personality, producer and business woman, Leeza has been entering America's living rooms for more than 25 years.

What do you do to stay fit and in shape while you travel?
I climb the stairs of the fire escapes and I always bring my resistance bands....they go in the outside zipper of my bag and are immediately put to use.

How do you stay fit when you are time-crunched in your travels? What if there's no access to a gym?
My Pilate's ring/circle is very handy for travel when there's no gym. It fits in my carry-on bag and I can get an entire full body workout!

What are some of your in-flight beauty-grooming/health tips and tricks?
I use my Sheer Cover facial mist when I'm on a flight longer than 50 minutes (www.sheercover.com). It keeps my skin hydrated and is a great pick-me-up for travel-weary arrivals.

What do you snack on when traveling? How do you handle meals on airplanes?

Just about the only thing that works for me is: "Just say NO!" Of course, that doesn't always come out of my mouth when they are opening up the bread basket and asking me if I'd like foccacia or sourdough! When I am religious about drinking my water, I can usually keep my cravings in check. If I'm having a glass of red wine on an international flight, I will have two glasses of water for every glass of wine. Breakfast on planes is usually an easy time to stay on target....cereal, nonfat milk and a piece of fruit is available on any flight across the globe it seems! When I don't have time to call ahead and get a low-sodium meal, or a raw veggie salad (hold the dressing) - I throw a couple of energy bars in my bag - just in case. Also, I always feel deprived when it comes to dessert, so I have been known to pack a small bag of dark chocolate-covered almonds!

What do you pack in your suitcase, as it relates to travel/health/beauty/fitness?

Sheer Cover mineral powder foundation. No matter how sleep-deprived I am, a little brush of the minerals will immediately give my dull skin a blast of luminosity! I have turned on lots of flight attendants to Sheer Cover because they always comment on my skin! And Neutrogena sesame bath oil. I lather it on, morning and night (www.neutrogena.com).

What are your favorite beauty-grooming brands and products that you use in your travels?

Well, I am NEVER without my Binaca breath spray…one in my purse, one in my suitcase (www.binaca.com). I usually have my OPI cuticle oil too since my nail beds get really cracked and dry when I travel (www.opi.com).

Do you have a beauty-grooming/health/fitness item/product that you swear by or can't live without?

Hands down, my Sheer Cover Base Perfector! It's really like a treatment because it soothes irritated skin and "fills in" my fine lines so that my concealer can glide on effortlessly. It also minimizes the look of enlarged pores.

Do you have an offbeat beauty/grooming/fitness tip?

I use BIG SEXY HAIR "Backcomb in a Bottle" spray and a few ornamental hair pins to create volume and lasting power when I won't have time for a blow-dry or hot iron (www.sexyhair.com/big.htm). I can put my hair up while I'm waiting for everyone to get their bags out of the overhead compartment.

How do you deal with jet lag?

One of my special skills is that I can usually be asleep before the plane has left the gate. I have a soft scarf that I often drape over my head (scary visual, I know!) but it cuts out the light and lets the flight attendants know not to ask me if I need anything. If I'm on a long flight, I will remove my makeup and put moisturizer on (I love Cindy Crawford's Meaningful Beauty, www.meaningfulbeauty.com). I have also started drinking ZAMU, it has tons of minerals and ingredients, which instantly make me feel better. I have to pack it in my checked bag, but I pour it over ice as soon as I arrive.

Courteney Cox Checks In

As reported in *InStyle*, Courteney Cox travels with men's pajama bottoms, which she pairs with a Petit Bateau tank top for sleeping, as well as a baby pillow and linens from D. Porthault. She prefers her face against her very own sheets.

What luggage do you use in your travels?

BURTON....I love these bags...they are designed for skiing, but they are so light with a simple design and separate compartments that make sense (www.burton.com). Mine are red plaid...so when I have to check a bag, mine is easy to spot!

What purse do you travel with?

My black, square Bottega Veneta....it's open on the top and big enough for me to throw my laptop in, along with research, passport, makeup, snacks, hairbrush, exercise bands, floss and facial mist....along with the occasional lavender-scented travel candle (www.bottegaveneta.com).

What about shoes?

My black, flat boots - always.

What's your favorite destination or resort/hotel/spa, and why?

The One and Only Palmilla in Cabo! Serene, good food, private butlers who are discreet, views that are magnificent and massages that will change your life.

Do you have a favorite bargain shopping tip, about some "fabulous find" you discovered during your travels – on cosmetics or fashion or snack foods?

I found this organic oil called "Glow" by Nature's Inventory. I use it at night on my neck and décolleté, but I rub it on my temples in the morning and I get a little aromatherapy lift! (www.naturesinventory.com)

Favorite airline and why:

Virgin Atlantic....Upper Class! It's like being on vacation at 30 thousand feet. The duvets are better than a five-star hotel and the minute I put on the black sleeping pajamas they give you, I'm totally gone!

Susie Coelho, Lifestyle Expert, Bestselling Author with four books, and Television Personality (host of two prime-time series: *Surprise Gardener* and *Outer Spaces* on HGTV), www.susiecoelho.com

"I travel a lot," says Susie Coelho, a former Ford model. "I travel anywhere from once a month to three or four times a month. It's a pretty grueling schedule with early morning TV, meetings, appearances and then late-night flights." Susie says she's been "into" nutrition since her twenties in order to keep her energy high and her body in top shape. "My mom was a vegetarian and taught me to eat well. I try and continue those good habits on the road even though it's hard sometimes to get healthy food in airports. I always buy snacks such as Fuji apples (they're hard and crisp) and fresh almonds. I love rice cakes with white miso spread and fresh raw sliced tofu! It's phenomenal. I've turned a lot of my model and actress friends onto it over the years. Everyone loves it and it's so low-calorie. I also love Liquid Aminos which you can buy at the health food store. If I'm trying to lose some weight, I use this on salads and fresh or steamed veggies instead of dressing. It's healthy and salty."

"The main thing about traveling on planes is that you get very dehydrated so you need lots of water. Sodas are not a great thing – too much sugar and chemicals. And the more water you drink, the less hungry you are. It fills your tummy."

She also never travels without a cashmere wrap. "This is a must-have item as far as I'm concerned."

One of her swear-by cosmetics is Dermalogica Renewal Lip complex (www.dermalogica.com). "It's amazing. A makeup artist turned me on to it. It feels like silicone. It's so thin but not a gloss or balm. It makes your lips feel like a million bucks."

Passport to Pretty

Actress Rachel Bilson Checks In

Rachel's must-have travel essentials are a cashmere shawl and cozy socks for the plane. She also makes and takes her own egg-salad sandwich, which she pairs with a Hershey's Cookies 'n' Crème chocolate bar, plus Bold Party Blend Chex Mix, because she loves sweet and salty.

"Your Look," as reported in *InStyle*, **Nov. 2009**

At home, Susie is a frequent exerciser. "I run, take classes, spin and do yoga. When I travel, I don't like working out in a gym. I prefer doing something different. I actually schedule flights so I have time to run or walk afterwards. In New York, I stay near Central Park so that I can walk or run around the reservoir. When I travel, I make sure I enjoy the trip – by taking a walk, meeting friends, going to fun restaurants or shopping. I make it enjoyable."

"I'm a big foodie," she continued. "I love experiencing good restaurants. I plan my meetings around my meals! I love Topaz Thai on 56th Street in New York and Pastis down in the Meat Packing District. But my favorite place that I never miss in New York is Soba Nippon next to Rockefeller Center on 52nd. Their chicken tofu noodle salad is to die for!"

She carries her own brand of luggage, which she designed for Mervyn's Department Stores, and carries a lightweight nylon bag, instead of lugging a leather carry-all when she travels. "And I always wear a Chanel black blazer that I found at a consignment store in Arizona for about $250. It's a great piece. Gorgeous! I throw on pearls and a white T-shirt and I'm ready to go anywhere."

Susie loves to shop at sample sales whenever she can, and lately, that's where she says she finds the most values. "I get the best prices and incredible designers! I love the Robert Rodriguez sample sale at the California Mart in LA. The most expensive piece I bought was a leather jacket that would have been well over $1,000 at retail. I bought it for $150. Now that's the way to shop during a tough economy!"

India Hicks, Crabtree & Evelyn Creative Partner, Author, Designer and "Mum of four," (www.indiahicks.com, www.crabtree-evelyn.com)

Photo credit: JOSEPH

You probably know India Hicks best as the host of the hit TV show *Top Design*. But she is also a fashion model and the goddaughter of Prince Charles, the Prince of Wales. In fact, she was a bridesmaid in the wedding of Prince Charles and Lady Diana. Here's how India looks so great in her travels.

What do you do to stay fit and in shape while you travel?

I am currently in training for the London Marathon, so I run, wherever I am! There is nothing more invigorating than an hour to yourself, out of doors, breathing fresh air, without the distraction of a BlackBerry or a cranky child. I recently ran in thick snow, dressed in my 12-year old's football kit, and an ancient pair of hiking boots (so as to preserve my marathon clothes and sneakers). There are no excuses for not getting motivated when traveling.

How do you stay fit when you are time-crunched in your travels? What if there's no access to a gym?

Time is an issue, after a late business dinner or suffering from jet lag setting the alarm clock for an early morning run can be intimidating. You have to show self-discipline. I have not seen the inside of a gym for over a decade. I need my runs to be outside, especially if I am spending the rest of the day inside.

What are some of your in-flight beauty-grooming/health tips and tricks?

Moisturizing is the most important thing – body as well as face. Before getting on the plane I apply moisturizer full of natural emollients – my favorite is my India Hicks Island Night Body Cream, which was formulated with heaps of coconut and olive oils as well as silk amino acids and crushed pearl.

What do you snack on when traveling? How do you handle meals on airplanes?

Bagels and twiglets (whole-wheat sticks covered in marmite, the yeast extract, an English favorite).

What do you pack in your suitcase, as it relates to travel/health/beauty/fitness?

I always take my Island Living scented candle. It was formulated to capture the scents of the Bahamian island where I live, and is a reminder of home.

What are your favorite beauty-grooming brands and products that you use in your travels?

Dr. Hauschka face creams (www.drhauschka.com), which are natural and the perfect size for a few days or even weeks. My Mason and Pearson hairbrush – familiar and excellent. I have brushed my hair with this brand of brush since the day I was born.

Do you have an offbeat beauty/grooming/fitness tip?

When on a beach holiday, I mix fine sand with olive oil, and few drops of peppermint oil. The result is a really natural, inexpensive, beneficial exfoliator.

How do you deal with jet lag?

I set my clock to the time at my destination when I get on a plane and ignore my body clock. Mind over matter.

Padma Lakshmi Checks In

"I always have a cashmere shawl in my carry-on to keep me cozy on flights."

"Guest Editor Padma's Picks," *Shape Magazine*, March 2010

What luggage do you use in your travels?
L.L. Bean carry-on cases, with an extendable zipper, essential, as I inevitably return to the island with more than I left (www.llbean.com).

What purse do you travel with?
A very old, tired, and battered, tanned leather wallet. No one is going to think this is worthy of stealing.

What about shoes?
Depends on the trip. A quick dash to Miami will be in Havaianas flip-flops. A business trip to New York: high-heeled boots. Taking my kids on holiday: Converse all-stars.

What's your favorite destination or resort/hotel/spa, and why?
This changes all the time. I am lucky enough to travel a great deal, and have seen most corners of the world, but the Jalousie Plantation in St. Lucia has the most remarkable spa, and treehouses set in a rainforest, where you can have a world-class massage.

Do you have a favorite bargain-shopping tip, about some "fabulous find" you discovered during your travels – on cosmetics or fashion or snack foods?
After a long-haul flight I will add two packets of Eboost to 1.5 liters of water. It offers brilliant all-natural results for energy, immunity, recovery and focus. A very inexpensive way to stay on track (www.eboost.com).

Favorite airline and why:
Jet Blue, blue terra chips, streaming TV and no class discrimination.

Cruising at 35,000 feet is quite different than cruising on a large passenger ship. Don't miss the boat – read Chapter Five to discover amazing ways to make the most of your voyage, while you stay thin, healthy, and beautiful. So, as the Fifties song says, "C'mon babe, you've got nothin' to lose, won't you let me take you on a Sea Cruise?"

Cruise Control

You may be shocked to read this, but the average weight gain when you cruise is one pound per day. One pound a day! That's due to all of the delicacies, treats, sweets and delectables that cruise ships offer, to tempt you, all day long.

I once interviewed cruise staffers, who told me that on 15-day Alaska cruises they can actually see passengers, who, in just two weeks, have gained 14 or 15 pounds. Some folks, they said, even bring one suitcase filled with clothes one size *larger*, so they have something to wear at the *end* of their trip, when they have piled on the pounds.

It's shocking to me that some people – and we have witnessed this ourselves – have breakfast in the main dining room, followed by one lunch out on the pool deck, followed by yet another lunch in the main dining room. Followed by afternoon tea. Maybe a slab of Sicilian pizza or ice cream between meals. Perhaps dinner in their suite, followed by another dinner in the dining room. A trip to the midnight buffet. And so it goes.

It certainly doesn't have to be this way.

In fact, my philosophy of cruising is that you can actually have the cruise company make and bake you whatever you want – so why not ask them for something you can feel good – and guilt-free – about eating? Before embarkation many cruise lines will ask you for your dietary requests and restrictions – and you can tell them you're on a lowfat diet, or you need a certain-calorie yogurt, or a special lowfat bread. (We do this all the time.) Then, when you get on the ship, usually the first night, you can meet with the Executive Chef – and tell him what you want during the course of your trip. Here's what we usually request, and what always "floats my boat."

- ◆ Lowfat tuna fish sandwiches on rye bread (we even bring our own diet mayo to give to the chef)

- ◆ Lowfat yogurt – 100 calories in 6 or 8 oz.

- ◆ Lowfat bread/rolls made with little to no oil

Want a guilt-free tuna sandwich? Bring your own lowfat mayonnaise onboard, and give it to the Executive Chef.

Then, one day in advance, we ask the chef to personally make us a couple of special meals, which might consist of:

- ◆ Lowfat-chicken cacciatore made with lowfat spaghetti sauce and lots of veggies

- Garlic shrimp made with a hint of olive oil

- Herb-crusted fish that is baked, not fried

- Ratatouille made with just a little olive oil (I love all those veggies)

- Lowfat ginger salad dressing

- Dry-grilled asparagus, artichokes and mushrooms, oh my!

- Raspberries for dessert

- Lowfat carrot cake for special occasions

- Flourless chocolate cake made with pureed prunes instead of oil

You have to look at it this way – the chef is there to make sure you have a superb experience! All the more reason to request wonderful, healthy foods that you don't have to cook yourself. This is an opportunity to indulge yourself with diet-friendly fare that is fresh, delicious, and guilt-free. (The chef can also create gluten-free and kosher fare, in most cases. The high-end, upscale luxury lines such as Silversea, Regent Seven Seas Cruises, Seabourn and Azamara, especially, are always ready, willing, and able to offer you specialized cuisine on their ships – I call them "the aristo-crafts.")

Here's what my typical cruise day consists of, meal-wise.

Breakfast:
- One package of shredded wheat, skim milk, raisins, melon and coffee

Lunch:
- Tuna fish sandwich (specially made with diet mayo) on rye bread, salad, apple for dessert

The Botox Boat

People with lines and wrinkles – are lining up! In June of 2008, Norwegian Cruise Line (NCL) in partnership with Steiner Transocean, announced that it would be the first cruise line to offer Botox, Restylane and Perlane facial aesthetic treatments in its Mandara-operated spas. The treatments are part of Mandara's medi-spa program, and are currently available on select NCL ships, including Norwegian *Dawn,* Norwegian *Gem* and Norwegian *Spirit*, with plans to launch fleet-wide later on.

All of the facial aesthetic treatments are under the supervision of Steiner's Medical Director, Dr. Brad Herman, a Miami-based, board-certified plastic surgeon and his team of medically-licensed doctors and who have trained specifically in the administration of these treatments (www.ncl.com).

At this writing, we got word that Princess Cruises would also be introducing Botox aboard some of its ships too. Watch for other cruise lines to follow suit (www.princess.com).

Snack:

♦ Half a piece of blotted cheese pizza, or a piece of fruit, or some dried Sunsweet plums, or PB2 powdered peanut butter on a slice of bread – before I head to the gym

Dinner:

♦ Roll with butter, 6 oz. of protein (chicken or fish), grilled vegetables without butter, baked potato with one small pat of butter. Dessert? Bowl of berries with skim milk. Two bites of decadent chocolate dessert if I feel like a treat.

You could even travel with your own bottle of lowfat dressing, or Butter Buds, or non-caloric spray butter (which I do sometimes) – if you really want to count calories and bring your daily calorie allotment down even further.

Bring your own non-calorie butter spray, or small container of Butter Buds, for your veggies and baked potatoes.

Believe me, when you walk off a cruise ship after a 7-, 14-, or 21-day (or longer) trip – or even a world cruise for months at a time – and your jeans are loose – it will be worth it. That's a feeling that money can't buy.

The Love Bloat

It should come as no surprise that the wait staff and personnel who work on ships struggle with the same weight issues as passengers; in fact they probably struggle more, since they live on a ship and have to constantly contend with shipboard fare. I met Emilie Jauffret, from Marseille, France, who was a waitress aboard a luxury cruise ship, on a trip that my husband and I took through the Panama Canal. Emilie found life at sea very tough, so much so that she retired from it after only one contract. "In my first month I gained five kilos," she told me. "I couldn't zip my pants. So then I stopped eating everything that had chocolate and sugar, and I stopped eating lunch. Now I just have a banana or a kiwifruit. It lost three kilos during my second month here. Then I ate chocolate because of the stress of life on ship."

Here are some great cruise-control tips from staff and passengers – the road warrior "dames at sea."

Maria Tancredi, Waitress, Luxury Cruise Line

"On my first contract I gained six kilos in the first two months…I was eating five times a day: breakfast, then more food on a break, working in a restaurant, trying to taste everything. Then lunch. Then at 3PM I'd still be hungry. Then I'd eat at 6PM. Then I'd finish at midnight and eat my fifth meal of the day. Now, I eat two times a day, with nothing between meals. I have a lot at breakfast: high-protein, and steak and hash browns and beans. I haven't been to the gym once. I lost all six kilos. This is now my third contract. I used to work 14 hours a day, straight, but now I work 10-11 hours a day, for five, six, seven months."

Karen Grainger, Singer/Impressionist on Various Cruise Ships, www.karengrainger.com

Karen Grainger of Ontario, Canada is a very talented singer/impressionist, who can belt it out just like Celine Dion, Cher, Reba McEntire and Michael McDonald – sometimes even doing duets *with herself*. I met Karen on the Regent Seven Seas Cruises *Mariner* (www.rssc.com) when she was one of the talents who performed for us in the beautiful theater. Here's what she told me about her diet/fitness routine while traveling and cruising.

"I use DVDs on my laptop – Billy Blanks (www.billyblanks.com) and P90X (www.extremebodyworkout.com) are my favorites. I also bring a Nike exercise band for different exercises – you can wrap it around your feet and do bicep curls." Karen, who has a lithe, lean body and looks stunning in her evening gowns, proves that her routines work. "Small portions; choose wisely; everything in moderation" is her motto. (As is walking on the top deck of the ship, which I saw her do on several occasions.) She also drinks LOTS of water – "64 ounces a day." When cruising she also uses Hal Higdon's half-marathon training schedule. Concerning snacking, "I try not to snack but if I do it will be fresh fruit." She packs tons of vitamins and throat remedies in case she needs them for performing. Beauty routine? "Clinique for my face – I love Clinique makeup (www.clinique.com) – and Rusk Hair Straightener (www.rusk1.com) are a must!"

Jeanette Haua, Spa Director, Regent Seven Seas Cruises Mariner, www.rssc.com

Jeanette knows all too well how cruising can pack on the pounds. "When I first started working on cruise ships, I gained six kilos in the first month; as management I can dine in the crew mess and in the fine restaurants. It's dangerous. I then started going to the gym, and doing everything in moderation, with plenty of water, water, water."

Lisa Anne Jones, Executive Chef, Azamara Club Cruises *Journey*, www.azamaraclubcruises.com

Lisa, as talented a chef as you'll ever find, has 58 employees who work under her. Hers is a demanding job, making sure that each and every passenger on the Azamara *Journey* has excellent, delicious food – and that task includes accommodating the wealth of special requests that she gets every day. As part of her job, she must taste everything, all throughout the day. In fact, she never eats dinner, as "Dinner is the small bites I have eaten all day long," she told me. She skips breakfast, and only eats a nice lunch every day – with a Diet Coke. "I've been on the ship four months now, and I've put on a few kilos. I cook Thanksgiving dinner every single day, and at the end of the day, I don't want to taste or eat anything. The desire is gone."

Mary Jean Tully, Travel Agent Extraordinaire, the Number One producer for Crystal Cruises and Silversea Cruises, the Number Two producer for Regent Seven Seas Cruises and Seabourn Cruises, and *Conde Nast Traveler's* "Luxury Cruise Expert" for 10 years in a row, www.maryjeantully.com, www.cruiseprofessionals.com

Mary Jean is the best at what she does; that's why she is constantly lauded and awarded for her achievements. This high-achiever also has a bevy of beauty tips to keep you classy on a cruise ship – "I'm a very girlie girl," she explains. "First, bring

Haute Couture Hair Care

One of the highlights of a recent sailing on Crystal Cruises, was – the hair conditioner! (www.crystalcruises.com) In fact, it was Red Flower Italian Blood Orange Softening Hair Conditioner. It's made with pure flower extracts, vegetable proteins, fruit oils, soy protein and avocado oil combined with blood orange juice and essential oils of orange blossom, grapefruit, lime and orange rind. My sun-parched hair came out looking – and feeling – like cornsilk. That's the kind of complimentary amenity we just love. All Red Flower Japan products use ingredients that are only 100% botanically based, and are entirely free of drying agents, dyes and harsh preservatives (www.redflower.com).

your favorite hair product, as chances are the ship has their own hair products." That means that if you're addicted to Fekkai shampoo, by all means, pack it up. Second, Mary Jean advises, "Pre-book all of your spa and hair appointments, to avoid disappointment." After all, you don't want to embark, and find out then from the spa that all your preferred times are already taken. "Third, consider bringing along your own hair color, if you're going to be on a ship for a couple of weeks. I do that if I'm going to be away for a long time." Adds Mary Jean: "If your hair doesn't look good, it doesn't matter what you wear."

"If you're taking a cruise," she also advises, "Go to the destination about two or three days beforehand, so you can sightsee, and get a massage right after you land."

Mary Jean, who has been a travel agent for 23 years, and has taken 200+ cruises, also has her diet routine down. "First, I ask the waiters to please not put any bread on the table." Then, she simply eats more healthy when she's on board – she'll eat far more fish, fruits and vegetables. "I might walk on deck in the morning, and then I'll eat oatmeal with fresh fruit. It's so easy, and wonderful, with so much variety. And I've been able to walk on deck, get fresh air and look at the ocean too." Mary Jean also stays away from desserts; doesn't eat late at night (when she says *adios* to tempting room service); and frequently orders spa cuisine, or entrees with the sauce on the side. "I frequently look at the next day's menu, the night before. I might order a kosher chicken because I simply love it…The luxury lines do everything possible to fulfill special requests such as low salt, soy milk, anything that you want that you know you want in advance. The portions served onboard are not large, so it's a nice balance and always a good variety."

Another tip: she hires a personal trainer when she's on a cruise ship, to keep herself focused. "On Crystal Cruises, I met with my trainer every day and customized what I wanted to do. I was committed to it, and paid for it, so I had to do it."

This intrepid, elegant traveler also travels with all the bells and whistles to make herself comfortable. "I travel with two Longchamp large duffels and a carry-on (www.Longchamp.com). I use Crème de la Mer before boarding the plane (www.cremedelamer) and in my carry-on is a change of clothing, makeup and jewelry. My purse – I'm a diva – is a Louis Vuitton black epi carry-on or a Bottega Veneta hobo bag." (www.louisvuitton.com, www.bottegaveneta.com)

Wyndham's The Way To Go

Here's where I sing the praises of the Wyndham Miami Hotel at the airport. When you're readying to take a cruise, you definitely want to check into a hotel at your embarkation destination several days in advance, to make sure that you're there with time to unwind from the commute. Well, when I found the Wyndham Miami Hotel at the Airport, I struck gold – and so will you.

The Wyndham Miami Hotel at the airport does a booming business with cruisers – and it's easy to see why. "We do a lot of pre- and post bookings," said Bob LePore, General Manager. There's a special Bon Voyage package, which charges about $189 per night for your accommodations, full breakfast, complimentary airport transfers, and complimentary one-way to the cruise port. "We work with a local limo company," says Bob.

He added that the hotel has lots of international travelers, who love staying at this particular property because of all of its attractive advantages. For example, the Melreese (city) Golf Course is right next door, so you can easily play 9 or 18 holes soon after checking in. In fact, "Many airline pilots store their clubs here," he added.

The hotel also offers free shuttles to Coral Gables and Coconut Grove, where you can enjoy the historic atmosphere and great shopping. "It is important to us that our guests aren't isolated," he says. "There's also a $5 shuttle to the Dolphin Mall outlet with fantastic shopping," he added. "Our international travelers love it – and we pack and ship their purchases out using FedEx and UPS." The hotel is also conveniently located just 20 minutes from South Beach, and instead of taking a $50 cab ride there, you can easily pick up a $4.25 shuttle bus to get there.

Let's hear it for this terrific property, which makes staying at the airport as good as it can possibly get (www.wyndhamhotelmia.com).

Mary Jean also admits: "I like the expensive stuff," when it comes to beauty products. She likes ReVive (www.reviveskincare.com) and La Prairie serum (www.laprairie.com). "I wear Lancome Oscillating mascara, (www.Lancome-USA.com), Bobbi Brown lipgloss and bronzer (www.bobbibrowncosmetics.com), Clarins or Lancome suntan lotion, and a special topcoat on my nails, so it won't turn yellow in the sun." (www.clarins.com, www.lancome-usa.com)

Heike Berdos, Hotel Director, Azamara Club Cruises *Journey*, Azamaraclubcruises.com

"On the ship I eat very small meals several times a day," Heike told me. "In the morning I have fruit, oatmeal and juice. Lunch is a salad. Dinner is lots of turkey and chicken. I could exist on cold meals. My weaknesses are cheese and bread." To maintain her very-svelte self, Heiki walks 75 minutes every other day. "I also do weights. I used to teach aerobics classes, and used to be a volleyball player." Her must-have beautifiers include Bobbi Brown makeup, and everything in the L'Oreal line. This transplanted German resident now lives in Athens, and when she's there, she always visits the Korres shop at the airport, to buy locally-made Greek cosmetics. "I love Korres products from Greece (www.korres.com)." In Athens, she also recommends making a trek to the factory-outlet mall at the airport, where she makes purchases from Diesel, Guess, Boss and Levi-Strauss.

Michelle Colligan, Senior Account Executive for Redpoint Marketing PR, who handles travel accounts such as Princess Cruises, a former client, www.Princess.com

Michelle Colligan handles public relations for Princess Cruises, and she also needs to cruise because of her work. Her techniques? "If I'm staying on a Princess ship I turn to the Fitness@Sea channel for stretching exercises." On flights, she snacks on fruits and nuts, and eats a turkey sandwich that she brings. And she's never without her LoBello chapstick – "I can't leave home without it, especially when traveling in dry airplanes to colder climates." When she gets to her land destination, Michelle asks the concierge for the nearest running trail.

"If there are no trails, just run out and back for the same amount of time each way, down the nearest street."

Susanne Volpe, Cruise Training and Development Manager

Weleda body oils – these are the top things that Susanne Volpe of Italy packs in her Samsonite – "There is nothing better!" she says. "If you don't know about them they are a Swiss product made of natural oils and essences and very afford-able. They make me instantly feel comfortable and refreshed after a long travel and with the nice aromatherapeutic smell every hotel room becomes a spa." (www.weleda.com)

Susanne also swears by Yves Saint Laurent Touche Eclat eye concealer - "The proven best" (www.ysl.com), Dior Capture cream (www.dior.com), and Chanel lipstick in Rouge Allure 60 – "It's the best red for day and night," she says (www.chanel.com). On the plane enroute to the ship, she brings Samsonite pillows (www.samsonite.com), a cashmere shawl, and good chocolate. "A baby fleece blanket is always in my suitcase," she adds. To help with leg cir-culation she also packs pressure tights and cozy fleece socks, which she uses on the plane as well as after taking a shower and putting lots of Weleda oil on her feet.

Show Me The Honey

Room service on a ship can be just what the beauty doctor ordered. For example, ask your room steward for a small cup of olive oil – you can rub it in your cuticles. Or, smother your hair in it, sit out on your verandah in the hot sun for 30 minutes to basically give yourself a hot-oil treatment; rinse it out; shampoo, and be left with silky-soft tresses. You could even ask your butler (if you're lucky enough to get one) for a bowl of sugar – just mix it with the olive oil, and rub it all over your body in the shower, for an extremely lovely exfoliating sugar scrub. Or how about some honey and oatmeal, for a facial mask? These beauty treatments are FREE, and somehow even more fun when you implement them on a gorgeous cruise ship. That's the rub.

Jennifer Cowley, Cruise Industry Manager

Here's an offbeat tip: Jennifer Cowley, a cruise industry manager from South Africa, can't live without her leg and ankle weights – that's her fitness tip. "When traveling, I wear ankle weights around my legs all day long. Even when going through customs and immigration! I also travel with a set of wrist weights. These are available from Nike stores," she says. Jennifer is also a huge fan of Essie products for her skin – "These are organic and natural-oil-based products made in South Africa. They are the world's greatest beauty products!" she says enthusiastically. "Plus," she adds, "They offer beauty without cruelty."

Jaqui Lacroix, Assistant Cruise Director, Oceania Cruises, www.Oceaniacruises.com

Have you ever considered whitening your teeth while you travel? That's exactly what Jaqui Lacroix does; she's an Assistant Cruise Director at Oceania Cruises, and frequently travels alone for business. That's when she grooms her teeth and gums. "I like to use my teeth whitening strips when I fly. I also like to give myself a manicure, but I skip the nail polish, because the odor can bother other passengers." Jaqui is big into self-pampering: "I always supply myself with a loofah, pedicure file, facial scrub mask, and eye cream, and I always bring Vaseline Total Moisture (www.vaseline.com) and Oil of Olay Total Effects." (www.olay.com). She adds: "I also travel with Bayer Aspirin (81mg). I fly internationally and sometimes have problems with swelling in my ankles. But if I take one aspirin the day before, and on the day of my flight, my ankles don't swell."

Make the most of your pearly whites – use teeth-whitening strips while you travel.

Front-Office Manager on luxury cruise line (who asked to remain anonymous)

This petite officer told me that on her first few cruise contracts, "I gained a lot of weight – about eight to 10 kilos (about 17 pounds). "I was eating too much and it wasn't healthy. I was eating a lot of meat, rice, pasta – everything you don't eat at home. Here, you see the buffet and eat everything you don't eat at home. At home I would just eat a sandwich. But on a ship everything is available. So, I started to go to the gym on the ship – every other day. I go at night and do bike, treadmill, Pilates and weights. I lost eight kilos – but I should still lose two-to-three kilos. Every time I'm on the ship it's the same fight. Everything is available. I'm 5'2" – I weigh 60 kilos (132 pounds) now. It was much worse. I was 150 pounds at my maximum. Now for dinner I have salads. I watch out. Maybe a chicken breast or fish. I have no snacks between meals, and I eat in the officer's mess. I actually thought I would lose weight on ships, but it's been the other way around!" So, what makes her cabin feel like home? "I always travel with my own duvet that I sleep on. And my favorite shampoo is L'Oreal (www.lorealusa.com). I buy six bottles at one time in Europe."

Lisa Heath, Dancer from Leicester England, on *Silversea Silver Shadow*

"We're weighed once a month. Some people go to the gym between shows. I go for walks and

that caters to your wants and needs with aplomb. Just like a five-star hotel, Silversea offers silken service and cashmere care that's designed to offer an ultimate travel experience. Silversea makes the "getting there" as wonderful as the destination, and if you're a gorgeous globetrotter, you'll appreciate that your special food requests are taken seriously.

Even before you board, Silversea wants to know all of your special dietary requests. Then, once on board, every guest has an opportunity to meet with the Executive Chef, to handle all details. We love this feature – before we boarded on our recent Alaskan adventure on the Silversea **Silver Shadow**, we informed Silversea that we would be celebrating our 9th wedding anniversary – and could the chef possibly make us a lowfat carrot cake? Faster than you can say, "I Do," Executive Chef Sean Emslie proferred upon us a guilt-free gourmet delicacy. (We also brought on board our own lowfat mayonnaise, which we

runs on the track. I eat everything. I buy rice cakes, snacks and pretzels to eat on the ship. We do four shows per cruise. I'm a big cosmetic fan of Benefit and MAC lipsticks – they stay on all night. We usually shop at a Walmart or a mall in San Francisco." (www.benefitcosmetics.com, www.maccosmetics.com)

Jessica Kaiser, Singer from New York City, on the Silversea *Silver Shadow*

"I do a lot of portion control. We've been eating the same stuff for eight months (she's on a year-long contract). You could eat cereal at every meal. We did Special K for lunch a lot. I actually lost weight, as I need a snack every two hours, so we get Special K bars for snacks. A lot revolves around your next meal. We keep the same things in our rooms that you would have in your dorm room at college, without a fridge. Goldfish crackers are great. In the beginning of this contract, I was hungry all the time, and we couldn't get snacks because the mess wasn't open. And you have to watch what you drink at the crew bar."

Jessica is just as careful of her diet when she's on a plane. "I'll take an apple to snack on. I was a gymnast for 15 years; I go to the gym when I want, and do the elliptical machine."

"I like Neutrogena for my face, and Cover Girl, and MAC. We use MAC on stage, and then use Neutrogena to get off our stage makeup." (www. neutrogena.com, www.covergirl.com, www. maccosmetics.com)

To make her cabin feel like home, Jessica brought photos of her family, and then shopped at Walmart. "We bought fun stuff at Walmart – a fluffy purple rug and a pink phone."

Trendy Tanning

Tanning came into vogue in 1923, when Coco Chanel unwittingly bronzed her skin on a cruise aboard the Duke of Wellington's yacht.

Natallia Korsak, Ballroom Dancer from Belarus, on the Silversea *Silver Shadow*

It's not often that you see perfection – but believe me when I tell you – it's evident in Natallia Korsak. She is a young, professional ballroom dancer, who has won numerous competitions and is a world-class dancer. Along with that, she looks like a model – long and lithe, with a stunning face, and an even more beautiful body. You can't take your eyes off of her, whether or not she's on stage. How does she stay trim? Read it and weep.

"I'm 19. I've been dancing ever since I was 4. I eat everything. No diet, never. I eat a lot of desserts every day. No free weights. Never. My favorite desserts are ice cream and chocolate mousse."

Natallia loves Neutrogena cleanser and lipsticks by Max Factor and L'Oreal (www.maxfactor.

gave to the Chef, so we could eat tuna fish sandwiches at lunch without guilt.) "Requests are made with your reservation through a travel agent," Chef Emslie told us. The requests are commonly for lactose-free and gluten-free menus, although the staff will move heaven and earth to see that you are satisfied. For us, it's like having your own personal chef. We also asked for special low-calorie breads and rolls, as well as entrees such as lowfat chicken cacciatore, stuffed chicken breasts and ratatouille– requests that were fulfilled deliciously without any problem. In fact, Chef Emslie told us that he welcomes a challenge.

One notable offering we loved were the wellness options routinely featured on all of the menus. Who said you have to gain weight on a cruise ship? The room-service breakfast menus all featured healthy options, such as delicious bran muffins weighing in at about 100 calories each. (We ate them with gusto every day.) A dinner menu might feature an iced beetroot soup for 31 calories; antipasti salad for 94 calories; and a grilled filet of halibut with shallot cream, all for just 187 calories. There are even separate vegetarian menus. No matter what you want, the staff is there to serve you. Chef Emslie told us that one guest wanted the specific blackened cod dish that is routinely served at Nobu, one of the world's most high-end restaurants. Chef Emslie looked up the recipe on the internet, and served the miso-marinated delicacy to the delighted guest. The most unusual request? Another guest insisted that his food be served piping hot, and in that case, "We served his meals with a thermometer, so that his meal was almost boiling," said Chef Emslie. And on world cruises, there's even a Special-Request Chef on board, to handle all of the inimitable dietary requests. My response to this type of stellar service? All I can say is, "Ciao bella!"

Ah, Spa!

I had the pleasure of enjoying a fantastic massage in

com, www.lorealusa.com). "It's easy to get cosmetics in Belarus, but they're much more expensive. A regular $25 mascara might cost $100 – and it's fake. Counterfeit. We can only get Pupa cosmetics from Italy in Belarus. I buy cosmetics in port at the duty-free, or in San Francisco." (www.pupa.it)

Evita Opara, Australian/Polish Journalist, Author of *Adventures of Bernie* (children's book, Richard Smart Publishing), *What You Don't Know About Your Man* (Klucze Publishing) and *Social Climbers* (Authorhouse Publishing)

I met the beautiful Eva Opara on a Silversea cruise to the Mediterranean. We actually met in the gym, as we are both very preoccupied with staying fit and trim. Eva and her husband Richard, a Polish doctor, take tons of cruises – they traveled on *The World of Residensea* a few years ago, and they also sail frequently on upscale cruise lines such as Silversea, Celebrity and Crystal, as well as the more mass-market Royal Caribbean line (with their six children). Says Eva: "I am obsessed with staying fit while traveling. First, I don't eat three meals a day. I eat fruit for breakfast; salad for lunch; and for dinner, when my husband orders appetizers, I order two appetizers for my main meal. My husband loves to eat and it is very difficult for me not to accompany him to a restaurant. Usually one or two hours after breakfast he starts to look for a good restaurant for lunch. It is very hard on a cruise. I avoid sweets or drink a glass of water before the meal."

For exercise, "I try to exercise whenever possible or book a private trainer. Usually there is a gym in most hotels or on cruise ships. I go swimming where it is possible – I hate cold water, so I am a bit limited. I take classes or simply stay on a bike. After each dinner I go for a walk or dancing if on a cruise (Richard and I take lots of dancing lessons together to keep fit). After all of that, I still usually put on two-to-four pounds on a long trip. If I don't take a taxi, I walk wherever possible. I try to do something every day, otherwise I lose momentum."

On planes (and she prefers Qantas), Eva takes aspirin to prevent blood clots, and uses a facial mask by Shiseido (www.shiseido.com). She always packs a pashmina and cuticle oil. Her luggage used to be Louis Vuitton. "Now I use Rimowa, a German brand – it is very light and you can pack a lot of things in it."

Her favorite bargain shopping tip is the Pearl Market in Jakarta: "You can spend hours finding the right pearls. They make necklaces on the spot, from pearls chosen by you. It is a great place for all presents."

the Elemis Spa located on the top deck of the Silversea *Silver Shadow*. Here's where you can enjoy a wealth of posh pamperings that will indulge and invigorate you. The Silversea spa features four treatment rooms, and if you want to save a few bucks, 20% discounts are offered on a regular basis on port days. The hot stone massages are the most popular treatment of all. I had the Swedish massage ($110 for 50 minutes) and sopped up every stroke like a sponge. You name it, there's a treatment for it – from the Elemis Tri-Enzyme Resurfacing Facial, to Exotic Frangipani Body Nourish Wrap, and even to a Go Smile tooth whitening treatment ($199 for 30 minutes) (www.gosmile.com). My masseuse, Lourika from South Africa, started her massage with a dry brushing, followed by massage with rosemary and lavender oils, plus an application of milk bath used on the décolletage. Said Lourika: "I love giving massages – I'm happiest when I'm in the treatment room." And you know what? I totally believe her!

The **Silver Shadow** also boasts a fitness center outfitted with everything you need to negate calories: treadmills, elliptical machines, Nautilus machines, workout balls, free weights, and more than enough Pilates and yoga classes – which are all complimentary, by the way. (On other ships we've been on, there's an added fee for such classes.) It makes a trip all the better, when you know that you can get in some exercise, to compensate for all of the delicious food that the ship serves. Each treadmill and elliptical machine also has a television, so you can tune in (and tune out) from all the hard work you're doing. Personal training is even available ($83 for 60 minutes). If you want even more exercise, follow our example and take a ballroom-dancing class, which was typically offered on days at sea– our cruise featured Natallia and Dmitry, two talented ballroom dancers from Belarus, who taught us how to do the jive. It definitely came in handy to know this routine, when we danced at night in the ship's disco – another great escape that burns calories.

The Full Monty At Sea

The Yachts of Seabourn, an ultraluxury cruise line known for its extraordinary service, offers "The Spa at Seabourn," which spans two decks. In fact, the spa, measuring 11,400 square feet, is the largest on any luxury vessel. Here you'll find unusual amenities including Thai massage as well as SkinCeuticals products and treatments – an award-winning and scientifically-proven line used by dermatologists and plastic surgeons. One highlight of the spa is the Spa Villa on Deck 10, which features a treatment area large enough for treatments-for-two, including a double daybed for relaxing. You'll also love the treatment rooms on Deck 9, including a Garden Villa room with a spa tub on the balcony. What a view! Two more fabulous features of cruising on Seabourn: the five-minute complimentary "Massage Moments" offered to guests at the pool, and the Molton Brown special baths that your room steward can prepare for you. That spells good clean F-U-N (www.seabourn.com).

What Would Jeannie Do?

Barbara Eden, better known as the gorgeous gal on the hit TV sitcom *I Dream of Jeannie*, loves to travel. She and her husband Jon try and include one cruise a year. "I recently took a Crystal cruise to Vietnam and it was great. Yes, other passengers do ask me about my career and some of the greats in showbiz with whom I've worked such as Elvis Presley, Paul Newman, Gene Kelly and Pat Boone. As you know, I headlined in Las Vegas for eight years – we traveled with steamers and vaporizers in those days, so my throat wouldn't get dry 'Vegas throat,' they called it."

To keep her genie-like figure, Barbara spins on a bicycle at the gym three times a week as part of her routine to stay in shape. "But when I travel, I don't go to the gym. There's no time for that. It's more of what I don't do, than what I do. I stay away from the ice cream bar. But I usually come back with a couple of pounds and work like mad to get it off. Plus we always go on the excursions. On a recent trip to China, we were so busy I lost weight. I even hiked The Great Wall."

Stay away from the ice cream bar — taste makes waist!

Barbara also maintains her svelte self by, unbelievably, not ordering any special meals when she's cruising. "I just don't eat a lot of it," she said. "Just an entrée and salad – that's it."

(cont. on next page)

Same for when she's on a plane. "I eat what they have available on the plane because I don't want to bring or carry anything I don't have to. It's the *quantity* of what you eat that matters. And I also don't drink alcohol on my flights."

Barbara packs her standard-issue, plain black luggage with liquids that have been double-bagged: sunscreen ("I swear by it"), mascara and lipsticks in pink and peach. When she wants a healthy glow, she dusts on a smattering of terracotta. "Otherwise I look really white," she said with a laugh.

Barbara loves to shop, especially in Paris, and she also had some beautiful silk clothes made for her in Vietnam. "But I got taken in Bangkok. I bought some sapphires that looked beautiful in the shop under the lights but I got home and discovered they were black, not blue. But I had them set anyway."

Alice Bloom, retired Event Planner for Hewlett-Packard

I met Alice on the Regent Seven Seas Cruises' *Mariner.* I noticed her because every night, she had on a beautiful dress, with fantastic shoes. I asked her to divulge her secret: "Zappos," she told me. "They're the best and they have free shipping, and you can ship the shoes back at no cost to you – and you get the goods in two-to-three days. Fantastic!"

Alice took seven cruises in a 10-year period, and most recently, the RSSC Cruise through the Panama Canal, where we met. With all that cruising, her weight never fluctuated. "I have never gained weight when I travel," she said. "The secret is to eat as 'normally' as I do when I am home. There is the misconception that just because you are traveling, there is an excuse to overeat and eat the wrong things at the wrong time, especially on a cruise where food is so readily available. So I have found that when I 'normalize' my eating routine during travel, then I do not have to worry about weight gain."

She continued: "As far as exercise, I do sit-ups, push-ups, and I get my cardio since I take along tunes that I can dance to. I am also a kickboxer and martial artist. A few minutes of kicking, and wall squats incorporated with martial arts poses/forms keeps me right on track."

On planes, she watches her weight by snacking on nuts, cheese, crackers and fruit. On cruise ships, her all-time favorite snack is caviar with strawberries.

Her beauty routine consists of Yon-Ka and Decleor products (www.yonka.com, www.decleor.com). "They are super hydrating and smell wonderful," she said. "Their aroma essences are also conducive to a soothing sleep as they are inhaled throughout the night." But the best way that she stays renewed and refreshed is through meditation. "It is my miracle fitness tip of all time."

Marni Nixon, the famous Voice of Eliza Doolittle in *My Fair Lady*, Anna Leonowens in *The King and I*, and Maria in *West Side Story*, author of *I Could Have Sung All Night: My Story* (Billboard Books), www.Marninixon.com

Marni has been performing since 1940, and has gone on numerous world cruises, on ships such as Holland America, Seabourn and Royal Viking. You know who taught her how to pack? The late, great, Liberace. "I toured with him and he designed the gown I wore – it had layers of colored chiffon, with a train. He had me buy a suitcase to his specifications – it was the size of a coffin – I had it made. Then, you'd take everything and roll it into the folds of the gown. I never ironed the dress once, and I toured with him for a year. He was very practical that way."

One of Marni's great secrets is a damp washcloth. "On the plane, and in a hotel,

The Love Boat

Ladies, I can tell you that there's no better way to profess your love for your partner, than to renew your wedding vows. At sea. A vow-renewal ceremony will remind you why you married your spouse in the first place, and you'll also be inspired to be on your best behavior. Bill and I have had numerous vow-renewal ceremonies throughout the world, but two of the best were at sea. One was on the Regent Seven Seas Cruises *Mariner*, complete with ceremony by the captain, out on deck, and a delicious lowfat carrot cake and champagne to celebrate (www.rssc.com). Another time, on the *Paul Gauguin*, we had a gorgeous ceremony as the ship sailed into Moorea, and I was covered in Tahitian tiare flowers (www.pgcruises.com). The backdrop of palm trees, azure sky and turquoise waters was truly awe-inspiring. These lovely ceremonies will make you feel like a bride again, full of zest and anticipation for the days ahead with your loved one. Make sure to say "I Do" to this wonderfully romantic idea. Many cruise ships offer vow-renewal ceremonies along with their wedding packages. And since you're already in a honeymoon destination, on the ship, you're sure to make time for romance.

I always sleep and breathe into a damp washcloth over my mouth, because the membranes in your mouth will swell up if they don't get enough moisture." She also takes a buckwheat pillow that is scented with lavender.

Her swear-by cosmetic is Stallex, available exclusively from Dr. Neil Schultz in New York City (www.parkavenueskincare.com). "I've been using it for 10 years and I love it. Everyone remarks about my skin, as it kind of glows."

Pamela Conover, President and CEO, Seabourn Cruise Lines, www.seabourn.com

Pamela has taken hundreds of cruises over the course of 25 years, so she's got her diet-and-exercise routine down pat. "For me, it's easier to stay fit when cruising – because the gym is right there. Cruise ships have fantastically equipped gyms. Just fall out of bed and you're minutes away. And *never* use the lifts (elevators). It gives you much more exercise…I also do cardiovascular exercise by running on the treadmill, and doing weights."

"When it comes to eating," she continued, "I just do it through portion control. A little taste of everything. Lots of salad and fruits. But potatoes and bread? I avoid them like poison. I also avoid nuts and snack foods. I might snack on an apple. For dinner, I tend to have grilled fish with sauce on the side, and I save my calories for chocolate."

When flying to her cruise destination, she swears by Rosa Graf Cerasome Regenerative Capsules (www.rosagraf.com); "My facialist in Key Biscayne recommended them to me. I put them on my face when I get on a plane. They're very good. And I love Chanel gloss in "Twinkle" and Chanel mascara." (www.chanel.com)

One of Pam's favorite shopping destinations is Hong Kong. "You can buy cus-tommade suits, one-of-a-kind, at reasonable prices. I most recently bought a silk jacket and skirt and pants, in cream. I got home and I ordered the same thing in black, for about $600. I wear them all the time."

Tiffany James, CEO and Founder, UnderCoverwear lingerie company, www.Undercoverwear.com

Tiffany is a "girlie girl" and loves clothes, jewelry, makeup and all the things that women typically love.

"Crème de la Mer is my Number One (www.cremedelamer.com)," she told me, although she also loves to use "a special Miracle Oil that UndercoverWear carries."

She and husband Walter frequently take world cruises – most recently they took the inaugural voyage on Silversea's new ship, the *Silver Spirit* – so she's quite adept at making herself and Walter feel right at home when they're cruising.

To fit into her 42 ball gowns and 16 bathing suits that she brought onboard the world cruise, Tiffany was careful about what she ate. Breakfast aboard ship (brought by the butler, of course, to their Grand Suite) was a bowl of berries, black coffee, egg-white omelet and piece of wheat toast. Lunch was a huge salad with chicken or tuna, with no bread and certainly no pizza, she told me. Before dinner, she typically would have a glass of champagne and some caviar. Dinner was chicken or fish with steamed spinach and no oil. At times however, she might have dined on some pasta in Silversea's Italian restaurant, or "small portions of something fabulous." To stay in shape, she walked the decks every day, and "I never took the ship's elevator," she told me.

On the world cruise, this intrepid traveler also brought "every kind of prescription and medicine for every ailment possible," she said. "We even figured out the exact amounts of saline solution and hair conditioner that we needed."

To make her stateroom feel homey, Tiffany also brought magnets – so her photos of children and grandchildren would adhere to the magnetic walls of the ship's suite. Brilliant! "If we go anyplace for more than three days, I take photos," she explained. "We also signed up for Skype," she said, so she could stay in touch with family, while cruising around the world. (That's a tremendous idea, www.skype.com) Another great tip: Tiffany always cruises with her own stationery, so it's easy for her to send thank-you notes during her travels. And she's just as meticulous about her appearance. "In port, I would get my hair done, although

I brought 12 wigs and hairpieces with me on the cruise, just in case I had a bad hair day or was showing roots."

And since she's in the lingerie business, Tiffany, of course, makes sure she has "black flowing lingerie and maribou slippers" packed in her suitcase. "How my husband looks at me is very important," she said. "I put a lot of time and energy into what I wear to bed."

Ana Valente, Owner, France Cruises, www.Francecruises. com, www.wlcvacations.com

Ana is part French – and her diet regime definitely fits into the "French Paradox." She says: "I've never dieted in my life. I try everything in this world but I look for small quantities and balance in my meals. Most important, I have red wine with my meals, to cut the fat. Do you know that secret?" This is how she stays slim, traveling 60% of the year, sometimes for months at a time, on her company's ships. "I rarely go to the gym," she adds. "But I do a lot of yoga and breathing exercises. I'm a size 7-8."

Ana is a former fashion designer, and actually, she still designs things just for herself. For example, she designs her own shoes, which she has custommade in Milan and in Mexico. "But I can't give you the name of my craftsman in Mexico," she said with a laugh. Her purse is also her own design, and she's currently working on developing her own line of luggage.

Ana is also a cosmetics maven. When she travels, she scours all the marketplaces, to find local, handmade, indigenous products. "I find them in small villages in Europe when I travel. I love to find these handmade, exquisite products." She adds, "I've done a lot of comparison shopping, testing a lot of products. I love Ahava products from the Dead Sea, which are made in Israel." (www.ahavaus.com).

Who else knows how to stay beautiful? Why, experts and professionals in the beauty business, that's who. Read Chapter Six to get the inside scoop about how these pros stay stark raving glad and gorgeous in their travels.

CHAPTER SIX
Insider Beauty Scoop

Who knows more about beauty than models – and women who work in the beauty industry? They were practically *born* with beauty tips, and luckily, I got them to share their secrets with me.

Linda Cole, *More Magazine's* 2002 "Model of the Year"

"I always carry snacks with me," says this beautiful 48-year-old Wilhemina model from the Boston area, whose clients include Saks, St. John, Loro Piana, Akris, Sonya Rykiel and Tiffany. "I always have 100-calorie packs such as Keebler baby fudge cookies, South Beach, Dr. Atkins or Pria bars, popcorn or fruit. If I eat dessert, I actually eat it for breakfast – say, a nice chewy muffin or brownie – so I have the entire day to burn it off. I was chubby as a kid, and I had to watch my weight. I eat a ton of grilled chicken, and I always use good olive oil and lemon. I eat about 1,800-2,000 calories per day, if I'm active."

On the road, Linda is partial to Au Bon Pain's salad portions of green apples, blue cheese, and cranberries, or the flame-grilled chicken with lettuce and tomato (hold the mayo) at Burger King.

On a plane, "I always use a lot of moisturizer, and that's when I do my hands and cuticles." She brings a cashmere blanket or pashmina wrap and a neck pillow. Linda is constantly traveling from Boston to New York for her work, taking the LimoLiner or AmTrak.

"I'm such a beauty queen," says this product junkie. The item she swears by is Neutrogena Micromist Airbrush Sunless Tan #3 – "I buy it at CVS," she says. (www.neutrogena.com). "I moisturize, hold the can away from me, and just spray it on. I do it every day. I put it on my face before I apply base, and even after I've put on makeup. I love to be tan. It's also great for your legs, and it covers spider veins."

Linda also loves Jemma Kidd's $12 eyeliner sold at Neiman-Marcus and Sonia Kashuk cosmetics sold at Target (www.target.com).

"The year I won the *More Magazine* contest, I won a year's supply of Crest White Strips Premium Plus. People can't believe how white my teeth are, and always ask if I've had them whitened professionally. You have to initially do it for two weeks. I swear by those, since 2002." (www.crest.com)

"I try everything. They gave me some of Estee Lauder's Advanced Night Repair – I definitely see a difference (www.esteelauder.com). Makeup artists always ask me about my skin. I also use it on my décolletage. It even lightens freckles."

This bargain shopper frequents the open-air markets in Italy, loves clothes-shopping in Montreal (where the dollar still has some clout) and can't live without Zara (the chic discount store from Spain). But by far her favorite recession-proof destination is Filene's Basement. "They have the best designer stuff."

Gretta Monahan, Style Guru on *The Rachael Ray Show*, Co-Host on *Tim Gunn's Guide To Style*, and the Founder and Co-Founder of GrettaCole, G-Spa and Gretta Luxe, www.grettacole.com

If you've seen Gretta Monahan on Rachael Ray's TV show, you know – she's tiny. "I'm 5'2" – I'm just making it – and I weigh 112 pounds. I'm petite. I have to work out three times a week. I indulge when I travel, though. I'm an explorer, so I'm not sedentary."

Gretta travels A LOT. "Lordie, I travel more than than half my life, I would say, 125 days per year, easily," she confessed. "My home is in Boston, I own two boutiques, plus five spas – the most recent one opened in Ledyard, Conn., at the MGM Grand. Plus, for buying trips, I go to Paris, Milan, London, four times a year. I'm also regularly in New York, taping the *Rachael Ray* show."

For ease when traveling, Gretta never uses liquid makeup. "I have a zip-up Filofax, and all the makeups are solids – a lot of my products are by Trish McEvoy (www.trishmcevoy.com). I carry minis of June Jacobs papaya enzyme scrub on the plane (www.junejacobs.com), with Dove moist towelettes (www.dove.us). I use Vickery & Clarke aloe vera and cucumber face tonic, and Clarins water-purified one-step cleanser, (www.clarins.com). I love, love, love Darphin tangerine face oil (www.Darphin.com). It's awesome. I'm wild for it. It gives me a nice aroma." Gretta also admits that she's "crazy for" duty-free shopping for makeup, and she also loves Boots stores.

Her luggage? "I used to have a Louis Vuitton set but it got stolen . But I always have a Louis Vuitton garment bag (www.louisvuitton.com). Now Brookstone is my favorite. I'm a shoe freak, so one-half of my luggage is for shoes. Even for a weekend in Miami, I take five or six pairs of shoes. But on the plane I never ever check baggage. I take a garment bag and roller bag, or I ship it."

So how does Gretta stay fit when she's away? "My exercise is to jumprope. My trainer also just gave me tension bars. I walk or jumprope for 30 minutes. I try to walk a lot."

Leah Wyar, former Beauty Director, *Fitness Magazine,* www.fitnessmagazine.com

Lucky Leah – as part of her job, she gets invited to a dazzling array of press events around the world, when beauty companies launch product introductions. "Recently I went to Paris – or I might go for a weekend to the Hamptons.....or I've gone to Bermuda for the weekend. I also have a lot of travel with my job, for photo shoots." Leah always has snacks on hand when she travels. "I am a realist but I also indulge," she says. "I always have Ziplocs with almonds in them. At the airport, I buy one or two Fage Greek yogurts after I go through security, and I also buy a banana or orange for the plane. I eat before I get on the plane. In London recently, before takeoff, I went to a Mediterranean food stand, and bought chicken with couscous." When she's thirsty, Leah sticks with to-mato juice – it has great antioxidant benefits – and "I try to eat more protein than carbs, because on the plane you can't even take a walk to burn it off."

In terms of beauty products, Leah says that sun-screen is "crucial" and highly recommends the incredibly popular La Roche-Posay Mexoryl products (www.laroche-posay.com). Her other favorite beauty item is Chanel Hydramax Active Serum (www.chanel.com). "It's under three ounces, and it's very cooling. It wipes out the slight rosacea I get sometimes. I have to bring lip balm. I like Yes To Carrots lip balm (www.yestocarrots.com) as well as lip balm by Kiehl's (www.kiehls.com). My favorite mascara is the Dior Iconic (www.dior.com) – throw on two coats and you look gorgeous."

For exercise at her destination, Leah uses resistance bands – "They're the easiest things to use, and they're Pilates-based. If you do a series the right way, you'll feel sore the next day. Plus, if you get stiff while traveling, they're great. Those bands are great for that. I try to walk – if you can be brave and walk in a city it's better than sitting in a cab." Her luggage of choice is a Kipling nylon bag on wheels, plus Stella McCartney's Le Sportsac (www.stellamccartney.com). "I just carry it and go." She adds: "I travel in loose cotton pants by J. Crew, one of my favorites – I'll never wear jeans on a plane – and three layers on top. You have to be comfortable and look nice too."

Nancy Houlmont, Creator, Beauty 411 Blog, www.Beauty411.net

Nancy's like me – she gets weak in the knees when it comes to cosmetics. Says Nancy: "I am a pharmaceutical sales rep in my real life, with no downtime during the week, so I blog on the weekends. I travel for work six to eight times a year, and my husband and I travel for pleasure, too. I pack my own snacks and avoid airline meals and snacks– they're nothing but salt, which can make your hands and feet swell. I take a Power bar, unsalted cashews, or a fruit cup bought at the airport."

Her makeup routine is simple. Because airplanes are so dry, she starts by moisturizing with Crème de la Mer (www.cremedelamer.com). "I try not to wear much makeup on the plane except for Laura Mercier tinted moisturizer (www.lauramercier.com) and a little bronzer. My favorite is by Bobbi Brown, in the Antigua shade (www.bobbibrowncosmetics.com). I usually take Boots No. 7 fresh wipes, and halfway through the flight I wipe my face and it really revives me."

Nancy also has her fair share of swear-by products. "I love the Crème de la Mer line (www.cremedelamer.com), including the Eye Balm – it's great at helping to reduce bags under your eyes. I've recently tried – and love – SK-II Signs Eye Masks (www.sk-ii.com). They're little saturated wings for under your eyes and are perfect after a long flight. I love products that multi-task and Yves Saint Laurent's Touche Eclat is an incredible product for highlighting and brightening." (www.ysl.com)

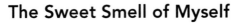

The Sweet Smell of Myself

Have I told you about *"Eau de Debbi?"* That's my custommade perfume that I crafted – with a little help from a master perfumer – in Grasse, France, at Parfumerie Galimard (www.galimard.com); $59 gets you a two-hour perfume workshop and a bottle of custom perfume. I spent two hours, assisted by the master "nose," who kept telling me to *"Melange, mélange"* (mix) my creations. I'm crazy about Vetiver by Guerlain, but in this instance I mixed my fruit and floral favorites. I started with the peak notes – and I included peach, grapefruit and cassis. "It's the first scent you smell – it's so light it flies away," the Master Nose told me. Then I picked the heart notes – peach, carnation, with some Oriental rose and violets, from all the many bottles set in front of me. "These are the most important," I was told. Then, for the bottom notes, I chose lilac, cedar and vanilla.

The result? A zesty fragrance that my olfactory glands gladly use, and which gets better the more I smell it. (You also have to give it two weeks to "set," before you use it.) But I also absolutely adore the custom label that the perfume factory put on my bottle – complete with Galimard's coat of arms of its name between two orange plants in urns. The bottle, with its rose-shaped top, looks absolutely *charmant* atop my dresser, and is a delightful souvenir.

Jean de Galimard, a friend of Goethe, lived in Grasse, where in 1747 he created the Parfumerie Galimard. He founded a corporation of glovemakers and perfumers and supplied the royal courts with olive oil, pomade and perfumes. The sources of all of these fragrances are the jasmine, roses, lavender, orange flowers and tuberoses found in Grasse.

Grasse (www.grasse.fr) is known as the "Silicon Valley of the Perfume Industry" and the "World Capital of Perfume." You can even tour a newly renovated International Perfume Museum (www.museesdegrasse.com), which is filled-to-the brim with flasks, room scenters, and incense burners. Here, in Provence, many of the world's most fragrant essences are produced, mostly from violets, daffodils, lavender, and jasmine. The legendary Chanel No. 5 – a blend of musk, Bulgarian rosebuds, and 100 other essences – was also born here.

I plan to spritz myself religiously with my own personal fragrance. So to that end, let me say: Let us spray!

Nancy doesn't normally use the hotel in-room generic bathroom amenities, preferring to bring her own. "I bring my Molton Brown travel size shower gel, Diptyque candles, and Aveda shampoo and conditioner (www.moltonbrown. com, www.diptyque.com, www.aveda.com). It's easy to find travel sizes of your favorite beauty products at Sephora (www.sephora.com), Nordstrom (www. nordstrom.com) and a new website, 3floz.com (www. 3floz.com), which has a great selection of beauty brands in travel-friendly sizes."

The site www.3floz.com offers TSA-approved mini beauty products.

And here's one of her best tips: after a long week of business meetings, she schedules her flight home to leave one day later, and uses that extra day just for spa appointments. "After days of meetings, I need to de-stress and a hot stone massage and a facial is just the ticket. It allows me to relax so that when I pull into the driveway, it's all good."

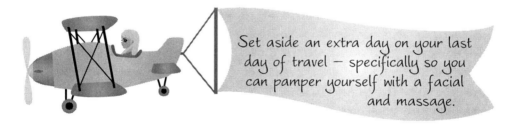

Set aside an extra day on your last day of travel — specifically so you can pamper yourself with a facial and massage.

Scent-Sational Souvenir

I'm sitting here at the award-winning Four Seasons Maui Resort at Wailea, having just spent the morning at the pool (and searching for celebrities, who always frequent this place). I spent the afternoon at the spa, a 13-room sybaritic center offering, shall I say, the Full Maui of pampering pleasures. Today I had the good fortune to have a demi-blending of Ajne (pronounced Aj-na) perfumes – a decidedly decadent experience that a slew of celebrities have raved about (Alanis Morrissette, Kate Beckinsale, Reese Witherspoon, etc). First, I filled out a brief questionnaire about my preferred fragrances, and my emotional type. (Am I a worrier? Not really. Do I have good intuition? Most certainly.) Then I met with Peggy Martin, who spent an hour with me, helping to customize my signature scent. She trained with Ajne's creator, Jane Hendler. (At Ajne Rare & Precious in Carmel, Calif., Jane crafts sophisticated scents that meld with the unique body chemistry of each client, using some of the world's most rare and precious pure plant oils.) Peggy, as my private "sherpa," and a "melangeur," helped me whittle down all the scents she showed me, to just five. One huge advantage? "People who are allergic to perfumes can wear these all-natural essential oils, which we put into a base of perfumer spirit," said Peggy. The five I liked were the Citron Regenerez ("It smells like Sprite would smell," said Peggy); Printemps (a mix of spring florals); Psyche (a mix of bergamot and Champaca Indian flowers); Savoir (a mix of bergamot and patchouli); and Sambac (containing tropical jasmine). Next, she sprayed my five favorites on my wrists, elbows and shoulders, to see which one I liked best. Hands down, it was the Citron Regenerez, which she then mixed separately with Sambac and Psyche, to offer more depth of aroma. And then, she asked, would I like to tweak any of them with linden blossom, Champaca or bergamot? I kept smelling my wrists, and truth be told, I liked my Citron Regenerez just as is. So that was that. This mix of lemon, pink-grapefruit, ginger, cypress and juniper will now adorn my wrists. The experience typically costs $150, and you go home with your own adorable 1/8-oz. gold-filigree bottle. Just like my scent, the experience was uplifting and totally refreshing. The Four Seasons Maui even boasts its own signature fragrance, Palena'ole, which Jane Hendler created for the entire resort, which is spritzed at various places throughout the surroundings. (www.ajne.com, www.FourSeasons.com/Maui)

Julia Anderson, Winner of ABC-TV's hit show, *True Beauty*, produced by Tyra Banks and Ashton Kutcher

Julia is a beauty queen from Dallas – and she's just as lovely on the inside as she is on the outside – that's why she earned the top title from the ***True Beauty*** show, and then went on to be featured in ***People Magazine's*** "100 Most Beautiful People of 2009." This 24-year-old native of Fort Worth was Miss Teen Texas in 2002, and later competed in the Miss Texas 2008 pageant. She's also a proud Native-American citizen of the Chickasaw Nation – and living proof that beauty is as beauty does.

Julia spends a lot of time in the air, as a correspondent for Tyra Bank's show. At the airport, she explains, "I usually get a Starbucks oatmeal – it's very low-calorie – and a piece of reduced-fat cinnamon coffee cake. It's sooooo good," she says. "I bring that onboard. If I'm starving on the plane, I'll get a cheese platter, but only if I have to."

She is definitely all about the comfort – "I wear sweatpants and a sweatshirt on the plane, and I bring a neck pillow and wear my Aveeno moisturizer." (www. aveeno.com). Julia "can't live without" MAC bronzer and blush, saying, "They instantly wake up your face. I also have eyelash extensions but when I don't, I love MAC Fiberlash (www.maccosmetics.com). It gives you thick, long, full lashes."

Her travel workout consists of dips, push-ups, crunches and butt lifts in her hotel room. "I typically do cardio and work out five times a week. I also love my candy and chocolate. I'm a chocoholic. I'm all about the candy. You know those round gummy peach rings? I get them at the airport every time I get on the plane, for a sugar rush."

Take It From Miss America

Kirsten Haglund, Miss America 2008, told **Woman's World** (Jan. 5, 2009) that her beauty-routine must is Victoria's Secret Vanilla Lace body wash. She told them: "I travel about 20,000 miles a month, and always have to be photo-ready. So I shower a lot more than usual, and I love my loofah. Especially with this wash on it."

Liz Mazurski, former Editor-in-Chief, *Spa Magazine*, www.spamagazine.com

"My travel varies – right now I'm on the road about 7-10 days every month or so, with short hops in between," says Liz. "We all know how miserable airline food can be so I try to be prepared. I either eat before boarding or I bring a stash of raw, unsalted nuts and fresh or dried fruit. On the ground between connections, my favorite comfort food is some kind of sandwich and a cup of tea. But, if the only thing open is a bar, I consider beer to be food."

When flying long-distance, Liz snags a pillow and blanket, and tries to make herself as comfortable as possible, which is difficult, because she's tall. "Seats on planes are miserable for me but I try to book aisle seats so I can at least get some leg room when I need it. To keep my back and body from freaking out, I get up and stretch in the back of the plane as much as I can. And drinking lots of water is an absolute must at all times."

To help avoid jet lag, Liz learned long ago to set her watch to the destination's time. "When I flew from LA to Sydney, I stayed awake for five hours after our midnight departure to get in synch so I could hit the ground running. It works like crazy for me. I eat according to my destination time zone, too. If it's time for breakfast where I'm headed, that's the meal I order."

One thing that's always in her carry-on is a tennis ball. "I roll it up and down my back. It's a great way to work out tension and it's super easy to carry along anywhere. And if you lose it, it's no big deal."

Pack a tennis ball, so you can "roll out" the tension along your spine and erase travel kinks.

Beauty products? "Yes," Liz said. "I'm obsessed with crystal deodorant. I love traveling with it. It's really small, it's not liquid and it lasts forever. A winning product. I always also travel with a tube of Kate Somerville Protect SPF 55 Serum Sunscreen. It's perfect – it moisturizes and blocks in one go. I never leave home without it (www.katesomerville.com). I also never go anywhere without a tube of Jurlique's rose hand cream, especially when I'm flying. I like the lavender, too. It's natural. Really refreshing and nourishing, even for my face. It's so pure and light (www.jurlique.com). Boscia's green-tea blotting linens are great, too. They blot up excess oil so you can look polished in a hurry. Very handy (www.bosciaskincare.com). My on-the-ground favorites include Kerstin Florian eye rescue pads – my all-time favorite product – I swear they de-puff and de-wrinkle your eyes. Brilliant. A killer product. Kerstin Florian also makes a Serum C+ Infusion day cream, SPF 30 that's really light and it's nice for travel. It feeds your skin (www.kerstinflorianusa.com). My other favorite skin reviver is Liz Earle's Super Skin Concentrate, (www.us.lizearle.com) made with argan and rose hip oils. It's so nourishing you can't imagine. It's brilliant stuff and relaxing to inhale, with a delicious smell. Great for the décolleté too."

Everything goes into Liz's Victorinox carry-on roller, and she tucks in a Longchamp fold-up tote for purchases on the road. "But my favorite travel bag is any Prada nylon bag in black," she says. "They're beautiful and practical. Right now I'm using a men's messenger bag as my travel handbag. You can't ask for more."

At her destination, Liz says she tries to never overeat. "But," she said, "when you're traveling it's tempting to fuel up. That's one of the challenges – you never know when your next meal is."

For exercise, "I'm a yoga practitioner, and I walk," she says. "It's easy to do both wherever I am. I start the day with Sun Salutations – as many rounds as I have time for. It's so completely awakening. If it makes sense, I might even rent a bicycle to sightsee and exercise at once. I need to wear my body out to get a good night's sleep."

Liz also has a preferred shopping site in every destination she travels to – the drugstore! "I shop pharmacies wherever I go. In Paris, you can get Fervex sachets that are great for suppressing flu symptoms. It's a miracle in a glass. I *beg* my friends to bring it back for me, when they travel to France. In Australia, I found the most delicious natural skincare products there, all based on rosehip oil and all locally made. They were beautiful and a real find. Pharmacies always have something interesting and they're a real window on what locals use. Plus, you can count on there being knowledgeable people there to answer your questions, so it's a win-win destination."

Shop the pharmacy for lovely foreign-made products.

Liz also shops flea markets and ethnic neighborhoods for textiles, which she collects. And she tries to get to Europe, when the annual sales occur. "I was in Madrid in early July when sales are on in Europe and I found fantastic shoe bargains. I won't need another pair of sandals for five years. International stores like Zara and H&M often have amazing things left on their sale racks that are great finds for tall Americans."

As a spa specialist, Liz has a long list of favorite spas to recommend. Rancho La Puerta and Golden Door are two West Coast favorites, along with Barberyn Ayurvedic Resort in Sri Lanka, (www.barberynresorts.com). Then there's the Como Shambhala Estate at Begawan Giri, in Bali, which she describes as "extraordinarily magical." (www.cse.como.bz.) "It's out-of-this-world gorgeous, with an Ayurvedic physician, nutritionist and even a psychologist to cater to you as a whole person. And the grounds, rooms and spa are supremely elegant, luxurious, and such a privilege to visit. You never forget this place."

Risi-Leanne Baranja, Palacinka Beauty Blog, www.Palacinka.com (pronounced PAL-A-CHINK-UH)

Risi-Leanne is a world traveler – who has her traveling beauty routine down to a science. She recommends: "The BEST exercise is using the stairs not only at your hotel, but also while taking public transportation – using the stairs to exit a station instead of the escalator or elevator. If you are in certain cities like New York, Washington, D.C., or London, which have deep underground stations, this can be quite a workout over several days!"

Her in-flight grooming tricks include Avene Eau Thermal Facial Mist, (www.aveneusa.com); Prescriptives Flight Cream, (www.prescriptives.com); La Mer Original Cream applied before the flight, (www.cremedelamer.com); Rohto Cooling Eye Drops, (www.rohtoeyedrops.com); Aveda 3-in-1 lip/cheek/eye pencil for touch-ups (www.aveda.com); Ted Gibson Hair Sheet for refreshing/moisturizing, (www.tedgibsonsalon.com); and Tarte Enbrightenment Lip Gloss Teeth Whitener, (www.tartecosmetics.com).

She says: "I never wear foundation or powder prior to flight – only light eyeliner and mascara. I use good-quality facial blotting papers to combat shine during the flight."

No matter what, Risi-Leanne always makes room in her budget for a spa massage. "It really helps to give me energy and relax me and get me focused, if it's a business trip."

For snacks, she's a high-protein, low-carb kind of gal: "Cheese cubes from Laughing Cow or Baby Bell; pre-cut salami cubes, pre-made turkey rolls with lettuce and Swiss or Havarti cheese; almonds or pecans; Vitalicious muffin tops; Fage or Oikos Greek-style yogurt cups; and water mixed with Emergen-C packs of vitamins (www.alacer.com). Another great low-cal snack I've discovered and swear by now are Jello Brand 60-calorie pudding cups in dark chocolate or double chocolate – so creamy smooth and satisfying with very nice chocolate flavor!"

Risi-Leanne also swears by Olay Pro-X Eye Restorative Cream, (www.olay.com); and Talika Therapy Eye Patches (www.talika.com).

Eye Say!

If you want to soothe tired, travel-weary eyes, you must try Talika's Eye Decompress, made in Paris. Just pop the tablet into the little vial of water and it instantly transforms into an eye mask! It will refresh and reduce swelling around your peepers, and transform you into one bright-eyed babe (www.talika.com). After all, that's why they named it the "red eye," right?

When traveling, she loves to use her Soap & Glory Clean On Me, because it's a two-for-one shower cream gel with lotion inside (available at Target). Her other secret weapon is SK-II Sheet Mask – individual packets that are perfect for travel, and a great skin treatment to apply *the night before* a big trip, especially if you're going to be in dry airplane air for more than three hours (www.sk-ii.com).

She also uses – are you sitting down? – Preparation H for eye puffiness. And her treat? Fresh flowers from the local market, or a florist, for her hotel room, when she's traveling. What a great idea!

Lots of women swear by Preparation H to shrink the swelling under their eyes.

Sarah Mays, Professional Hollywood Makeup Artist

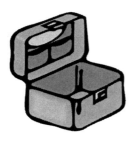

Sarah easily acknowledges that she does a great deal of traveling. She works on at least three Hollywood films a year, "so you can imagine how much travel is involved," she says. "It requires moving to a city where a film is being shot – I've been everywhere, including traveling with the press junkets afterwards, from city to city. I've been quite the globetrotter."

Sarah handles meals onboard by avoiding them. "I normally bring a favorite snack, and I like the Greens bars (www.greensplus.com). Otherwise, I'll pick up a salad or chicken salad at the airport. On occasion I might eat airline food."

Being a professional in the beauty industry, it's no surprise that Sarah has numerous favorite products and a routine in the sky. "I like to bring a small Evian water so I get a little mist. I keep moisturizer and sunscreen in my bag." There's one product that she says she is in love with, above all else: Yves Saint Laurent's Touché Eclat (www.yslbeautyus.com). "It's the fastest alterative, to get a quick brightener….I also don't leave home without DuWop's clear, reverse lip liner, to prevent lipstick from bleeding (www.shop.duwop.com). I also love Julie Hewett makeup – she offers classy colors and lovely packaging." (www.juliehewett.com)

Sarah adds that she's "madly in love" with Dr. Hauschka's lipcare sticks, for just $12 a tube (www.drhauschka.com). "They should be in everyone's purse." And she recently got some offbeat advice from a prominent Atlanta dermatologist, who told her to use prescription-strength Premarin cream (a hormone made from pregnant mare's urine, used as hormone replacement) – for her under-eye area. "He says it keeps the fine lines from showing up." Sarah also says, "The greatest moisturizers are by La Mer and Jurlique – highly emollient and effective." (www.cremedelamer.com, www.jurlique.com)

Sarah also has some great tricks up her own sleeve. If you emerge from the airplane looking and feeling parched, Sarah recommends tapping under-eye cream under your eyes, to plump up the area and keep it "glowy." Another tip, for your hotel room, is to use Bliss' Triple Oxygen Mask (www.blissworld.com) – "It will plump your skin like there's no tomorrow. It's the Number One thing I keep with me when traveling."

She keeps her weight in check by using her hotel's bathroom sink for push-ups and by walking everywhere. Her footwear of choice is MBT – the anti-shoe (www.mbt.com) whose curved soles make it easy and fun to walk – they offer a positive effect on the entire body, not just your feet. "These shoes motivate you. They're pretty special," she says.

She's also a big fan of her Zuca luggage (www.zuca.com) – the award-winning line that includes mini pouches in which to pack your belongings. "It's like having a filing cabinet of clothes in your suitcase," she says. (Each piece of luggage also doubles as a small chair, and easily navigates stairs.)

Jennifer Wayland-Smith, Spa Director, Golden Door Spa at the Boulders Resorts, www.TheBoulders.com

Whenever Jennifer flies, she takes along Wheat Thins, which she stashes in her carry-on. Among all of her favorite products, the one she can't live without—especially in the air – is her Kerstin Florian Neroli Spray - "It comes in a one-ounce bottle so it is very convenient. It refreshes the skin during travel and afterwards." (www.kerstinflorianusa.com)

Angelina Jolin, Fashion and Advertising Producer-Coordinator and Contributing Editor, *ELLE, ELLE Food and Wine, ELLE Décor Magazines*

Angelina has residences in Sweden and New York and is always on the go. On airplanes, she orders vegetarian and brings along Swedish salt licorice and dark chocolate for her sweet tooth. "I also have my Tempur eye mask, I sleep with it every night!" (Tempur-Pedic eye masks are comprised of pressure-relieving material that conforms to the shape of your face, to block out the light.) "I also use a special facial cream from the Czech Republic Called AB. (These facial creams, such as the Natural Almond Nourishing Cream, are bestsellers in Slovakia, www.ab-cosmetics.com.) She also swears by two Swedish creams from www.ldb.se and www.helosan.se. On the plane, she also uses a cucumber vitamin spray by Katarina Hakansson. (The Swedish brand makes gorgeous vitamin sprays for your face, in the flavors of cucumber, rosemary, kiwi, rose, passion fruit and orange blossom, www.hakanssonskin.com). She also takes Weleda Skin Food (www.weleda.com), her handmade ultrasuede slippers, good books, her own movies for her Mac, and some fashion magazines. Angelina carries the status-symbol luggage of choice – Louis Vuitton, as well as a Manolo Blahnik briefcase that fits her Mac. Shoes? Why, Cesare Paciotti cowboy boots, *pardner.*

Judy Goss, TV Personality, Former Ford Model, Author of *Break Into Modeling For Under $20* (St. Martin's Griffin), www.judygoss.com

Judy Goss began her career in the fashion/entertainment industry as a high-fashion model for Ford Models in New York City. She later went on to become an agent at Ford and NY Models, a casting director, producer and editor at *Cosmopolitan* and *More* magazines.

"I used to live on a plane when I was modeling and lived in Miami, Brazil, Germany and Italy and traveled all over the world," says Judy. "I usually ate something bought at the airport – a fresh turkey sandwich or tuna, and fruit, and three or four bags of munchies – everything from popcorn to raisins, and potato chips."

"It's hard to have a routine when traveling, so I like products that do double-duty," she adds. "Philosophy Real Purity Cleanser is a cleanser, makeup remover, and toner (www.philosophy.com). And I use Stila tinted moisturizer with SPF (www.stilacosmetics.com). I love products with more than one purpose. And I can't live without my Maybelline eyelash curler. If I were to take nothing else on an island, that's it." (www.maybelline.com)

Her exercise routine? "For me, I have to do crunches in hotel rooms – leg lifts, stretching, push-ups. At the gym I do cardio on the treadmill. I lift light weights for toning and I love yoga."

Jet lag is never a problem for Judy – lucky her! "I used to commute between Miami and Italy. I would adjust my watch as soon as I got on the plane. When I got to my destination, I wouldn't sleep until bedtime."

Helen Powers, Fit Model formerly with Ford Models, www.Helenpowers.com

Helen is a professional fit model, which means that she is a "vanity size 6" or a "standard size 8." She has been featured in numerous magazines, including *O, The Oprah Magazine*, and was seen in January 2008 in *More Magazine*, having her long hair cut by none other than Frederic Fekkai, the renowned style-maker (www.fekkai.com).

"I'm not crazy about food on an airplane," says Helen. "I eat animal crackers or granola bars. No carbonated drinks or coffee. I usually bring a protein bar or trail mix bar with me. They satiate me if I can't eat lunch. I might buy a turkey sandwich at the airport."

Helen has an idea that might even help you, dear reader. "It's always been my dream to make an exercise DVD for traveling and working women," says Helen. "I work out in my home. I ride my Exercycle. I use Jane Fonda's first exercise video – it still works for me. I know the routine by heart. I might do some weights. I don't like gyms or the time it takes to get there. I get my exercise walking from place to place in Manhattan every day. Today I was in Florida, at my Mom's, and I ran up and down the stairs, did 100 sit-ups. I just needed to get my body moving."

Her luggage is a Swiss Army wheelie (with a lifetime guarantee), with a special compartment for shoes (www.swissarmy.com). Helen herself designed a special Travel Bag, called "The Power Bag," and she had more than 2,000 of them sold at Saks, Equinox gyms and various other retail stores. It was written up in *O Magazine* and in *The Wall Street Journal.* "Women in New York always carry two bags and it bothered me," Helen says; that's why she created her Power Bag. It featured different compartments for shoes, wet bathing suits, wallets, a water bottle and cosmetics.

Helen likes to fly American First Class, but when she shuttles to Florida she takes Jet Blue. "I pay $69 more for the extra legroom in an exit row." She frequently travels to Hong Kong on Cathay Pacific Business Class – "I've never experienced such amazing service, on a plane with such privacy in Business Class along with First Class service. I actually slept 10 hours because the seats recline totally flat. I hate flying, but on this specific flight, it's unbelievable. The 16 and one-half hours just fly by. I fly to Hong Kong for Talbot's, and I have fit for them for over 20 years, and I love their completely new and fashion-forward style. Even Michelle Obama is frequently photographed wearing Talbot's clothes."

"On my last flight to Europe I read Michael Tonello's ***Bringing Home The Birkin*** book. I've never laughed so hard. People on the plane were looking at me."

Her swear-by cosmetics? "I have freckles so I use something old-school: Elizabeth Arden Flawless Finish (www.elizabetharden.com). I also asked my dermatologist and he recommended Oil Of Olay (www.olay.com) – I use Regenerist Eye Lifting Serum, Night Recovery, and UV Defense Regenerating Lotion SPF 15."

Helen's best beauty tip is as follows, and I couldn't agree more: "I try to stay in a place of gratitude and joy, and to be grateful to be where you're at and where you're going. If you're beautiful on the inside, it will project on the outside and you will glow."

Genevieve Monsma, Beauty Director, *MORE Magazine*, www.More.com

As Beauty Director of one of the most high-profile women's magazines, Genevieve gets to try a wealth of new products – and travel the world for new product introductions. "Each year I go on two to three press trips," she told me. "When Sunsilk haircare launched in the United States, Unilever sponsored a press trip to Sun Valley during the Sundance Film Festival. I've also been to St. Bart's with Dove, and I just got back from Tokyo for Shiseido."

Genevieve travels with snack foods. "I have an aversion to airplane meals, so I usually stash trail mix, a banana and water in my bag. I was happy to have my own food supply when, on a recent Japan Airlines flight, they served only seafood. On a plane? I don't think so. I also like hard candy when I'm traveling—it fights boredom. Some of my favorites are Brach's Butterscotch and Charms Blow-Pops."

Genevieve's beauty routine is to wear as little makeup as possible. "I feel like a face full of foundation is a dirt magnet in the air," she says. "So I try to get on the plane wearing just moisturizer, some tinted lip balm like Fresh's Rose and a little water-resistant mascara (www.fresh.com). I don't go anywhere with-

Make The Best-Tressed List

What to do when the hair dryer just isn't hot enough, you don't have the right-voltage curling iron, and your hair's dirty? These travel woes can put you to the test, but Alex Safar, owner of the ultrachic Salon Acote on Boston's fashionable Newbury Street, offers these tips. Here's how to make your hair the "mane attraction" anywhere in the world (www.salonacote.com).

1. If you're going to be away for a long time, or taking a world cruise, "Buy color and developer at your salon, so you can tap it on your roots while you're away," Alex says. "Don't ever get your hair cut or colored at your destination unless you have a personal recommendation and bring a picture with you."

2. Always have a special adapter with you, so your hair equipment will be the right voltage. Call your hotel ahead of time, to see if they supply hair dryers and any other equipment, so you can avoid bringing anything at all. Or, bring a universal-voltage GHD flat iron – to make your hair straight or curly.

3. Ask the best hotel in your destination for a referral to a top hair salon in that area. The concierges there will gladly make recommendations for your salon visit. Salon Acote, for example, works with the concierges at the Four

out mascara. If I'm on a long flight, once we're in the air, I stick on hydrating under-eye masks by Shiseido or Lancome, slip on a sleep mask, and take a nap. I also carry La Mer lip balm and slather it over my lips and cuticles repeatedly." (www.shiseido.com, www.lancome-usa.com, www.cremedelamer.com)

Genevieve also admits that she gladly pays the extra $25 per checked bag, because she loves to take all of her hair appliances with her—and they take up serious space. "I don't go anywhere without my Solano blowdryer. Too often, the one provided by the hotel provides as much air flow as a kid blowing out candles on a cake. But product-wise, I keep things simple and I try to stick to multipurpose products to conserve room. I love DDF Dew Ultra Light; because

Seasons Boston and even makes in-room visits to do clients' hair in private.

4. Visit Sally Beauty Supply to purchase a small color wand, which you can draw onto your gray hairs. "It works for one day, to hide things," says Alex. "You can also do the same with black mascara, for a quick touch-up."

5. Purchase mini plastic bottles, so that you can pour your favorite shampoos into them. "We use Rene Furterer and Kerastase at Salon Acote, but those brands don't come in travel sizes," Alex explains. "But you can easily transfer these high-end products into small plastic portables."

6. Never travel without bobby pins and hair elastics – they're indispensable.

7. The best-ever dry shampoo is Kerastase Naturia, says Alex. "We sell more of it than any other product. It will make your blow-dry more bouncy, and absorb oil. If you're in a pinch, baby powder or cornstarch will do the trick," adds Alex.

And here something else: if you want lots of volume and bouncy, big beautiful hair, try Bump-Its. Just attach these little plastic pieces to your crown, smooth them over with hair, and you've got va-va-vavoom volume (www.bumpits.com). You'll have Hollywood hair in just minutes!

it's both a moisturizer and sunscreen (www.ddfskincare.com). And Bliss makes a good 'all-in-one' exfoliator, cleanser and toner (www.blissworld.com).

Exercise? "I always stay somewhere with a gym and I'm usually the first person there at 5:30AM, reading a celebrity tabloid and sweating on the elliptical machine. Plus, I'm a New Yorker so I walk wherever and whenever I can. In Beverly Hills, I walked from my hotel to Fred Segal. It was about three miles. The locals passed me in their BMWs and stared at me as though I was deranged."

Her luggage is a Stella McCartney Sportsac rolling duffle (www.lesportsac. com). Her purse is an Yves Saint Laurent caramel tote – "It holds a lot, keeps

Jackie Oh!

Before Jackie Kennedy, the standard of American beauty was defined by Elizabeth Taylor, who possesses a heart-shaped face.

But Jackie Kennedy started the current, ongoing trend that defines beauty by a wide face, says Dr. Anthony Weikel, director of Boston Cosmetic Center in Newton, Mass. (www.bostonfaces.com), who specializes in surgery on faces. Dr. Weikel believes that Mrs. Kennedy popularized a new image of beauty that still prevails today. "She possessed a wide face, where the gonial angle of the lower jaw, on the outside, was rather large," Dr. Weikel says.

Dr. Weikel has also observed that Mrs. Kennedy had, in comparison to other beauties of her time, a short face that was frequently complemented by bangs. "Nowadays, starlets and supermodels have short, wide faces – everyone from Christie Brinkley to Michelle Pfeiffer," says Dr. Weikel.

its shape and isn't too flashy – something I think is important when traveling. Nothing says 'steal from me' like an overtly expensive bag," she says (www.ysl.com). And her favorite shopping find is the jewelry designer Becky Thatcher, in northern Michigan, where Genevieve and her family vacation every August. "She makes things with local gems and stones. From her, I've gotten some of my favorite accessories: a ring carved out of a Petoskey stone and a cuff bracelet created from a piece of broken china bearing my son's name."

Her favorite airline? Any one with business class. "My recent trip on JAL was pretty fabulous. You've got to love a seat that fully reclines."

Angela Doyle, Spa Manager, Fairmont Kea Lani Maui Resort, www.Fairmont.com/kealani

"For traveling I love to have a little bottle of hydrating flower water to mist my face any time I can....in the restroom, before the plane, or after. Kerstin Florian's Neroli or Rose water are both amazing." (www.kerstinflorianusa.com)

"Having a facial before you travel is great; when you get off the plane your face still looks and feels nice."

"Take along a travel pack of mineral salts. Kerstin Florian or Tara Spa Therapy are two great options. As soon as you can, take a mineral bath to relax your muscles and rejuvenate after the travel....It makes a huge difference."

"I really like Skinceuticals (www.skinceuticals.com). It's the best Vitamin C on the market. And B. Kamins products give instant results." (www.bkamins.com)

D'Andra Simmons, Creator of the cosmetic brand, Hard Night Good Morning, www.dandrasimmons.com

D'Andra, who has been involved in the skincare and nutrition industries for much of her life, travels up to four times a month from her home in Dallas, and follows a strict regimen of travel techniques guaranteed to make her feel good.

"I have my housekeeper cut up vegetables and fruits for me," D'Andra says. "Or I take vegetarian sushi. I don't want sugar or iodized salt, and I don't drink alcohol when flying, especially if I'm going overseas. I take antioxidant vitamins. After landing I'll double or triple the amount. And I'll take up to six packets of Emergen-C to make up for my depleted antioxidant levels. The liquid C assimilates faster than a tablet." (www.alacer.com)

D'Andra also might take a chicken breast and raw almonds, for the protein, and swears by a product her other company makes, called Green Miracle. "It's from my mother's and my company called Ultimate Living. It has 70 ingredients. It gives you your fruits and vegetables...there are 30 calories in three scoops." (www.ultimateliving.com)

And here's a little beauty trick I just love: D'Andra buys Vitamin C powder at the health-food store, and mixes it with toner, to give her face a burst of fresh antioxidants. "I spray it all over my face," she says. She also mixes the Vitamin C powder with her moisturizer. "It's a natural sunscreen and you won't burn. I used it in Cabo and I was white as a sheet when I left."

She has several favorite airlines – Virgin, Singapore, South African and British Airways – that's because they offer full fold-out beds. "I travel First Class when going overseas. But Virgin has more entertainment features – they're fun."

D'Andra says, "One of my favorite shopping destinations is Marché aux Puces Saint-Ouen de Clignancourt in Paris, France. At this famous and gargantuan flea market, you can find everything from vintage Chanel handbags and clothes to junky knock-offs and fabulous antiques." (www.parispuces.com)

Add Vitamin C powder to water, to create a tonic that you can mist on your face. Add it to moisturizer, for an effective antioxidant sunscreen.

Emily Katz, Department Head and Celebrity Makeup Artist for Film and TV

Emily is constantly traveling between her home in Los Angeles and Hawaii, for her work. "I'm allergic to a lot of foods, so I usually just get a salad on the plane. But on Virgin Atlantic to Europe, I had a great food experience. They are very generous. I highly recommend Virgin Atlantic – and the ongoing ability to have fruit whenever you want on the plane is quite a plus. Their flight attendants have great senses of humor, so it's very enjoyable."

"Before I get on the plane, I overload on eye cream and moisturizer. I use ChapStick and Caudalie lip balm (even on my cuticles) (www.caudalie-usa.com); many Jan Marini products (www.janmarini.com); and La Mer SPF 18 (www. cremedelamer.com). I like Jan Marini's sunscreen and her Age Intervention – in fact I love it. I'm big on La Mer – I use their eye concentrates and eye balms. One of my staples – and one which I use on set – is Clarins Eye Revive Beauty Flash (www.clarins.com) – it refreshes and brightens, and it does take the puffiness away. I always have a tube with me." Emily has other favorites including B. Kamins Bio-Maple Revitalizing Booster (www.bkamins.com) and anything by Jurlique (www.jurlique.com). "In my kit I like the Biodynamic Refining Exfoliant, and their Silk Dust in rose, lavender and citrus. They are exquisite and gorgeous. I love Jurlique products."

As far as exercise goes, "I'm a runner," Emily says. "I wear Nikes. I get on the treadmill in the gym or run outside at my destination – such as Kensington in London. Or I might just do a little kicking workout in my room."

She can't say enough good things about her Samsonites (www.samsonite.com): "I use the semi-hard case with 360-degree wheels. God bless whoever invented the 360 wheel. They're brilliant. I've been around the world with my Samsonites and they're still in decent shape."

Jennifer Walsh, former Owner of The Beauty Bar chain of retail stores, former Makeup Artist and Freelance Beauty Writer, www.jenniferwalshonline.com

As Jennifer's website says, she is well-versed in all things beauty. "I like lots of products on-the-go" she explains; these include Freeze 24/7 Freeze and Go (www.freeze247.com). "It replicates what Botox would do. It helps plump up the lines. I just love it. You can even put it on over makeup, I don't go anywhere without it. I also love Crème de la Mer cleanser and moisturizer (www.creme-delamer.com). I buy it at Saks or Neiman-Marcus. I also love Kate Somerville products for travel (www.katesomerville.com). I also love Bobbi Brown make-up (www.bobbibrowncosmetics.com). They have great kits for eyes, lips and cheeks, and great palettes."

She is also a big fan of Flight 001 (www.flight001.com) – a store that carries everything for travelers. "I love it and everything is under two ounces."

Exercise? "I've been a runner for 30 years and I run when get to my destination." Her snacks on the plane include a chicken or tuna sandwich, and a 16-oz. bottle of water. "I stay away from the mile-high Mojitos."

Wendy Bazilian, Doctor of Public Health, Registered Dietitian, Author of *The SuperFoodsRx Diet* (Rodale Publishing), and Nutrition Specialist for the Golden Door fitness resort and spa, www.wendybazilian.com

"I travel about twice a month on average, but as much as four times a month," says Dr. Wendy. And she tells me she has lots of health and beauty insider secrets, especially when traveling. "I bring—and wear—my pedometer. I do serious leg lifts while blow-drying – it's a ritual. I do arm swings when I wake and before I go to sleep – which stretches me out and gets the blood flowing. I march in place watching the morning shows or CNN in the hotel. I also take a five-minute walk multiple times in a day. Walk and talk with people, for meetings, instead of sitting down for tea or a break. Just keep moving, that's my motto."

She always flies with a Martin & Barnett (San Francisco) eye mask, which comes in silk/velour, and comfortable ear plugs. "I know I've got to use my travel time to work or get rest for my good health and productivity."

Her other recommendations? "Water, water, water—honestly it helps the skin, actually minimizes swelling, and because you are drinking water, it provides a built-in reminder that you should get up to walk on the plane and stretch when you get up to use the restroom." Wendy also recommends green tea –"It increases water (hydration), and I love it for its metabolic and antioxidant boost."

The cosmetics she craves are Golden Door Crisis Cream II with AHA (www. goldendoor.com). "It feels so smooth, but not oily and smells subtle but amazing." She also likes Jurlique Rosewater Balancing Mist (www.jurlique.com) – "It fits easily in my 3-oz. liquid quart-sized bag. I spritz during the flight. It feels moist, smells nice and makes me feel like I'm keeping the stale flight air away. I also like Burt's Bees Beeswax Lip Balm – all natural, with a nice fragrance, and not sticky." (www.burtsbees.com)

Naturally, you would expect Wendy to stress good health and hygiene when flying. "Wash your hands, keep hands away from face, and wipe down surfaces before settling in. That means all surfaces I might touch – seatbelt, tray table, head rest, lean-back button, window shade. It's saved me from getting even a single cold (not one) from a plane flight in over three years (probably a couple hundred flights at least). And when I'm traveling with my business partner and husband, Jason, who happens to be one of the foremost doctors of acupuncture and oriental medicine, my secret health booster is two tiny acupuncture needles inconspicuously inserted in points on both my hands."

Being a registered dietitian, Dr. Wendy also knows what to eat, when in the air. "Walnuts and dried cherries – two natural sources of melatonin – in a home-made trail mix! A great, portable snack, offering some protein, healthy carbs, a crunchy and sweet/tart flavor, great energy and they can be added to my oatmeal if I have to make a meal on the fly." Her other standby is a peanut butter and low-sugar fruit preserves sandwich, cut in quarters or a PB and sliced-fruit sandwich (apple, banana, nectarine, or blueberries). "It accomplishes two things – I get great, nutritious travel food and I don't let the fruit in my kitchen go to waste as I head off on a trip." She also recommends oatmeal packets – "I always travel with instant oatmeal packets – McCann's or Uncle Sam's. You can get hot water anywhere. And don't forget green tea bags – my husband and I make tea-times central to our lives. We're like a traveling tea house sometimes with the variety of tea bags."

"Meals on airplanes? What are those?" Wendy asks. "I don't even go there. I bring something. Often I pack an organic salad or make a healthy wrap or stop by the evening before a flight to a great market and get something amazing to carry on. It's so worth it (and you're the envy of the flight, too – so sometimes I bring an extra something if I'm going to sit next to someone so I can share a bit of what I have)."

Wendy's beauty routine when traveling starts with vintage Clairol Hot Rollers – the travel set, of course. "Sure I get laughs, but the curls are terrific. One of my fabulous friends, Nancy, in New York makes such fun of me about these – but they are quick, easy and awesome!" Wendy also loves Estee Lauder Intensive Eye Lifting Cream (www.esteelauder.com). "I wear it at night and though I'm only 'almost 40' and they say this is for 50- and 60-year-olds, I can really see a difference in moisture and fine lines."

"I also love Jane Iredale cosmetics – all natural, no paraben, mineral makeup and color. Her products are amazing and I feel good about using them frequently (www.janeiredale.com). I also like the Skyn Iceland Relief Eye Cream (www.skyniceland.com). I can be a puff-ball in the morning for about an hour after I wake up and this calms everything down. Another must if I'm going to wear foundation and be out all day on television: Smashbox Photofinish Foundation Primer." (www.smashbox.com)

Wendy's also never without Lancome Rouge Sensation Luxe (www.lancome-usa.com). "I wear it practically every day and I get so many comments and compliments. Another tip when on the road: "I lightly brush my teeth with baking soda about once a week – it removes any of my normal tea stains and really brightens me up (without the expensive teeth-whitener strips that actually make my teeth a bit sensitive even after a single use). About 50 cents a box and lasts me all year. On the road, it's an unusual, but always available item from room service or from the restaurant."

Her luggage is the Victorinox Werks Traveler series – because of the lifetime warranty (www.victorinox.com). "They'll fix anything – zippers, tears, whatever. Plus it's super lightweight so you can pack more in the allowable weight." She also owns a Black Tumi carry-on roller bag (www.tumi.com) and an L.L. Bean classic canvas tote – XL size – folded into another piece of luggage (www.llbean.com). And her bigger than average Coach purse, with classic brass toggles in go-with-anything vintage brown leather, holds everything from the laptop and file folders to more dainty items like lipgloss and a travel toothbrush while always looking smart (www.coach.com). Another of her fab finds: Ecco London Mary Jane shoes. "They have a modest heel, about 2-2 ½ inches – They're a go-anywhere day shoe, but really nice looking. I get stopped and asked about them all the time because I can literally walk all day in them comfortably and they look professional and fashionable, too." (They were founded in Denmark in 1963, www.ecco.com.)

Finally, here are her super secret weapons: her health remedies. Yin Chiao powder – the traditional Chinese Medicine formula. "I take it at the first signs of sore throat, dry throat or slight fever. It's been used for generations in China at the first signs of cold. I just mix it in room-temperature water. And my favorite is White Flower liniment oil – I use it topically if I sense a headache coming on or if my neck or shoulder muscles ache. It's simply amazing."

Eva Malmstrom Shivdasani, Former Model and Creative Director, Six Senses Spa, www.sixsensesspa.com

Eva is a fashion designer by schooling and a fashion model by chance, as well as an amateur photographer. She also owned her own dress manufacturing company in Paris and designed for companies like Sergio Rossi shoes.

"I live between the Maldives and Bangkok and go twice a year to London and Sweden where I have a summer place by a lake," Eva says. "There are a few things one can do to make one's journey more safe and comfortable when fly-ing. I always put a thick oil (like jojoba) into my nose, as the air in the plane is very dry. I always wear my special travel outfit, which is made of linen and consists of a pair of wide pants with elastic waist. Over that a sleeveless top that covers the hips, and finally an ample shirt/blouse with long sleeves. Being dressed like an onion is practical as one can easily adjust to different tempera-tures. I have this travel outfit in several colors."

"I usually wear support stockings, which look exactly the same as any nude color stocking, to prevent deep vein thrombosis. All makeup and amenities I use are 100% natural. (I keep a list of toxic ingredients and check labels when I go shopping). I also put what vitamins I need for the trip in tiny containers, and my makeup – from Aveda and Dr. Hauschka. The shampoo and conditioner I use is from Louise Galvin in London; it's totally natural and she was the first hair-dresser in the world, I believe, to become 'carbon neutral.'" (www.louisegalvin. com; she is one of the UK's best hair colorists.)

"My favorite airline is Singapore Airlines – they let you take two bags (without fees). I fly it so much that it feels like a second home. Singapore Airlines has fantastic service, always so kind and helpful. The planes are very clean and new, the loos are super clean (and kept that way during the whole flight) and the food is always good. I fly Qatar Airlines when I go from the Maldives to Europe."

"As I never have time to go shopping, I have all my clothes made by my tailor in Bangkok and buy my sandals at 'Charles and Keith' at Singapore airport. I buy all my travel handbags from the German company Bogner (www.bogner. com). They are by far the most practical handbags for traveling and every-day use. They are beautiful and have thousands of pockets, which for me is essential."

Carmela Arcolas-Gambola, Beauty Title Holder in The Philippines

Carmela has held three different beauty titles in The Philippines – "MassKara Queen 1995," "Miss Western Visayas, 1997," and "Miss Philippines Centennial 1998," which is the jewel in her crown. I met her in Westwood, Mass., (my hometown) when she was part of a Group Study Exchange sponsored by Rotary International. Here's what she told me.

"When I held my title, I traveled a lot around The Philippines, and I took a lot of planes and ferryboats." Staying thin? "Our staple is rice, so it's hard to stay thin because of the starch. I usually do a Continental breakfast, a salad for lunch with only a quarter-cup of rice, and a lot of greens. On this particular trip (to the Boston area) I've been not so good. I order kiddie meals in restaurants or share with a teammate. I drink a lot of water but no soda or chocolate. I take sugar-free gum and candies with me. We've done a lot of walking here – one host family even had a gym in their basement, so I did weights and used a treadmill for the three days I was there."

"I like Oil of Olay," Carmela continued (www.olay.com). "I used Mary Kay a lot before (www.marykay.com) and now I use a travel makeup kit from Lancome (www.lancome-usa.com). At home, I get a facial every week at my dermatologist, and a Diamond Peel twice a month. It's great, because I can get a massage at home, once a week, for just $4. That's how it is in The Philippines."

Marie Lowrance, Certified Laser Specialist, Consultant to JTav Clinical Skin Care & Laser Center, www.youngskinforever.com

Marie, who lives in New York, travels all the time, and when I interviewed her, she had just returned from a two-week trip to Italy. "We always fly First Class. I'm very careful and stick more to carbs, water and red wine. I use Evian spray on my face. I eat snacks such as blanched almonds and dark chocolate." Her favorite airline is Air China – "I absolutely loved the healthy food, and the very calm stewardesses. And I love Swiss Airlines – they're great. Comfort is important to me – I'm 5'10" and you could lie down flat on Swiss Airlines. I was so comfortable and the food was great."

Ten years ago Marie was on a plane when she got an attack of deep-vein thrombosis – and survived. "So now I always get up and walk around and drink much more water. My entire right side was paralyzed. It could happen to anyone."(Deep-vein thrombosis is the formation of a blood clot ("thrombus") in a deep vein, which can dislodge and travel to the heart and the lungs.)

Her beauty regimen is to use a nice moisturizer – "or I might make my own," she told me. She also might use some youth serum from Is Clinical (www. isclinical.com).

Her exercise routine? "I have it down pat," she said. "I do a lot of stairs, and work out my arms. I might take my smallest bag and lift it. I'm very concerned about legs and arms. I do some squats and lunges. Or I might use the gym."

On a recent trip to Venice, she had a spa treatment at the legendary Hotel Cipriani. "They have the neatest spa, with mood lighting that changes – it's really interesting. I had a massage with blue lighting. It's really well done. And in China, the way that they shampoo your hair is amazing. They work the shampoo into your head until the foam is a foot high. It was fabulous."

Her luggage is Tumi (www.tumi.com) and she always travels with just one purse. On this trip it was a black-patent leather Marc Jacobs. And her ultimate beauty secret? "I always travel with a sonic peel – a handheld device for your skin. It's very small. I use it every other day. I swear by it. It takes everything off your face. It's rechargeable, and it's the best little tool there is. It's even great when your Botox starts to wear off – if you use it over the Botoxed areas, you can get another month out of your Botox, before it wears off."

Bed Voyage!

Going to an inexpensive hotel or motel? Do yourself a favor and pack high thread-count sheets and pillowcases, to make the experience more of a luxury. BedVoyage is an eco-luxury brand that makes all-in-one linens for your travels. Made of 100% organic bamboo, the linens consist of a top sheet secured to a deep fitted sheet with beautifully embroidered and zippered pillowcases. Soft as silk or cashmere, BedVoyage bamboo sheets are naturally antibacterial, odor-resistant and anti-mite. Sheets come in twin, double, king and queen. Menopausal women may also find the coolness of the bamboo helpful for their night sweats. These sheets are definitely swoon-worthy (www.bedvoyage.com).

Jennifer Devlin, International Beauty Therapist, Author, Educator, International Makeup Artist and Master Esthetician, www.beachbeautymobileday-spa.com

Jennifer has one of the best – and one of the most unusual – travel tips I've ever heard – she travels with her own set of 800-thread-count sheets. "I would rather use the room in my suitcase for sheets, rather than shoes. You spend one-third of your life sleeping. I go to Tuesday Morning, where they carry $500 brands from Italy. You can score those sheets for about $149. I also spray my own lavender oil on my sheets. The dumpier the hotel, the more you need those sheets and pillowcases. They are well-appreciated."

Jennifer used to be the online beauty director for the website Eve.com and a result, "I had products sent to me all the time – we would test-drive the products." But she's been in love with just one product out of all of them, for more than 10 years – Emu oil contained in Dremu (www.dremu.com). "It's a product that does everything – you can use it on your lips, cuticles, hair – it doesn't smell – you can add essential oils to it – it's transdermal, so it disappears into the skin, making your face look plump and radiant." So when Jennifer travels, she takes her Dremu oil. She also is faithful to Angel Organics' coconut oil – "It's nature's magical elixir – I even take it internally, two teaspoons daily. If I was stranded on *Survivor,* I'd take coconut oil." She used to work for Colorescience (www.Colorescience.com), and says she never goes anywhere without their Sunforgettable powdered sunscreen. "I'm never without it – it has the highest percentage of zinc and titanium dioxide than any other product. I really like it – I would never use anything else. I have one in my car, in my purse, and at home." She also purchases nothing but therapeutic-grade Rocky Mountain Oils (www.rockymountainoils.com); she soaks them into a cotton-ball, and tucks it into her bra. "It instantly makes you feel good." Jennifer also purifies her own drinking water by using a reverse-osmosis machine – "It takes all the junk out of your water and turns it into high alkaline water," and this is the water she travels everywhere with. She doesn't eat airline food and instead, packs almonds and raw fruits and vegetables, plus Clif bars. Her exercise routine is yoga – "It oxygenates your body and all your vital organs." Jennifer's mom worked for PanAm Airlines for 30 years, and that's how Jen learned to take carry-on for everything. "I've traveled my whole life and I multi-task my wardrobe. Wear your pashmina, and wear flip-flops through security. Virgin Atlantic is my favorite airline – they give you lots of goodies."

And when it comes to souvenirs, when she goes to flea markets and bazaars, she purchases fabrics, which she has made into pillows and blankets. "I have drawers filled with fabrics. I have things made for me. In Sydney I bought fabric, and I made stuff for my yoga altar."

Sheree Fletcher, Founder of Whoop Ash, www.whoopash.com

Sheree does a great deal of commuting between both of her homes in Los Angeles and San Diego. (Her husband is former NFL running

Bee Beautiful!

Sheree Fletcher, creator of Whoop Ash – now a Hollywood must-have – was inspired to create her product after seeing the hit movie, *The Secret Life of Bees*. Sheree became inspired to learn more about the healing properties of honey; she discovered that honey, a humectant, has the ability to attract and retain moisture. White honey, in particular, has a rich, smooth, creamy texture, not unlike icing on a cake. After more than six years of research, concocting creations on her stove, and working with chemists, Sheree perfected her formula; Whoop Ash contains white honey, grapeseed oil, organic shea butter, mango butter, and organic coconut oil. It's destined to defeat all dry skin, which is why celebrities who include Queen Latifah, Alicia Keys, Cameron Diaz, and Vivica A. Fox all use it (www.whoopash.com).

back Terrell Fletcher). And, in the next few months, she'll be doing much more traveling by plane, to promote her skincare product Whoop Ash (see sidebar). "I never leave home without a neck pillow," Sheree says. She snacks on raw, unsalted cashews, munches on chocolate-graham Zone bars, and always has her iPod with her, to listen to podcasts and audio books. Her must-have makeup? "I just discovered Nars, and they offer an amazing foundation (www.narscosmetics.com). I also like the Black Opal brand, which is made for African-Americans (www.blackopalbeauty.com). I stock up on it a Duane Reade in New York. I love their foundation stick."

At her destination, Sheree is apt to do sit-ups and push-ups in her hotel room. And she makes a point to hold her tummy in, all day long. "It works my stomach muscles," she explains.

Her luggage is bright red Swiss Army and Tumi (www.swissarmy, www.tumi.com). "But I don't check my Louis Vuitton," she says with a laugh. "It always stays with me." (www.louisvuitton.com)

Packing tips? She only has one – and that's to have someone else pack for you. "Hire someone to do it for you," she says. "My housekeeper packs for me."

Diane Ranger, Inventor and Founder of Colorescience Pro, www.colorescience.com

Diane travels 12 weeks a year on business. When she's on a plane, she's never without her lavender baby pillow. "As you lie down, it crushes the lavender inside the pillow and releases the lavender oils. It keeps me relaxed, along with my iPod and Sony noise-reducing headphones." Diane doesn't eat airline food, and instead carries Power bars, trail mix, beef jerky and a lot of water. "I try to eat as much protein as I can."

"I always walk in my destination in my MBT footwear – they make them in 'Mary Janes' – and I wear them at the airport. You can even wear them with dress pants. Since using them the dimpling in all of my legs went away, and I have better posture." (www.Us.mbt.com)

One thing that she swears by is her Obagi blender, which she says is proven to help activate Retin-A. "Obagi really offers dramatic results," she says (www.obagi.com). And the other thing that has transformed her life is having her hair straightened with Keratin (www.keratincomplex.com). "It gave my hair volume and control. You'll feel like a rock star. I have naturally wavy hair. Now I can swim and let it dry naturally. It cost me $100/hr., and I do it every four to six months. It is a big deal. It's so amazing, it should be sold as an anti-aging hair treatment." She also got a prescription for Latisse, just two days after it went on the market (www.latisse.com). She swears by this lash-lengthener, saying, "You won't even need to wear mascara. I can't go without Latisse."

Wavy hair? Curls? Frizz? For rock-star, stick-straight hair, get a Coppola Keratin Complex Treatment.

Dawn Fitch, CEO of Pooka Pure and Simple, www.pookapureandsimple.com

Dawn travels at least once a month, and follows a special diet wherever she goes. "No sugar, red meat or diary. I might order the diabetic meal on the plane. I bring trail mix and nuts. I do a lot of brown rice and sushi, lots of fish and salads. I practically live in Whole Foods. On the plane I just drink water and eat my snacks. At my destination I do yoga. It helps you fight fatigue and jet lag." And here's her greatest travel tip: Dawn swears by Tom's of Maine toothpaste – for pimples. "The tea tree toothpaste cleans out bacteria, and the peppermint toothpaste dries it out. It always works. That's my secret travel tip." (www.tomsofmaine.com)

Dawn always packs her yoga DVD, soy candles, laptop, iPod and ceramic Chi flat iron. "I love it – no matter what, it doesn't burn your hair. I might even run it through my hair at the airport, in the bathroom, if I have to rush into a meeting after a flight." When she's looking for a bargain, she finds it at Marshall's. "I'm a Marshall's fanatic – I can always find a store, because I am always forgetting something in my travels."

Decorate-On-A-Dime With Cosmetics

Beauty products and cosmetics can be a wonderful way to decorate various rooms in your home. My home, a former ShowHouse, is called My Faux Chateau, because I decorated it to look like a villa in the South of France – but I did it all with bargains. In my toile-decorated French bedroom, for example, I showcase a container of Benefit's "Kitten Goes to Paris" powder, books on France, tins of French designer candies, and French perfume. In my South Pacific bathroom is a slew of spa products, including a wealth of gorgeous gelatin soaps from Hawaii, beauty creams from Bali and Bora Bora, imported candles, and Tahitian monoi oil. Remember, when you see an adorably packaged beauty product or interesting item (like champagne-flavored toothpaste), add it to your décor. You'll have a constant reminder of your terrific travels.

Helen Brown, Spa Director, the award-winning Mobil-Five-Star Mayflower Inn and Spa, www.mayflowerinn.com

Helen has a great tip for all women: do Kegels! Everywhere and anytime you can. "You should do Kegels for all kinds of different reasons," says Helen. "It's a muscle like every other muscle, which needs to be exercised, and it also enhances sexual pleasure for both sexes." Helen also advocates, when you're traveling, to discreetly stand on one leg, to work on your balance. She also travels with resistance bands.

Beauty tips? "Make sure to have a facial the week before you travel – that way your skin will look great, and you can ask your facialist for samples that you can take on the flight," Helen advises. She takes almond butter, almonds, carrot sticks, protein bars and apples to eat on every flight, although she might order a vegan meal. She's also never without her travel candle, and a sleep spray made by Nectar Essences (www.nectaressences.com). At her destination, she might ask room service for some honey for her face – "Just put raw honey on your face – raw honey used as a facial mask works wonders – it's a natural exfoliant, and very hydrating," she explains.

Miss Louisiana 2010, Sara Brooks

We all know that traveling can be an ordeal – imagine what it's like lugging your luggage – AND your case for your crown. "I have a crown case, yes ma'am," says Sara, who, when I spoke to her, had been in five different states in the last five weeks. Sara tries not to check her luggage, however, and puts everything in her Longchamp luggage (www.longchamp.com).

Her packing tip? "I lay everything out and roll it." On the plane, she only eats pretzels and water. "I also try to find a Subway for a sandwich, and load up on veggies. I get turkey with lots of veggies, or chicken with marinara and cheese on wheat bread, with no mayo." But her biggest beauty secret is to get enough sleep: "I try to make sure I don't skip out on sleep. If I don't get enough, I don't look good."

She walks a great deal at her destinations. "Today we're going to do a four-mile hike in Sedona. But my usual is to go to the gym and do 30-40 minutes on the treadmill or elliptical."

Sara is a big Sephora fan. "They have great sales. But I swear by The Perfect Face Makeup, which I got through the pageant (www.theperfectface.com). I love L'Oreal lipglosses – they're my go-to item. I buy the mini-packs at Christmas and load up (www.loreal.com). And I buy the Obagi skincare system through a dermatologist (www.obagi.com). I use their cleanser and sunscreen – it's awesome. I make sure I always have sunscreen on."

Need to hit the hotel gym? Want to stay svelte and slim? Read Chapter Seven, Gorgeous Getaways, to make your stay sensational and fit-tastic. After all, you want to be a *femme fatale* frequent flier, don't you?

CHAPTER 7
Gorgeous Getaways

There's nothing like working out in the privacy of your home – or your favorite gym. But now, hotels want to make your stay a haven of fitness and comfort, with a wide range of programs and choices that make working out a breeze. They also want to make sure you're rested, relaxed, and dining on nourishing fare. Take this armchair expedition right now, and discover hotels that are fitness – and health and well-being – wonderlands.

Affinia Dumont – New York's First And Only Executive Fitness Suite Hotel

The **Affinia Dumont**, New York's first and only Executive Fitness Suite Hotel, is designed to meet the needs of today's active and health-conscious business traveler. It offers an array of special fitness features and services that you're sure to love. There's even a Fitness Concierge to assist you – imagine that! Guests at the Affinia Dumont can choose between using the Oasis Day Spa, or working out in their room (you know, like Madonna). All rooms are equipped with full-sized wall mirrors and ample workout space, and a variety of exercise equipment can be delivered to rooms free of charge. Take a look at these attractive options:

◆ The Fitness Concierge oversees the Oasis Day Spa and is a resource for guests seeking to enhance their fitness and wellness experience during their stay. The Fitness Concierge arranges appointments with personal trainers, educates and assists guests with the fitness equipment, leads spa and fitness seminars and workshops (for both guests and hotel staff), recommends appropriate running/walking routes upon request and often leads these tours for guests.

◆ Fit Kits are four different types of packaged exercise equipment available to guests for in-room use: Running, Walking, Strength-Training and Yoga. The Fit Kits are free-of-charge during the stay and will be delivered to a guest's room upon request. The kits' contents are based on the activity; the strength-training kit, for example, includes hand weights, ankle weights, mat, exercise ball and resistance bands.

◆ Fitness Locker service features a Fitness Valet and Sneaker Valet to provide prompt refreshing, laundering and storage of workout attire for a nominal charge.

◆ The Affinia Wellness Library has CDs and books available for guests to borrow or purchase.

- The Fitness Suite is a 1,100-square-foot one-bedroom suite located on the 26th floor of the hotel. The suite includes a private gym with cardio and strength-training equipment, as well as a sauna.

- Stretch of the Month introduces new stretches to staff and guests every month to help with relaxation. Instructions for the stretch are posted in the spa, front desk and throughout the hotel.

- A healthy mini-bar in every suite includes energy bars, water bottles and low-fat snacks. (So you can say goodbye to fattening sodas and chocolate bars.)

- An "On-The-Go" pack available for purchase at check-out includes items to refresh travelers while in transit.

- "Black Book" of NYC fitness resources is a comprehensive directory of health- and fitness-oriented facilities (such as yoga, Pilates, swimming pools) and restaurants compiled especially for the Affinia Dumont so the staff can help guests find any type of health/fitness service throughout Manhattan.

- Running and walking route maps are available for guests who enjoy these outdoor activities. Staff can direct guests to the best running or walking routes and will be ready with a towel and bottle of water upon their return.

Here's what else Affinia Hotels offer to their business and leisure travelers:

A pillow menu of six choices; a signature "Affinia Bed" with down comforter and triple sheeting; and a rotating library where guests can exchange their book from one of Affinia's library of bestsellers and top-picks (www.affinia.com).

AKA – For Serious Shuteye

Here's news about a hotel that's a real snore – and I mean that as a compliment. AKA, a luxury extended-stay brand, has taken serious shuteye to the next level with the AKA Sleep School. In partnership with the New York University School of Medicine Sleep Disorders Center and the New York Sleep Institute, AKA is creating a comprehensive program to ensure guests get a good night's rest during their visit. Guests can choose customized accommodations, participate in evening Sleep School seminars and benefit from in-room screenings with board-certified sleep specialists.

"We are addressing guests' sleep concerns and helping them find solutions that go beyond the pillow and the bed," said Larry Korman, co-president and director of general operations for AKA, who struggles with getting enough rest himself. "While many in the hospitality industry focus on the bed, we learned from our partners at NYU and the New York Sleep Institute that all aspects of the room, from the lighting to mirrors to alarm clocks, must be taken into consideration," he continued. "Since AKA's extended-stay guests typically stay 30 days or more, our sleep-school students will have a healthy amount of time to put what they learn into practice."

In-room sunlight plays a significant role regarding one's sleeping habits. At AKA United Nations, guests who have trouble falling asleep are placed in a southwesterly-facing suite on a lower floor with minimal exposure to the sun, while guests who have trouble waking up in the morning will feel the rays coming through the window in a front-facing suite on a higher floor. For those with stronger sleep aversions, AKA properties will be outfitted with light boxes, blackout drapes and light-sensitive alarm clocks. Since televisions and bedroom mirrors can also be a distraction, each can be removed or covered upon request. Customized suite selection is available free of charge. Guests will also receive a complimentary AKA Sleep School amenity kit upon arrival including a sleep mask, ear plugs, aromatherapy oils, sleep CD and the highly-acclaimed book, *The Promise of Sleep.*

The AKA Sleep School is available at AKA's four Manhattan properties in Central Park, Times Square, Sutton Place and United Nations (www.stay-aka.com).

Cambria Suites: Refresh, Reflect and Refill

Many affordable hotels cut lifestyle amenities to cut costs. Cambria Suites was designed with the healthy traveler in mind from the beginning, and has made the following efforts to promote guest health.

1. All properties include a minimum 1,200-sq.-ft. gym with state-of-the-art Precor cardiovascular and weight equipment, as well as medicine balls, agility fitness balls and bosu trainers, items not commonly found at most hotels. Design and equipment choices were led by a world-record-holding training and extreme fitness expert to create the **Refresh** fitness center.

2. **Reflect,** the bistro dining area at Cambria Suites, features a full barista coffee bar that serves Wolfgang Puck coffee, Numi organic teas and healthy light fare to-go items. In addition, guests can indulge in a full breakfast and dinner menu, both of which contain a wide array of healthy, organic and local food choices. What's more, Reflect's menu does not offer any fried foods, providing guests healthy and delicious dishes as opposed to traditional items like french fries. Cambria Suites guests don't have to sacrifice taste to have a healthy meal.

3. In addition to Reflect, all properties offer **Refill** – a 24/7 sundry shop that stocks freshly prepared "grab 'n' go" gourmet salads and sandwiches as well as health-conscious energy drinks and organic foods. Cambria Suites provides healthy alternatives such as Luna and Clif bars, grab-and-go fresh salads, Numi Organic tea, and Amy's microwaveable organic meals.

4. All Cambria Suites hotels offer guest suites that are 25% larger than the industry standard; offer separate working/living and sleeping areas; are 100% smoke-free; and feature luxury amenities including upscale bedding and linens, a hospitality bar with microwave, a refrigerator and premium Wolfgang Puck Coffee and Numi Organic Tea.

In addition, the design of the guest baths in each suite provides a comfortable and tranquil, spa-like experience, offering a place to melt troubles away. Giving guests the feeling of being pampered and relaxed, the baths offer plush towels and upscale Bath and Body Works toiletries, along with a functional space where colors and patterns are kept to a minimum to soothe the senses and create a peaceful haven. A spacious, walk-in glass shower with luxury shower heads completes the ultimate retreat (www.choicehotels.com).

Element Hotels: An Eco-Chic Experience

A hotel group that offers free shuttles to Whole Foods and local farmer's markets? Now that's a hotel that we can get our arms around – in fact, that's a hotel we want to hug. The free shuttles are just part of the fitness/wellness initiatives at Element, created by Starwood Hotels & Resorts Worldwide. Element is an eco-chic experience designed for longer stays and consisting entirely of new-build hotels. The flagship is in Lexington, Mass., and it earned the U. S. Green Building Council's LEED gold certification, an internationally recognized, third-party certification for the design, construction and operation of high-performance green buildings. "Our whole culture is about living well and staying whole," explained Chris Hartzell, general manager of the Lexington flagship.

Rise is the Element signature – and complimentary – healthy breakfast, which includes egg-white burritos and wraps; organic granola and fresh fruits; hard-boiled eggs; smoothies; and filtered water. At Relax, offered four nights a week, an evening reception offers guests the perfect chance to mingle with fellow guests. "We offer healthier options here too," Chris explained; these include organic chips; hummus; organic meats; veggie burgers and fresh organic veggies. And in the Restore "grab-and-go gourmet pantry," guests can purchase some of Whole Foods' ready-set-cook meals, healthy snacks and indulgent treats. Cooking demonstrations also occur in Relax as well.

The Fitness Center is a generous 1,000-sq.-ft. facility offering top-of-the-line cardio, machines, free weights, Nautilus, "You name it," Chris adds. "It's larger than the typical hotel fitness center." Element also boasts a saline pool (instead of using chlorine), and even has a borrow-a-bike program. "You can ride on the bike path all the way through Minuteman National Park, all the way to Boston,"

Chris added. There's even a free shuttle to a nearby Aveda Concept salon, as well as a local fitness center that offers personal training.

Oh yes – and you can also get a massage in your room. In your glorious Heavenly Bed. Each Heavenly Bed is made up of 10 layers of plush sheets, bedspread and duvets with four large pillows, so you can indulge in sybaritic sleep (www.elementhotels.com/lexingtonhotel, www.starwoodhotels.com/element).

Element Hotels in Lexington, Mass., offers free shuttles to Whole Foods and farmer's markets.

Fairmont Fit

We recently stayed at Boston's Fairmont Copley Place, and realized that the entire brand offers an incredible Fairmont Fit program. Begun in 2007, the program "is absolutely successful – the responses have been phenomenal," explains Sharon Cohen, Executive Director of Loyalty Marketing, Fairmont Raffles Hotels International. Here's how it works: Sign up for the President's Club program (it's a free loyalty program), and there's a minimal charge of just $10 for Club level members (higher tiers of membership get it for free). Here's what you get:

- ◆ Adidas workout apparel and footwear delivered directly to your room – shorts, T-shirts and athletic shoes

- ◆ Creative Zen MP3 players to use during your workout, pre-loaded with music from EMI featuring "the latest and greatest artists"

- ◆ Yoga mats and stretch bands

Wheeled Wonders

Want to bike on your next trip – without lugging your equipment? Visit www.rentabikenow.com, to browse bicycles in every size and description, which you can rent from shops in North America, to make sure your thighs – and lungs – get a workout.

Fairmont understands that maintaining a fitness routine while traveling is difficult but often key to maintaining a healthy lifestyle. Fitness enthusiasts can add their sizes to their on-line member profile to ensure that their items are waiting for them when they arrive. Your apparel can also be replenished during your stay. After you leave, the items are washed and the shoes are sanitized, and put back in inventory. If you wish to purchase some of the Adidas gear – which many travelers do – you can do so at the hotel. "Many businesswomen purchase the capri pants to wear on the way home," says Sharon.

With airlines charging for your first item of luggage, it's great to know that you can leave behind your workout gear – and cumbersome sneakers – and still be ready for a workout. This means that you can use Fairmont Fit in such diverse locations as Boston, Bermuda, Hamburg, Montreaux, St. Andrews, and Dubai – to name a few (www.fairmont.com).

Furthermore, some of the shoes from the Fairmont Fit program will get a second life with Soles4Souls, a non-profit organization that collects gently worn and new shoes for redistribution to those in need (www.soles4souls.com).

In its continued quest to provide guests with a healthy environment to stay fit and maintain a balanced lifestyle, Fairmont has also announced an extension of its partnership with German automaker BMW to include a complimentary hotel bicycle service featuring BMW Cruise Bikes. Fairmont hotels across Canada have introduced these state-of-the-art bikes as the newest benefit for guests, granting active and adventurous travelers the opportunity to explore the vibrant cities and stunning landscapes of Fairmont's distinctive locales. In addition to offering a selection of BMW Cruise Bikes, each hotel boasts a variety of child-sized BMW bikes, allowing families to enjoy the great outdoors together.

Four Seasons Finest

I recently had a two-night overnight stay at The Four Seasons Boston, only to realize that the property featured a pool. A gorgeous indoor pool. And I had not only forgotten my workout gear, I didn't even think to bring a bathing suit. Well, it was not a problem! The attendant in the fitness center provided me with a complimentary disposable bathing suit in my size (their pattern resembled Hawaiian board shorts), as well as shorts and tank top on loan. Mission accomplished!

The Four Seasons is famous for taking care of its clients at all of its properties around the world, and has been a major innovator by providing many features free of charge, which would be considered extras at other hotels. Here's just another typical example. At the Four Seasons Resort and Club Dallas at Las Colinas, these are some of the complimentary services and amenities for fitness enthusiasts:

- Rental equipment for tennis, racquetball, squash and golf

- Workout attire – shorts, T-shirts, tennis shoes

- Heated hand towels for winter golfers when they come off the course, and complimentary hot coffee

- Apples and bananas on the golf course marshall's carts

- Daily fitness classes such as yoga, spinning and Pilates

And the crackerjack complimentary services go on and on. Chocolate-chip cookies for departing guests, plus a "sunglass butler" at the pool, at their resort in Scottsdale. A Hawaiian outrigger canoe paddling program four times a week, and fitness classes, at their resort in Maui. A basketball court, morning fitness walk, exercise and tennis attire, and aromatherapy candles, at their resort on The Big Island. And at all properties, you can have the exercise equipment placed

Airport Exercise

Want to work out while you wait for your plane? Airport Gyms offers FREE listings of airport gyms, airport exercise clubs, and airport fitness centers available in and around select popular US (and Canadian) airports (www.airportgyms.com).

in your room – if you're sorely seeking privacy. You can even get free repair of your sandals and golf shoes. This is just the tip of the "excellence iceberg," making sure that all guests wish to return. (And we do.) (www.fourseasons.com)

Fairmont and Four Seasons Resorts offer complimentary workout gear – in case you forget yours.

Healthy Menus At Hilton

With more of today's traveling women recognizing the important of maintaining a healthy diet on the road, Hilton Hotels Corporation has launched new menu programs across three of its brands. The Hilton, Doubletree and Embassy Suites "Eat Right" menu programs offer meal choices that are rich in nutrition. Eat Right recipes have been specially created by the Hilton Eat Right Culinary Team in conjunction with Johnson & Wales University for Hilton Worldwide and embody the Hilton Eat Right concept of balance, variety, and moderation. The hotel corporation has also partnered with fitness equipment leader Precor, and has launched "Fitness by Precor" facilities at Hilton, Doubletree and Embassy Suites Hotels in North America, and also in New York at the legendary Waldorf=Astoria. The specially designed facilities offer Precor-developed strength, cardio and entertainment equipment, to include cardio theater so you can watch TV while you walk on the treadmill (www.hiltonworldwide.com).

Hyatt Health and Wellness Programs

Hyatt hotels and resorts has instituted several initiatives to foster the well-being of their guests. StayFit@Hyatt is a dynamic selection of workout programs that cater to fitness-conscious business and leisure travelers. There are 24/7 gyms as well as in-room on-demand yoga videos; a 24/7 StayFit Fitness Concierge Service to offer workout attire in less than an hour; complimentary GPS armbands to help runners and walkers easily monitor their heart rate; plus palm-sized route cards offering directions. A StayFit Cuisine program offers guests tasty, well-balanced and nutritionally sensible menu options. And so everyone can enjoy a good night's sleep, there's the signature Hyatt Grand Bed – a Sealy Posturepedic mattress with Grand Bed mattress pad, super topper, grand pillow, allergen-free goose-down bedding, and 300-thread-count Egyptian cotton sheets. Sweet dreams! (www.hyatt.com)

Kimpton's Mind.Body.Spa Program and Women InTouch

As a boutique hotel company, Kimpton's nimble ability to customize each hotel experience to meet the needs of its guests and local community are what make Kimpton one of the healthiest hotels in the country. Whether it's the freshly picked produce from the restaurant's own organic garden at the Poste Modern Brasserie in Washington D.C., or the recently garnered Green Seal Certification at many Kimpton hotels from coast-to-coast, Kimpton is in-step with the way guests live their lives.

Through Kimpton's brand-wide **Mind.Body.Spa.** program, guests have access to:

- Complimentary in-room yoga totes that include mats, blocks and straps

- Complimentary use of in-room 24-hour on-demand Yoga, Pilates and Meditation channels

- In-room massage treatment program that includes the use of organic and paraben-free spa products by Kerstin Florian

♦ Organic in-room mini-bar food and beverage options

♦ Every Kimpton hotel offers a complimentary nightly wine hour that takes place in the hotel's living room-style lobby. During this time, guests often choose to relax by the fireplace with a glass of red or white and a good book, or socialize with other hotel guests after a long day of exploring.

All Kimpton hotels feature fitness centers. Some are very expansive and include indoor or outdoor pools with exercise equipment ranging from cardiovascular equipment to weight-lifting machines, exercise bars, medicine balls and stretching/mat zones. Many hotels offer in-room maps with the safest running routes through the city, and concierges can additionally map out a customized running route, based on a guest's individual needs. Kimpton will also store fitness gear at no charge, such as sneakers and workout clothes, for frequent travelers.

Kimpton's "Women InTouch" program anticipates women's needs and provides services and creature comforts to make life on the road easier. The "Forgot It? We've Got It" menu offers a wealth of complimentary essentials, such as spray wrinkle remover, Static Guard, eye makeup remover pads, shaving cream and toothpaste. Available for a nominal fee are goodies such as sunscreen, tweezers, lint brushes and clear nail polish. Kimpton also has a "Quick Concierge" service to let women know insider tips on local haunts – from the best "updo" to the city's best view! (www.Kimptonhotels.com).

Live It Up At Loews

Loews' Hotels promises a supremely comfortable and vibrant travel experience, including health and wellness. The Loews in Denver, for example, offers complimentary access to Bally Total Fitness, plus complimentary transportation there. And in New York, in partnership with Verve, one of Manhattan's most sought-after personal training facilities, the Loews Regency offers one-on-one private training by well-known personal trainer Mary Ann Browning (www.loewshotels.com).

Omni's Get Fit Rooms

Travelers who wish to stay in shape can stay at any of Omni Hotels' 45 locations in North American, and reserve a special "Get Fit Room." The specially designed rooms feature a treadmill, and a "Get Fit Kit" that contains 2-lb. dumbbells, a floor mat, stretch cords, a mini AM/FM headset and a bottle of water. The room's minibars will also be stocked with healthy snacks such as sports drinks, energy bars and trail mix. I had a fabulous visit to the Omni New Haven Hotel, deep in the heart of Yale University in New Haven, Conn. After a great workout in the hotel gym, I had an excellent gourmet lunch, and then a massage at the spa right next door. I highly recommend it! (www.omnihotels.com)

Peninsula Wellness

The Peninsula Hotels continues its tradition of exceptional, personalized service with the launch of Peninsula Wellness – a lifestyle program that touches every aspect of a guest's well-being. This program rolled out in 2007 and is still going strong. As well as staying in luxurious hotel accommodations with the finest amenities, guests can renew themselves in mind, body and spirit through an integrated approach to help them escape stress. Along with various spas, the Peninsula Wellness program includes "Naturally Peninsula" light and healthy cuisine options introduced at all Peninsula dining establishments, The hotel sources fresh, organic produce from local farms for this new range of

Women-Only Wonderlands

History repeats itself. When I was younger, I stayed at the Barbizon Hotel for Women in New York, because it was a women-only hotel where men were definitely not allowed. (I felt totally safe when I stayed there as a college student, while interning at WNYW-TV.) The hotel eventually became an anachronism, and totally out-of-date, and was turned into a condo. But now, in an interesting turn of events, with the numbers of female business travelers exploding, more and more hotels are catering specifically to business women, with special "women-only" floors designed to make them feel pampered and protected. One such hotel is the Hamilton Crowne Plaza in Washington, D. C., where female travelers find special pampering amenities such as plush slippers, spa bathrobes, seven-layer pillow-top beds, fresh flowers and more. Rooms also include oversized counter space in the bathroom, allowing ample space for cosmetics bags and styling tools (www.hamiltonhoteldc.com).

The Fit-Lifestyle Lowdown

If you travel and are searching for a healthy restaurant, or simply wish to find out about hotels with great gyms, log onto www. Athleticmindedtraveler.com. For a small monthly fee, you can get the shapely scoop in major US cities and even some in Europe. This web travel guide eliminates the guesswork and uncertainty of trying to stay active and healthy while on the road by providing specific and reliable recommendations for: fitness-focused hotels, health clubs, running routes, lap pools and places to eat. Now you'll never have an excuse for staying in your hotel room and eating pizza.

dishes, which offer light healthy dining options without compromising taste (www. Peninsula.com).

Go Westin, Young Woman!

With incredible "Running Concierges," workout guestrooms, and health-infused Super Foods, you should run – not walk – to the nearest Westin Hotel and check in! Get a load of these services and amenities.

runWESTIN is a growing program from Westin Hotels & Resorts that enables guests to learn about the destination while participating in guided runs (great for women on the road). These "discovery" runs are led by Running Concierges who also serve as cultural guides, highlighting distinct points along the three-mile route. The Running Concierge also leads warm-up sessions with Reebok training tips and distributes water and towels. Guests staying in Beijing, for example, jog past The Sculptures of Financial Street, the Temple of Immortal, and the Thai Chi Gardens. The runs are tailored to fitness level and free to guests. And, if guests prefer to run solo, runWESTIN also provides guests with pocket-sized local running maps.

In April 2009, Westin announced a partnership with Nintendo under which it became the first hotel company to introduce a specially designed Wii console that's meant for use in hotel fitness centers. Guests can play with WestinWORKOUT trainers or face-off against each other, using a console that requires no pre-loading of games and is meant for public use. Westin was also one of the first spots in the United States to unveil Wii Fit.

Passport to Pretty

Sleep Tight At The Benjamin

What gorgeous globetrotter doesn't need a full night of beauty sleep? With that in mind, The Benjamin in New York City has gone to extraordinary lengths to back up the guarantee of a good night's rest in The Big Apple, "the city that never sleeps." The hotel has added a Sleep Concierge to the staff, who will make sure that guests get everything they need to sleep peacefully. "We offer our guests a selection of 12 specialty types of pillows from which to choose: upper body, buckwheat, satin, hypo-allergenic, water-filled, Swedish memory, magnetic therapy, a jelly neckroll, a five-foot body cushion, maternity and a special anti-snore pillow," says Sleep Concierge Anya Orlanska.

In addition to the pillows, the hotel features The Benjamin Bed: a Serta mattress created exclusively for The Benjamin, with specially engineered convoluted foam cushioning and layers of fibers quilted to the mattress for a luxurious surface feel. The custom-designed Benjamin Bed is covered with 100% Egyptian Cotton 400-plus thread-count sheets by Anichini (divine!) and a down-filled comforter with luxurious triple sheeting (the pillows, sheets, and mattresses have become so popular that they are now offered for sale to guests who want to sleep as well at home as they do at The Benjamin!). Aromatherapy bathroom amenities help guests relax and prepare for bed. In addition to the luxurious sleep amenities, The Benjamin's windows are double-glazed with argon gas between the panes to help keep rooms quiet and restful.

The Sleep Concierge can also arrange a relaxing massage at the hotel's Wellness Spa to help guests unwind, a bedtime snack of milk and cookies or other sleep-inducing room service choices, or loan a bedside white-noise machine that electronically drowns out any stray background noise.

"We're not doctors. We don't cure sleep disorders. But we'll do everything we can to make sure that our guests get the rest they need for the next New York day," says Anya (www.thebenjamin.com).

And here's more that you'll love: Customized WestinWORKOUT guestrooms. They feature in-room state-of-the-art, full-body equipment for all levels of performance where guests can elevate their well-being with a challenging and exhilarating workout. WestinWORKOUT guestrooms are great for female travelers who may not be familiar with their surroundings and would like to work out in the comfort of their own room. The WestinWORKOUT room features:

♦   Treadmill or spinning cycle

Send Jet Lag Packing

The fact is – you won't want to work out at all if you're exhausted and suffering from jet lag. That's the worst! All you want to do is sleep – if you can. To find out how to avoid the dreaded JL, I spoke with naturopathic physician Dr. Coleen Murphy, of Natural Medicine Works in San Francisco, who has this advice.

"Jet lag is when your body is in the old time zone, but you're presently in the new time zone. Traveling during the day is the best way to avoid jet lag. It's better because you're not getting a disturbed night's sleep."

To eliminate jet lag, "At your destination, soak up the sun from your window, for about 15 minutes, so the sunlight can jolt your circadian rhythm," Dr. Murphy advises. "Have a smoothie with protein, even mixed with juice, to get your body started."

"The first night, take melatonin to get to sleep. Most healthy people need about 1-2 milligrams. And take it every night of your trip. Anxiety and fear can also cause jet lag, and to alleviate that, try the natural remedy known as Bach Rescue Remedy (www.bachflower.com). Valerian and passion flower tincture can also help you to sleep along with a tincture of California poppy," she concluded.

Along with Dr. Murphy's recommendations, above, here are some other formulas that I discovered, which you may want to try.

- ◆ Reebok® Pilates and Cycle DVDs

- ◆ Adjustable dumbbells and Reebok core training equipment

- ◆ *Bicycling* and ***Runner's World*** magazines and a fitness library

- ◆ ***Runner's World*** maps

- ◆ Complimentary bottled water

FlyRight Jet Lag Formula is a product that supports travelers against the full spectrum of jet lag symptoms. Just take two capsules on takeoff, then two capsules every three hours during your flight. FlyRight was developed by Ted Ray, a licensed acupuncturist and herbalist in California, with organic and wild harvested herbs. For example, to counteract the dehydration and headache caused by dry cabin air, FlyRight contains feverfew and wild oats. For time zone changes and disrupted circadian rhythms, there are linden flowers, along with ginkgo, gotu kola and mushrooms. And there is a whole boatload of satisfied business travelers who swear by it (www.jetlagformula.com).

For those who prefer a homeopathic remedy, Boiron (who makes the much-beloved Oscillococcinum for colds) has its own proprietary Jet Lag CareKit. The three tubes contain nux vomica for heartburn; cocculus indicus for motion sickness and sleep pattern disturbance; and arnica montana for muscle soreness. Since you just dissolve the pellets under your tongue, and they don't require water, they're ideal for travel (www.boironusa.com).

You can also send jet lag packing with two dairy-based, all-natural sleep dessert beverages that use ingredients such as Lactium, PharmaGABA (a naturally occurring ingredient to promote relaxation) and a low amount of melatonin. Dreamerz makes sleep dietary supplements that claim to help you fall asleep faster without feeling groggy in the morning. There are packets of drink mixes in flavors such as berry and peach, plus 45-calorie dark chocolate "pillows" that you take one hour prior to going to bed. Imagine eating chocolate and still getting a good night's sleep! (www.dreamerz.com)

Hotel Horror Stories

Yikes! Sometimes you really can wind up at a "roach motel" (or the Bates Motel in *Psycho*) only to have a horrible experience. These testimonials come courtesy of BedVoyage (www.bedvoyage.com), creators of luxurious linens you can take in your travels. (They're like sleeping on a cloud!) These examples are from their website, as BedVoyage had sponsored a contest for the worst hotel experience. Ladies, don't let these things ever happen to you!

"During college I was on a trip to Nice, France. Seven of my friends and I traveled through Europe and found ourselves on the French Riviera during one of their busiest times of the year. We didn't arrive until 11PM so the pickins' were slim on a room and we all ended up having to bunk together. When we pulled back the bedspread the sheets were covered with matted hair, mysterious stains and greasy spots, UGH! There was no bathroom, just a toilet that was right next to the bed and it would not flush and was filled to the brim. If anyone had been brave enough to sleep in that bed and accidentally flung an arm out it would have ended up in that mess! Eight years have gone by yet the horror of that has never faded."
Lindsey B.

"I rented a room at a well-known hotel in Hurricane Mills, Tenn. The room was dirty and shabby but I was tired so I used my Clorox wipes I always travel with to clean the toilet and sink. The sink was dirty and had hair in it, but that was nothing compared to the bed! When I got into bed I sat right in a wet spot, upon looking further I was horrified to learn I had sat in someone else's urine! The sheets had a big wet yellow circle on them. Needless to say, I went to the front desk; they didn't give me my money back but gave me another room. I'll never get the feeling of sitting in someone else's urine out of my head."
Linda P.

"Let me tell you about a peach of an experience! We went to a hotel in Wildwood, N.J. The place was ON the beach, it was supposed to be a wonderful getaway. Right after we checked in, I pulled back the retro bedspread. Oh, what a glorious sight! The sheets were so thin that you could see through them and there were random hairs all over the pillows and sheets. And, there were yellow

stains all over them. Obviously I complained immediately and this is where the story gets good: I was told to get out and that I had some nerve complaining after getting a special promotional deal. I left, but not after taking dozens of pictures, which were then submitted to my credit card company in conjunction with my dispute of the hotel charge. Yes, that was a super getaway!"
Kris W.

"My fiance proposed to me the day before he was to leave for military duty, and we had an amazing day with a final celebration at a hotel on the beach. It was a pricey hotel and the entire day my fiance told me about it because he was so excited about the room he'd booked us. But we got there and it was a dump! I have asthma so it was important that we get a non-smoking room, but this room reeked like smoke and the sheets were folded up and on the floor. We called the front desk and were informed that we were to make our own bed with the sheets from the floor. We mentioned our non-smoking room request and we were hung up on. It was a nightmare and we ended up sleeping in our car because the room was unbearable for me to sleep in due to my asthma."
Tiffany H.

"The worst experience I ever had with a bed in a hotel was in London, England. My husband and I were about to go to bed when we turned down the comforter and noticed that there were footprint marks all over the sheets! They had never been changed from the previous occupant, we were so disgusted that we checked out right then and went to another hotel."
Stephanie N.

"Travel with me to a beautiful cabin deep in the woods. My wife and I snuggle into a beautiful wood-carved bed in front of a crackling fire. Flash forward to the next morning when our entire family was scratching and had horrible bites all over our bodies! BED BUGS! Our fabulous vacation was ruined by these pesky critters and my wife and I vowed that we would always travel with our own fresh, clean sheets thereafter."
Gregg R.

"My husband and I got a motel room in a rural town in Texas, as our son was attending a Boy Scout camping trip and we stayed nearby in a hotel as semi-

chaperones of the camp out. The only motel was not even a one-star but we had to stay there so we tried to make the best of it. But we kept waking up feeling like something was crawling all over us, we finally got up and turned on the lights and our bed was full of tiny black ants!"
Annette D.

"My worst hotel bed experience actually took place on my wedding night! My husband and I were broke and only had $50 for a room. I booked a motel room that I found near the airport. It was located between a bar and a strip joint, and the room had a vibrating bed. When we pulled back the bedspread the sheets looked like they hadn't been washed in many, many nights....and they were so scratchy. We both woke up with a scratchy rash, mine was on my back and my husband's was on his face! Upon further inspection, there were bugs in the bed, which just made us sick to our stomach."
Angela O.

Care to visit the gym? The sleek, airy surroundings of WestinWORKOUT gyms are the perfect setting for guests committed to maintaining their wellness routines while traveling. Featuring the finest exercise equipment from Life Fitness, Precor, and other brands, WestinWORKOUT facilities are designed to accommodate a full range of exercises, including:

- Running, Jogging, Walking

- Bicycling

- Weight-lifting

- Calisthenics

- Swimming, where available

- Yoga

Last but not least, as part of Westin's ongoing commitment to personal renewal they have teamed up with SuperFoods Partners LLC and founder Steven Pratt, M.D., to become the first hotel brand to create a SuperFoods-focused menu for their guests. SuperFoods, which are health-enhancing and rich in antioxidants and phytonutrients, are the main ingredient in Westin signature dishes such as banana oatmeal brulé, green-tea-infused salmon and molten dark chocolate cake. I'm there! (www.westin.com)

Passport To Pretty

Y-a-w-n. Feeling sleepy? If you're in New York City, you can take a nap for 40 minutes in a dark, cozy pod – just long enough for you to feel refreshed. ($28 for 40 minutes) Just visit Yelo, a wellness center in the city (www.yelonyc.com).

Wyndham Clear Air

Health-conscious travelers – especially those suffering from allergies and asthma – can breathe easier at Wyndham hotels, thanks to the upscale chain's Wyndham ClearAir initiative, to offer allergy-friendly guest accommodations. How does the program work? Utilizing a comprehensive purification system designed by New York-based Pure Solutions NA, guest room walls, carpeting, bedcovers and fabrics are sanitized and treated with a long-lasting microbial shield, making them free from odors and resistant to bacteria and viruses. Next, a medical-grade air purifier is installed. Air-handling units and vents are deep-cleaned and equipped with a tea tree oil cartridge, which acts as a natural antiseptic and disinfectant.

Wyndham ClearAir guest rooms are designed to remove 98 percent of allergens. In hotel meeting rooms, air is purified at a greater intensity and filtrated eight times more frequently than standard air-handling systems. The goal? To achieve 99.9% effective treatment of air and surfaces (www.wyndham.com/ClearAir).

Wyndham's "Women on Their Way"

Want to find a wealth of wonderful information for women travelers? Here's the secret.

Women on Their Way (www.womenontheirway.com) is Wyndham Worldwide's online resource for business and leisure travelers to find everything they need to plan and book their next trip. The website includes expert advice on destinations, hotels, timeshare resorts and vacation rentals, plus special deals and packages. There are even special columns on Health and Wellness, Budget Travel, Weddings and Honeymoons, and Business Travel. You'll love reading it all!

Women on Their Way is the hospitality industry's longest-running branded program entirely dedicated to female travelers. Since the program's launch in 1995, Wyndham has supported women travelers as they've emerged from a niche market to a formidable force, listening and responding to women's feedback, which has resulted in a better hotel experience for all travelers, including the addition of various amenities to hotel rooms such as coffeemakers, full-length mirrors and healthier room-service menus.

When you stay with Wyndham, your room is equipped with the following amenities and services:

- High-speed Internet access

- Voice mail

- Cordless phones

- Herman Miller ergonomic work chair

- Coffeemaker

- Complimentary weekday **USA Today**®

- In-room iron and ironing board

- Premium pillow-top mattresses and bed linens

- Hairdryer

- Shower massager

- ◆ Real hook hangers, including skirt hangers

- ◆ 100-watt light bulbs

- ◆ Bath and Body Works True Blue spa amenities

Forgot something? Don't worry. Wyndham takes care of everything with a "We Remembered What You Forgot" program. Every Wyndham Hotel and Resort offers a whole menu of indispensable and complimentary items that you may have forgotten to pack in your suitcase.

Wyndham ByRequest, the Wyndham brand's free-to-join signature guest recognition program, caters to the individuality of each guest with complimentary benefits that ladies will love, including free high-speed Internet access, choice of welcome snack and beverage, preferred pillow type, express check-in, guaranteed late check-out, local and long-distance calls within the 48 contiguous United States, best available room upon arrival, photocopies, faxes and online receipts. Members also earn Wyndham Rewards points, which can be redeemed for free hotel stays, airline tickets, name-brand merchandise and dining and shopping gift cards, among other options. Wyndham Rewards is the world's largest lodging loyalty program based upon number of participating hotels (www.wyndhamworldwide.com).

Now that you know where to stay, you'll want to bring the very best lotions and potions with you. In the next chapter is a dazzling array of some of the world's most dynamite skincare and beauty treatments. If you want to be a traveling bombshell, well, these are all the bomb.

CHAPTER EIGHT

Quest For The Best

There are so many skincare and beauty treatments on the market, it's hard sometimes to figure out which ones are right for you. Sometimes if you know the back story behind the product, or a little bit of its history, it can help in your decision. Here's a look at some remarkable beauty companies – many of them right under the radar – offering excellent products – and those that even come in travel sizes, which is just what the doctor ordered. These chic, boutique brands are your visa to a vivacious, vibrant face.

Black Opal – Great For African-American Skin

Black Opal is a ritualized set of beauty treatments treating the specific skin-care needs of African-American skin. These can include hyperpigmentation, acne and pseudofolliculitis. With this targeted focus, Black Opal has solidified its position as the trusted brand for transforming its consumers' desires into their beauty realities. The brand was created in 1994 by BioCosmetic Research Labs, in conjunction with renowned African-American dermatologist Dr. Cheryl Burgess. The first launch was the industry legend Advanced Dual Complex Fade Gel, designed to effectively combat the dark spots of hyperpigmentation. Today, you'll find Black Opal products that are uniquely formulated for the chemistry of African-American skin, including the Total Coverage Concealing Foundation that contains "skinerals," skin-protecting minerals. It's the Crown Jewel in this cosmetic line. (Insert applause here!) (www.blackopalbeauty.com)

Blinc – It's Tube Technology

When it comes to mascara, there are oodles of options that make your lashes look long and lovely – as long as you don't sweat during your workout, cry at a wedding, rub your eyes at work or have oily skin. Oy! That's why everyone's excited about **Blinc** mascara, which forms tiny tubes around each lash, amplifying the volume and length. Once set, the tubes bind to the lashes, and they will NOT run, smudge, clump or flake. Blinc offers a lash-a-palooza! To remove, simply wash off with water and a little pressure. It's amazing for busy executives – and soccer Moms – who want to coat their lashes in a little mascara and forget about it all day long. And if you're distressed by dead skin on your face, try Blinc's resurf.a.stic – an unusual microdermabrasion roll-on-type stick featuring medical-grade, diamond-shaped crystals to instantly exfoliate dead skin cells. It'll easily store in your Samsonite, and I find it to be pure genius! Just roll it around on your face with gentle pressure, and instantly, your visage will become squeaky clean and brimming with color. *Fan.tas.tic*! (www.blincinc.com)

How Bourjois!

In the 1860s in Paris, makeup was largely used by stage actresses, and consisted of greasy, thick creams that were uncomfortable to wear and damaging to the skin. French perfumier Alexandre Napoleon Bourjois saw the opportunity to develop a range of expert cosmetics and devoted his time to creating a superior quality of theatrical makeup. It was in this pursuit that he created the world's first powder blush, Pastel Joues, in 1863. This was the start of something big – **Bourjois** cosmetics – which I purchase every time I'm in Paris, at my beloved Monoprix store. The blush was a great success with the actresses, and as makeup usage became fashionable off-stage it did not take long for the word to spread, making women *everywhere* eager to experience the magic of the Bourjois brand.

Color, one of the strongest values of the brand, is at the heart of everything Bourjois does. Ranging from neutral shades to the most vivid hues of the rainbow, Bourjois has colors to fit every mood, occasion and personality.

The packaging is even color-coded to match its contents – how adorable is that?

Lipsticks That Make You Look Younger

It's blue for you! That's right. Any color lip shade with a blue undertone, such as rose, red, burgundy and plum will make your teeth look their pearly whitest. At the other end of the spectrum are nasty orange shades of lipsticks with an orangey or peachy undertone – these are terrible for the appearance of your teeth, and only make them appear yellow. Yuck! "It is the shades with the bluest hues that really bring out the whites of your teeth," says dentist Dr. Laura Torrado (www.drlauratorrado.com).

You'll love the **travel sizes** – the Mini Bourjois range of items that include mascara and lip glosses – they all are lovely, Lilliputian and lovable. And for the longest lashes ever, try Coup de Theatre 2-In-1 Mascara – first you apply the white fibers, then dress your lashes with black mascara – for an ultrachic style. No wonder fashion mavens and makeup artists worship this beloved brand that's so quintessentially French. These are cosmetics with cachet (www.bourjois.co.uk/content/view/full/316).

G.M. Collin – Distinguished Products For Your Dermis

Here's a Canadian brand that offers all the key ingredients – plus a little *je ne sais quoi* – making beautiful skin a breeze. I'm psyched about **G.M. Collin,** because all of its products are derived from natural plant and marine extracts. This boutique brand has won a slew of awards, including kudos for its Aquamucine Cream SPF 15, and its Puracne Oxygen Cleansing Gel. What you are guaranteed to love, right now, is the new Bio Organique line, which uses 99% natural and certified organic ingredients, with no mineral oils, alcohol, parabens or silicone, and was made to respect the environment. Start with the luxurious Revitalizing Mist, containing orange water, concord grape, pumpkin seed-cake, fig extract, and green tea. It smells divine when you spray it on your face. Then follow-up with the Treating Serum –it offers a little wake-up call to your wrinkles, and smells lusciously of lavender and Barbados cherry. Just using it feels like a day at the spa. After that, apply a light touch of Nourishing Cream made with olive, avocado, and argan oil. If you have hormonal issues, try the H50 Therapy Serum and the H50 Therapy Cream in the traditional G.M. Collin product line, to restore the structural integrity of fragile skin. If you're into anti-aging, nothing beats the bota-peptide eye contour containing five peptides including argireline and lipo-arginyl tyrosine – the whole shebang is clinically proven to erase lines and wrinkles. I put it on my plain little pudding face and it pampers my entire outlook on life. There's a whole lot to love in this line. What can I say? G.M. Collin is killer (www.gmcollin.com).

Combray – It Takes Two, Just Two

Combray is a unique antioxidant skincare product with just *two ingredients.*

The antioxidant Oxofulleram is one of the two ingredients in Combray (grape seed oil is the other), and the primary reason that Combray is distinctive. It is a result of years of research and development by Solenne, a science company based in The Netherlands, where Combray is a huge success. Combray represents a significant scientific achievement in the application of antioxidants in skincare. The *NRC Handelsblad,* a national newspaper of record in The Netherlands, featured Solenne and Combray in a full front-page feature in the Science Section. The *NRC* said that Oxofulleram "beats as it sweeps as it cleans" free radicals, invoking the famous vacuum cleaner ads, and called it "a beautiful hybrid of Vitamins E and C."

If you've been searching for an effective, natural, anti-aging moisturizer or relief from the redness associated with inflammation-related conditions such as psoriasis, eczema, acne, or rosacea, then you should try Combray. It has no added colors, perfumes, emulsifiers, stabilizers, or any other chemical. Combray is for any skin type, including oily and combination skin. Combray is a complement to any vanity - the bottle is made by Verreries Brosse of France, the creators of the first Chanel No. 5 bottle in 1921 and one of the world's finest glassmakers. Call it the original Dutch Treat (www.solenne.eu).

Sole Survivors

Planning to do plenty of walking on your trip? To prevent blisters, and to keep feet smelling sweet, roll anti-perspirant on your tootsies. The anti-perspirant prevents your sweat glands in your feet from producing moisture and odor. It also creates a barrier between your feet and socks or shoes, to decrease friction. Blisters, be gone!

Cor Silver – Give It The Gold Medal

Wash your face with silver? That's the secret of the **Cor Silver** line, containing a soap, eye cream, wrinkle serum, and anytime moisturizer. All of the products contain the patented formula of nano-silver with silica. Why silver? It is fast-emerging as one of the best natural anti-bacterial agents. Silver blocks the bacteria's ability to transfer oxygen through its cell walls. Silver also has healing properties and has been used by doctors and hospitals to speed cell repair. Silica, the other ingredient, prepares the skin to accept the ingredients of Cor. The sponge-like nature of silica draws the silver and all of Cor's active natural ingredients into its particles so that it can richly nourish the skin. Other ingredients in the Cor soap include glycerin and pomegranate extract. This cocktail of cool ingredients offers a dewy complexion with an even tone, replenishes collagen, and results in a bright, luminous complexion. Start with the soap – rub its foam into your face and let it sit for a minute or two. The company claims you'll see results in one week. In 2007, the soap (which retails for $125 for a full bar) received *Self Magazine's* Health and Beauty Awards for Best Normal Skin Cleanser. Why not test-drive it? The consensus is that it's the Rolls-Royce of rejuvenators (www.corsilver.com).

Classy Crabtree & Evelyn

A pioneer in botanical formulations for more than 30 years, **Crabtree & Evelyn** blends the very best of nature, science, tradition, and innovation, to create bene-fit-rich bath, body and home care. In fact, the company's heritage is reflected in its name: Crabtree comes from the crabapple tree, which is the original species from which all cultivated apple trees have derived. And Evelyn comes from John Evelyn, the 17th-century Renaissance Englishman, who wrote one of the first important works on conservation. Today, you'll find fabulous treats from C&E's Creative Partner India Hicks, such as her Island Living Spider Lily Body Collections. India's passion for natural beauty led her to work with island plants, fruits and flowers – the cornucopia includes avocado, mango, hibiscus, coconut, aloe vera, grapefruit, sea salt and seaweed – which all help to nourish and pro-tect the skin. For example, her favorite island flower, the delicate Spider Lily that grows out of the pink sand – is the heart of the Spider Lily fragrance, which is also a blend of citrus, orange blossoms, tropical fruits and night-blooming jasmine. There's also India's Casuarina Collection that includes fragrance dif-fusers, candles and room fragrance, which capture the scents of a West Indian breeze. Aside from India's line, there's also much more in store. Want more zest in your life? Look no further than C&E's Citron, Honey, and Coriander Hand Therapy that is bursting with tangy lemons and rich shea butter, as is the Hand Recovery treatment that exfoliates and moisturizes in one easy step. My little nose, however, is quite partial to the Lily of the Valley perfumed bath soaps (great for travel) and the scented **travel kit** of four lovely Lilliputian items: soap, shower gel, body lotion and perfumed powder, which will make you feel like a rock star. Yes, Elvis has left the building – and he took these goodies with him (www.indiahicks-islandliving.com, www.crabtree-evelyn.com).

Super Skincare From Jane Iredale

Now you can take in the sun and stay healthy doing so.

Iredale Mineral Cosmetics, Ltd., manufacturer of **Jane Iredale** – The Skin Care Makeup – recently received the Seal of Recommendation from the Skin Cancer Foundation for *five* of its most popular products. The Seal of Recommendation is awarded to products the Skin Cancer Foundation recommends as an effective ultraviolet (UV) sunscreen. The five products that proudly wear the Seal include Iredale's Amazing Base, PurePressed Base, Dream Tint, LipDrink and Powder-Me SPF in Tanned and Translucent. Take that, traditional cosmetics – you're fired!

Products were evaluated by the Foundation's Photobiology Committee, composed of leading U.S. dermatologists who are experts on sun damage and sun protection. Each product underwent extensive testing to obtain the value and interaction between UV rays and the skin to ensure that each product did not cause irritation and phototoxicity on the skin.

Jane Iredale is a comprehensive line of mineral cosmetics that provides products with the utmost integrity and the ability to enhance the lives of women though its effectiveness, simplicity and beauty. You can wear these mineral marvels in the sun and even during your workouts, with the utmost of confidence. Founder and president Jane Iredale has worked with world-renowned plastic surgeons and dermatologists in the development of her line because she believes makeup should be as good for the skin as it is aesthetically pleasing. Beauty-istas, rejoice! (www.janeiredale.com)

Crème de la Mer: We Love A Good Broth

Here's information on the cult cream that has a devoted following among sophisticated skincare aficionados. **Crème de la Mer**, a cosmetics classic, was conceived under extraordinary circumstances. Years ago, aerospace physicist Dr. Max Huber suffered a horrific accident – a routine experiment exploded in his face – covering him with severe chemical burns. Neither science nor medicine offered sufficient promise of help, so Mr. Huber decided to help himself.

Twelve years and 6,000 experiments later, he perfected the cream that would give skin a dramatically smoother appearance. At the heart of the cream is the Miracle Broth – composed of sea kelp, calcium, magnesium, potassium, iron, lecithin, Vitamins C, E and B12, plus oils of citrus, eucalyptus, wheat germ, alfalfa and sunflower. Through fermentation, these ingredients transform info a whole far greater than the sum of its parts. This is why so many who have tried every cream on the market are steadfast in their devotion to Crème de la Mer. To activate the broth, remember to warm a small amount between your fingertips, and then pat it onto clean, dry skin. A fabulous **travel kit**, called Miraculous Beginnings, contains six products and retails for $350. Also advisable for travel-weary skin is The Mist, which creates a negative-ion-rich environment to boost skin's energy level, $55 (www.cremedelamer.com).

Sonya Dakar: All Things Bright And Beautiful

What do Britney Spears, LeAnn Rimes, Jaime Pressly, Mariah Carey, and other celebrities have in common? They all sing the praises of **Sonya Dakar Skin Care**. And why not? Back in 1999 when the company began in their home kitchen, family patriarch Israel Dakar and his son Nate never imagined their creation would attract an impressive list of A-list clients. Today, celebs – and mere mortals – love Sonya's Total Skin Fitness philosophy, and a line that includes more than 70 results-oriented products that combine cutting-edge ingredients with nature's purest botanicals. Dad and Son – the sultans of skincare – also source their ingredients from all over the world, from the Brazilian rainforest to the Dead Sea, to the vineyards of France and Spain. Sonya's products address a variety of skin issues, including anti-aging, acne, scarring, discoloration, irritation, and more. You'll swear by the fabulous **Jet Set Ultraluxe Travel Kit**; in this TSA-regulation black-satin bag come the UltraLuxe 9 Age Control Complex (containing nine of the most potent anti-aging ingredients known to science as well as essential oils of bitter orange, apricot and pomegranate); a lovely nourishing wash made with grapefruit and verbena; active mask; and more. And if you're prone to breakouts, try the award-winning, cult-fave treatment known as "Hollywood's secret weapon": the Drying Potion that contains Dead Sea sulfur, sage and peppermint. It was the first Sonya Dakar product that was launched, and Drew Barrymore says it's the only zit cream that works. Bravo! (www.sonyadakar.com)

Dremu – The Great White Hope

Actress Jenny McCarthy loves **Dremu.** And why shouldn't she? This skincare line, which uses the oil of American emu birds, has many advantages. "It's very penetrating, and it's an anti-inflammatory," explains CEO Julie Brumlik. "Emu oil is also very similar to human fat, with no allergic properties. It helps to re-store the barrier function of skin to plump up the skin." Julie says that airline pilots in the cockpit, and female soldiers in Iran and Afghanistan, constantly send her love letters about Dremu, because it has worked wonders on their parched skin. "Dremu takes three weeks for the skin to turn over, but it takes years off the appearance of your skin. I'm 61 and I have no wrinkles," Julie told me. The Airbrush eye cream also made Oprah Winfrey's "Favorite Things" list some years ago. The product line includes a terrific daily lotion called Daylight; a cleanser called Whistle (as in clean-as-a-you-know-what); Deception, a wrinkle-filler with a special formula to retract light into the shadows of your wrinkles, so you don't see them; and the triple rich Face Paste ($270 for a little under 2 ounces). *Vogue Magazine* also reported that Cashmere, a hand and body lotion containing micronized mica for polished skin, is Beyonce's favor-ite. As the marketing materials say, expect a miracle! (www.dremu.com)

Dremu skincare is made from the oil of American emu birds.

Epicuren: Started By A Flight Attendant!

Epicuren's president, Colleen White Lohrman, was a flight attendant with Continental Airlines for 43 years. She first learned about **Epicuren** from its owner, Robert Heiman, one day, while on a flight. When she mentioned she was about to visit the La Prairie Spa in Switzerland, for their sheep's-placenta facial for her ever-dry skin, he told her about his new company that uses enzymes (from New Zealand- and Colorado-raised sheep's hooves or fur that is sheared) to reinvigorate the skin. (The enzymes increase the metabolic activity of skin cells, allowing them to take in more of three nutrients that are also present in the human mouth – biotin, niacin and riboflavin. These three nutrients, among others, are why the inside of your mouth never ages.) (Mr. Heiman also claims that his Epicuren line also cured his vitiligo). Colleen took his samples, put them in a drawer for six months and forgot about them. But when she eventually did try them, she was instantly impressed. It led to her to mix conditioner and water into her own "protein mist" that she sprayed on her face during extended flights. Fellow flight attendants and captains were so impressed that they clamored for some for themselves. So did her brother, who is also an airline captain. Eventually, Colleen was so enthusiastic that she quit her job and took the lead at Epicuren, which today offers a wealth of enzyme-packed products for face and body. **Travel kits** are also available.

Epicuren's colostrum cream comes from the breast milk of cows raised in Nebraska. Colostrum is known for its growth factor and ability to speed the growth of new cells. I interviewed the farmer, who claims that it also works wonders on rosacea and eczema. The farmer has worked with Epicuren for 20 years. Colleen asked me never to name him: "His work is a trade secret."

She also claims that the Epicuren products made with bee propolis (from killer bees in the Rainforest) are even more healing than the colostrum cream.

Today you'll find that Epicuren is a word-of-mouth secret used by A-list celebrities and models whose names are too numerous to mention! Use Epicuren and you'll feel like a VIP too (www.epicuren.com).

Epicuren is craved by Hollywood A-list celebrities.

Episciences: Move Over, Renova!

If you're seeking a product that has taken on some of the leading skincare products on the market, look no further than **Epionce.** This brand claims to be the only cosmeceutical line that has 14 independent clinical studies done to prove both efficacy and safety. "We were so confident that we went ahead and took on the No. 1 prescription anti-aging product, Renova, and were found to be statistically equal," says Trish Stack, Epionce's Communications Coordinator. "We have since taken on most of the non-prescription market leaders including Prevage MD and Obagi C20 and have been statistically superior across the board." The product's fact sheet says that Epionce delivers ingredients to reach targeted cells with minimal barrier disruption; the active formulas repair, fortify and strengthen your skin's natural protective barrier while helping to block destructive inflammatory factors. I personally love the sweet-smelling Intensive Nourishing Cream, which is non-comedogenic and made with proprietary ingredients. Available in a **travel size** is a TSA-compliant kit in a plastic bag containing the showstoppers of Epionce's regime: Renewal Facial Cream, Gentle Foaming Cleanser, and its special Lytic lotion; the kit has a suggested retail price of $79. Want some? Epionce is available only in physician offices and medical spas. It will add TLC to your travels (www.epionce.com).

Kerstin Florian: The Swedish Secret

Kerstin Florian International develops and manufactures a range of European facial, body and bath products, and treatments for the spa industry, based on natural resources including thermal mineral water, mud, algae, herbal extracts and essential oils. The family-run company is based in Southern California and was founded in 1978 by Swedish-born Kerstin Florian, a spa expert with more than 40 years of experience in the industry. Today the company produces more than 100 retail and professional products and more than 25 treatments. You'll love the two anti-aging lines. The Caviar Collection contain Sevruga caviar as well as Chinese herbs, caffeine and Coenzyme A, a healing antioxidant. The Correcting Skincare Collection is based on hyaluronic acid (which binds and attracts water to the skin), vitamins, and glycolic acid, to treat, repair and refine the skin. For **travel**, try the mini sizes for face and body, including cleansing gel, moisturizers, body lotion, shampoo and conditioner, or the weightless Eye Rescue, a velvety eye pad to hydrate delicate skin around the peepers. (The Hyaluronic Serum, which smells delightful thanks to lavender and bitter orange oil, is also a keeper) (www.kerstinflorian.com).

Sally Hansen Is A Great Girlfriend

I love **Sally Hansen** – always have. I always find that her nail products are awesome, and totally reliable. Take the Ultra Smoothing Growth Treatment – and please do! Just pump the brush, and it works wonders on my short, thin nails that break easily and bend in weird directions. This smoothing solution adds a heavy coat of clear polish that makes my nails look and feel healthy – like using a polish with silk fibers to strengthen your nails, but this has none of the muss and fuss. I swear by it. What else I love about Sally is that she's always thinking outside the bottle. You'll love the Color Quick nail color pens as much as I do – the color glides on, just like you're using a Sharpie, and the pens pack well in your suitcase. You can also get an artful French manicure, also with the push of a pen. After you've given yourself an expert manicure, nothing can match the Double Life base and topcoat – it will protect your nails and grip the color for about 10 days. And I would be doing Sally an injustice if I didn't rave about her Airbrush Sun, the spray-on tanning perfection that dries in just 60 seconds and is devoid of that telltale "self-tanner" smell. Sally – well, I guess you'd have to say she's been my BFF (www.sallyhansen.com).

Hard Night Good Morning: Filled With Berried Treasures

Wouldn't you just love to use a cleanser that's filled with wild blueberries, raspberries and their seeds, strawberries, bilberries, cherries, and prunes? Well now you can. **Hard Night Good Morning** makes an AM Cleanser enhanced with these ingredients and jojoba beads, to gently slough off dead skin cells and leave skin with a healthy glow. The smell is so fruity, your follicles will love it! The line is the brainchild of D'Andra Simmons, who has been involved with nutrition and skincare much of her life. To create her line, Hard Night Good Morning, she traveled the globe in search of the most effective natural ingredients and breakthrough technologies, to create a formula that would strengthen, restore and heal damaged skin. From Africa, to China, and South America, D'Andra sourced – are you ready? – acai, honey bush tea, dragon fruit, tonka bean, papaya, green tea, aloe vera, jojoba oil, macadamia nut oil – and a lot more. Her products are unusual in that they all list aloe vera (and not water) as their first ingredient, and they are all pharmaceutical-grade, made in small batches without parabens. The bestseller is the Facial Cocktail Serum (sold at Whole Foods Market and online at her own website), which contains rooibos tea, calendula flower, acai and green tea. "I try to bathe your skin in antioxidants," she says. She claims that one of the ingredients in the Facial Cocktail Serum has been clinically tested to show a 51% reduction in the skin's wrinkled surface, in just one application (www.dandrasimmons.com).

Dr. Hauschka: Holistic Beauty

Loved by Gossip Girl Leighton Meester, Debi Mazar (a fan for more than 30 years), and Jennifer Aniston, **Dr. Hauschka** is the holistic skincare line that celebrities rave about. The celebrated line has also been used by professional makeup artists in such movies as *Julie & Julia, Enchanted,* and *Crazy Heart*, as well as TV shows such as the *The Rachael Ray Show*, and *Desperate Housewives.* What's the fuss about? From the beginning, Dr. Hauschka Skincare based its approach to personal care on an in-depth understanding of the power of healing plants to restore and maintain healthy skin. That's where Biodynamics comes into play. Biodynamics is a holistic, sustainable form of agriculture that dates all the way back to the 1920's. It takes into account everything from the cycles of the moon and stars to the soil, plants, animals and people, with the ultimate goal of making each garden or farm a healthy self-sustaining ecosystem. Dr. Hauschka manufacturer WALA Heilmittel has owned and maintained its own certified Biodynamic gardens for more than 60 years, and a number of the botanicals used in Dr. Hauschka preparations comes right from these very gardens. You'll find a wealth of posh preparations in elegant metal tubes, which smell fantastic, including Rose Day Cream that contains rose oil, extracts from wild rose hips and rose petals (and which smells like The Real McCoy) in addition to rose wax. There's also a Soothing Mask containing healing botanicals such as lady's mantle, borage, buckwheat and mullein. Dr. Hauschka also receives the Triple Crown for NOT containing these three: synthetic colors, preservatives or fragrance. This line is a winner in more ways than one. To Dr. Hauschka, we all say a heartfelt "Danke." (www. drhauschka.com)

La Roche-Posay For Complexion Perfection

Recommended by more than 25,000 dermatologists worldwide, **La Roche-Posay** is the dermatologists' brand of choice for their patients' skin. The brand continues to be at the cutting edge of research, demonstrated by breakthrough innovations, highly concentrated ingredients, and clinical testing. One of its dynamic breakthroughs? Anthelios SX Daily Moisturizer SPF 15. This revolutionary moisturizer contains Mexoryl, a unique, stable, organic sun filter that is highly protective against short-wave UVA rays. This moisturizer also contains photo-stabilized Parsol 1789; L'Oreal patented the ratio of Octocrylene to Avobenzone in the product, providing coverage against UVB and long UVA waves, respectively. (It represents the first time since 1988 that the FDA has approved a new sunscreen formula.) This sunscreen is free of fragrance and PABA, and is suitable for sensitive skin. You'll also find Anthelios 60 Melt-In Sunscreen Milk, offering high UVA protection to face and body thanks to Cell-OX Shield, which treats the skin right down to the cellular level, from exposure to harmful UV rays. Perhaps the most exciting advancement for the Anthelios franchise is the Anthelios 60 Ultra Light Fluid. One is sold every 15 seconds, making this sunscreen a cult favorite of women. Of course, I'm partial to the Active C line, including the deliciously fragranced Anti-Wrinkle Dermatological Treatment containing active and stable Vitamin C, as well as the Active C Fluid for your eyes. (I've used other Vitamin C emulsions, which only burned – that's right – **burned** my face. These, by comparison, will caress your complexion). And they'll juice up any journey. (www.laroche-posay.us)

Living Proof, Inc. – The Science Of Beauty

Are you flat-out longing for flat, straight hair?

I would kill for straight hair – or the kind of tresses that let you wash-and-go and still look gorgeous. Well, I'm almost there, thanks to No Frizz – an unprecedented formulation developed by Dr. Robert Langer, one of the world's top biomedical scientists – and a Professor at the Massachusetts Institute of Technology.

Dr. Langer partnered with Polaris Venture Partners, a venture-capital firm with an extraordinary 25-year track record of business development, to launch the company **Living Proof.** To achieve their vision, Living Proof assembled a scientific team with experience *outside* of beauty that could break new ground – without any preconceived notions of what could and could not be done. This team spent more than three years assessing new molecules that have been used in the past in medical applications, but never in the beauty industry. The scientists created products that push beyond existing limits to change how we think about beauty today.

What they found is that most of the current products on the market to solve anti-frizz problems treat it with silicone – a technology in use for three decades. The problem? Silicone doesn't address the causes of frizz – as it doesn't prevent humidity from entering the hair shaft and it doesn't reduce the surface friction on hair. Rather, silicone works by weighing down hair with oil.

Instead, the scientific team asked: *"How can we reduce the surface friction of hair, and how can we prevent the hair, and its surface, from absorbing water?"* The answer: produce a hydrophobic material with low surface energy that can coat the hair without weighing it down. The search led to the discovery of PolyfluoroEster – a smaller molecule than the traditional materials used for frizz control. It creates a weightless shield on the hair to prevent moisture flux in and out. In fact, repeated use after shampooing improves the hair's own ability to resist humidity changes, so No Frizz works even better! The non-greasy coating also makes hair more repellent to dirt and particles than natural hair, so you can actually go longer between shampoos.

I've tried the product and I love it. I let my hair air-dry for 45 minutes after applying No Frizz, and even before I used my blow dryer, it appeared straighter. Afterwards – *wowza* – it was super straight, and on the second day, it looked even straighter. I am continually amazed at how well this product works on my hair. I have always said that I don't blow-dry my hair – *I beat it into submission* – but no more, thanks to this wonderful product.

It's available in two formulations: Straight Making for women who prefer straighter styles, and Wave Shaping, Curl Defining, for women who prefer to refine their natural curls and waves. Want a pocket-sized potion? Just $14 for each **travel-sized** spray (www.livingproof.com).

You'll Love LUSH

Millions of bottles of water, perfume, lotions, shampoos and conditioners have been confiscated at airports around the world since the ban on liquids, gels and balms. Fortunately, 70% of **LUSH** bath and beauty products are in solid form – that's right – solid form. With LUSH you can pack your toiletries, pamper yourself, and breeze through airport security. There are numerous solid options: Godiva shampoo and conditioning bar; Jungle solid conditioner; vegan Buffy body butter; Olive Branch solid perfume; Therapy massage bar, and many more. Some of the other solid perfumes include American Cream (strawberry); Honey I Washed The Kids (honey toffee); and The Comforter (blackcurrant). And if you love serums – but hate toting any liquids – pack your carry-on with Lush's Solid Facial Serum called "Full of Grace." This little almond-shaped beauty bar is chock-a-block with almond oil and murumuru butter (an oil from the murumuru fruit found in the Amazon; the lipids present in the plant material hydrate and moisturize skin and hair). It will deeply moisturize your face, without making it feel greasy. All of these innovations come packed in their own recycled aluminum tin, which keeps your travel items tidy. If you don't know about LUSH Fresh Handmade Cosmetics already, every store is a veritable cosmetic-deli, with products that are 100% vegetarian, 74% vegan, 65% preservative-free, and which are made from fresh organic fruits and vegetables, and the finest essential oils and ingredients. If you also like to pack your own soap in your Samsonite, there's no end to the beautiful bars available such as: Gingermen (in ginger of course); 17 Cherry Tree Lane (mimosa and orange blossom); and Tiptoe Through the Tulips (violet and lavender). And their balms are the bomb, especially Chocolate Whip Stick (chocolate-orange). Vegans, you'll go bonkers for the Sweet Lips Scrub, a crème-brulee creation that tastes as good as the results it gets. LUSH makes the perfect little items to lust after (www.lushusa.com).

Luxtural – Can You Spell Luxury?

At the age of three, skincare became Pnina Vilinsky's passion. As a young child, she met the elegant sister of the renowned skincare pioneer, Helena Rubenstein, and it was a milestone. As she got older, Pnina witnessed her own grandmother's anguish over her skin's premature aging, which made Pnina even more determined to create her own skincare formulations. The result? **Luxtural,** launched in

2009, "when luxury meets nature at your skin." Luxtural claims to capture the best qualities of cutting-edge cosmetic technology and holistic medicine from ancient cultures. What sets Luxtural apart is that is uses pure Pacific rainwater, collected in a fresh, clean location before reaching the ground – untouched by toxins and contaminants. It is this rainwater that leaves the products light and velvety soft on your skin. Three formulas exist – I love them all – and you just can't beat their sweet fragrance. (Put it on your skin, and the amazing aroma will delight your senses for a long time.) There's a deep hydrating mist, an anti-aging lotion, and my favorite, the anti-aging deep-moisturizing serum, which really does the trick. And they all come in **travel sizes**. Luxtural products also do not use any parabens, mineral oil, or synthetic or chemical fragrance. No wonder celebrities including Demi Moore, Angelina Jolie, Mariska Hargitay, Jenny McCarthy, Lucy Liu and Debra Messing are fans. For travelers, Luxtural is just the ticket (www.Luxtural.com).

Jan Marini: As Good As It Gets

A product researcher for more than 35 years, **Jan Marini** is an "ingredients expert" who is always on the lookout for "medically validated technologies" that she can incorporate into her products, resulting in numerous patents. Her Age Intervention Cream, for example, includes Interferon Alpha 2B that's applied topically, while her Transformation product line of creams and serums uses Thymosin beta-4 that contains 43 peptides. "I have the ingredients you won't find anywhere else," says Jan. I love to use her remarkable hair rejuvenator, Marini Hair ($170) "which addresses issues that contribute to male- and female-pattern baldness." In other words, it makes your hair look and feel *young* – big, bouncy and full of shine. I am amazed at my hair after I use it – it's like it looked in high school. This fantastic product is an *absolute must-have* for everyone. For travelers on the go, consider the Skin Care Management Travel System ($48) featuring **travel sizes** of C Esta Serum, Antioxidant Daily Face Protection, Bioglycolic Facial Cleanser and Cream, plus Age Intervention Face Cream. It's all skin-tastic! (www.janmarini.com)

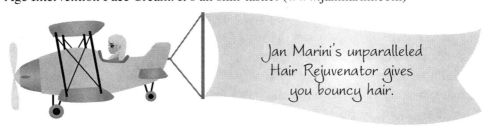

Jan Marini's unparalleled Hair Rejuvenator gives you bouncy hair.

Dr. Howard Murad, How Do I Love Thee?

Well, let me count the ways. First, I'm seriously addicted to – and swear by – **Murad** pomegranate lip gloss, which goes on like silk and keeps my smackers firmed up and juicy – and even offers SPF 15. There's also a sweet foaming pomegranate cleanser, and a moisturizer to offer complexion perfection. In the Resurgence line (which broadcaster Joan Lunden loves), there is a wealth of wonderful products – including day moisture SPF 15, age-diffusing serum, night-balancing cream, renewing eye cream, and even a **travel kit** of the Evening Renewal Regimen, all containing antioxidants, anti-inflammatories, moisturizers, peptides and phytoestrogens.

Speaking of **travel kits**, Murad also makes an Essential-C Environmental Defense Kit to help you fight free radicals, plus yet another containing Age Reform Essentials.

What sets Murad products apart? Plenty. Dr. Howard Murad, a board-certified dermatologist, is also a pharmacist – "It's how I worked my way through medical school," he told me – who has established himself as an international authority on the aging process. As a pharmacist, he was creating compounds of his prescriptions for his patients, which led him, naturally, to develop his own line of products – probably the world's first cosmeceutical line. He pioneered innovative treatment concepts that are now commonplace, including the use of alpha hydroxy acids, antioxidants, pomegranate and durian, into the world of skincare.

Dr. Murad's products are all based on his Science of Cellular Water, which looks at the ability of cell membranes to hold water as the fundamental marker of youthful good health. "The Murad Recipe" is at the heart of all of Dr. Murad's formulas, which include hydrators to improve the skin's ability to attract and hold water (at the surface and cellular level); anti-inflammatories to discourage redness and edema; and antioxidants to protect against UV radiation and other environmental assaults. Using insights gained from his discoveries, Dr. Murad developed an integrated multi-disciplinary approach, which he calls "Inclusive Health," to help the body create stronger, healthier cells. Today, Dr. Murad continues his innovative research and holds 18 patents for advances in the science of skin health. In many locations, including Sephora and Ulta, Murad prod-

Would You Pay $449,127 To Look Good Over Your Lifetime?

For women aged 30 to 49, beauty costs for the face include: $100 per month for cosmetics; once-a-year skin smoothing/anti-aging microdermabrasion treatments at $834; eyebrow shaping at $43 per session, six times year; Botox injectable wrinkle treatments for forehead creases at $443 per session, three times a year; deep line filler treatment, once a year at $566; and yearly lip plumping at $1,246 per session. This brings the face maintenance total in this age range to $108,660. That's the average cost that a woman will spend on beauty treatments for just one year. If she's a diva.

For women aged 30 to 49, body treatments include bikini waxing at $41 per session, six times a year; tanning at $300 per year; and laser varicose vein treatments once a year at $345. This brings the body total over this age range to $17,820.

The lifetime costs a diva will pay, from tweens up to 50+ year olds, for treatments that include hair, face, body, hands and feet are estimated at $449,127. This is what a **lifetime** of cosmetic maintenance will cost a dedicated beauty aficionado.

From *Newsweek.com* on April 1, 2009 (and it's not an April Fool's Joke)
www.newsweek.com/id/187758?GT1=43002

ucts are the Number One-selling clinical skincare brand. When Dr. Murad first opened his dermatology practice in California in 1972, he started out with two rooms, one nurse and one patient. By the time he moved his offices to their existing location in the Southern California location of El Segundo, he had built a patient base of nearly 50,000. Impressive! (www.murad.com)

Murad's pomegranate lipgloss is silky on your smackers.

The Sweet Smell of Hotel Success

Several years ago, my husband Bill and I stayed in the "lapa" luxury – better known as the Lapa Palace, an ultraluxurious hotel in Lisbon, Portugal, which actually used to be a palace. A member of Leading Hotels of the World, the Lapa Palace offers European elegance in a rarefied atmosphere. I'll never forget the experience of just having a Monday-morning breakfast there – silken service and cashmere care oozed from every pore of the breakfast room, where silver trays held fruits and croissants as though they were jewels. One of the more unusual things this charming five-star hotel offers is its own signature scent, **Eau de Portugal**. It was the favored scent of Maria Pia de Savoia (1847-1911), the daughter of Vittorio Emanuele II, King of Italy. She was married to Luis I, one of the Portuguese kings. Today, the hotel Lapa Palace, in cooperation with Helleboro, has recreated the queen's fragrance. Its main notes are black gooseberry, mandarin and orange, while the body is violet, apple and peach. And yes, it's available for sale in the gift shop for about $100 (www.lapapalace.com).

Take These Travel Sizes With You

Some of the best things come in small packages, don't you agree? I discovered some of these travel kits, and now you can easily tote these little treasures.

Leonor Greyl of Paris, with a famous institute in the City of Light, offers its distinctive haircare products all in travel sizes. The kit includes 2-in-1 volumizing and detangling shampoo; hair mask with a jasmine-orchid scent; and 100% natural palm oil used on dry hair to protect hair from excess sun, UV rays, salt and seawater. $38. (www.leonorgreyl-usa.com)

Sampar of Paris makes five of its Essentials products available in petite plastic vials. You'll get velvet cleansing milk, skin quenching mist, foam peel, hydrating fluid and nocturnal lifting mask in .17-ounce formulations that are easy to carry on. $40. (www.sampar.com/USA)

Molton Brown offers travel-ready packs in a security bag with a luggage tag. I got the "Relaxed Traveller," which ensures that you are de-stressed and soothed. The scent, a mix of vanilla, ylang ylang and rose oil, is present in bath and shower gel, body lotion and even a sleep mist, plus a pulse-point balm. $60. (www.Moltonbrown.com)

June Jacobs, a favorite of spa-goers, features an Intensive Age Defying Travel Kit of products including cleansing milk; mandarin polishing beads; hydrating serum; oil-free SPF 30; moisturizer; and eye cream. All come in an adorable cream quilted cosmetic case. $165. (www.junejacobs.com)

Organic Apoteke: Where Beauty Is More Than Skin Deep

Imagine yourself starring in a feature-length movie – with a pure, effective and luxurious skincare line that holds up to its claims and delivers powerful ingredients to your dermis. Well, that would be science fiction, wouldn't it? Guess again. If you try **Organic Apoteke**, you're likely to become hooked. The line was started by Dr. Nitasha Buldeo, who, as a young girl, helped tend her grandmother's herb garden and watched as she prepared therapeutic remedies for a wide range of skin conditions. Nitasha went on to get her degrees in homeopathy and Ayurvedic medicine and launched a line that incorporates ancient healing arts with cutting-edge science. Organic Apoteke has many things to set it apart: The entire 17-product line is certified organic by ECOCERT (an organic certification organization, founded in France in 1991); it is vegetarian, kosher, cruelty-free (as well as alcohol-free); and it's fair traded with ethically sourced ingredients. The brand is known to stimulate microcirculation – that's why when you use Organic Apoteke, you feel a warm, tingling sensation on your skin. "Our products stimulate blood supply to the skin – when you put them on, you are penetrating to

How Many Clams Would You Shell Out For Pearl Cream?

Supreme Pearl Cream from *Swissline* contains crushed mother-of-pearl from the *pinctada maxima* oyster, the largest and most precious oyster of the South Seas, as well as silk protein, and a seawater concentrate. The parent company, Swissline by Dermalab, claims that Supreme Pearl Cream produces a 30% increase in skin hydration, a 12% increase in firmness, and a 47% reduction in visible fine lines and wrinkles. The president of the company, Prince Michael Massalsky, is a former president of La Prairie, who launched its popular Caviar Cream, another posh preparation (www.euro-essentials.com).

the deeper layer," says Nitasha. She adds: "Everything we say is backed by research to prove it." The most popular product is the Rasayana Rejuvenating Serum – it has a funky, organic smell, but it lightens age spots and improves skin tone. "It's the amino-acid smell," Nitasha says. "There are also palmerosa and rose geranium oils in it, but we don't fragrance any of the products….I used it on a third-degree burn, and in three months the scar was barely visible." Made in the UK, Organic Apoteke has also won a slew of beauty awards, and was a winner in the 2008 Natural Health Beauty Awards and the Pure Beauty Awards, making it an Oscar-worthy choice in our book. There's also an excellent **travel size** of the Droseros hydrating mist containing rose water, homeopathic belladonna and damask rose oil. Use it and follow the 11th Commandment: Thou Shalt Spritz (www.organicapoteke.com).

Patyka: Unbelievably Organic

Patyka, made in France, is famous for the ingredients it *doesn't* contain: no silicone, petroleum products, sulfates, parabens, synthetic fragrances or colorings – and there's a whole laundry list of a lot more that *doesn't* go into its certificated organic products. All Patyka products are certified organic by ECOCERT and COSMEBIO (the professional association of Ecological and Organic Cosmetics, www.cosmebio.org). Founder Philippe Gounel spent more than 10 years formulating and developing beauty products for many major companies throughout Europe. After discovering some old Hungarian skincare recipes, which were made from natural products, he created an organic approach to beauty – with Patyka, which was launched in 2002. The first product created was the Huile Absolue, an organic face and body serum containing organic rosehips, geranium and rosewood. Another standout: Biokaliftin, the first line of certified organic cosmeceuticals of which the Crème Miracle Reparatrice is the highlight. This cream contains hyaluronic acid, and a new advanced peptide – Acetyl Hexapeptide-8 – which reduces fine lines and wrinkles. Patyka has also recently introduced an affordably priced Family Line, and all items retail for $19 and less. They're all joy in a jar (www.patyka.com).

Ren: Beauty And Brains

Founded by Robert Calcraft and Antony Buck, **Ren** was created to offer the best of both worlds: to be as pure as it is potent. The two founders describe their products as bio-active skincare, because it lacks any of the nasties: synthetics, parabens and various animal ingredients. It's smart, savvy skincare with a fresh point of view. A **travel size** introductory kit contains six products including a Vita-Mineral Day Cream, Omega-3 Overnight Lipid Renewal Serum, and a Radiant Eye Gel containing hyaluronic acid. Other distinctive products in the entire Ren line include Moroccan Rose Otto Bath Oil; Perfect Lip Honey; and Neroli-And-Grapefruit Shower Wash. Here's what my ace tester, Sally Shields, had to say: "The Ren Cleansing Gel was very gentle and I loved the coolness. I could actually feel the aloe vera included in the product. It did a fabulous job removing my makeup, and even my mascara came off easily, which I love. I was expecting The Skin Renewal Mask to burn or sting, but it was very, very lightweight, and gentle. I felt a little bit of tightening, but overall it was a very mellow experience and I actually wanted to leave it on longer than the recommended 10 minutes because I could feel my pores tightening up and knew it was doing great things for my skin! I LOVED the Day Cream. I have dry skin, and this stuff just gave me a ton of moisture. It didn't take long to sink in, but did a fantastic job under my makeup, leaving me with a smooth look for the first time in ages. The Omega Renewal Serum is liquid gold. I love it. Overall, I give Ren five stars!" (www.renskincare.com)

Rimmel – Get The London Look

Who wouldn't want to look like Kate Moss? I seriously love, love, love **Rimmel** products – find 'em at Walgreen's and you'll pay a fraction of the price of department-store brands. And if you only buy one mascara this year, please make it Rimmel's Sexy Curves Full Volume and Curve Mascara in Extreme Black – it is aptly named. I don't know what they put in it, but this magical little mascara will instantly make your lashes stand at attention and look long, lush and full. It's become my brand new favorite. If I only had one thing to take on a desert island, it's my Rimmel in the purple-metallic container. Rimmel's purple reigns! (www.rimmellondon.com)

There's Something About Hairy

Manuscripts at the Louvre bear witness to the multitude of recipes for shampoos, soaps, toothpastes and depilatory creams, in ancient times. For instance, all-over hair removal caught on – for both sexes – after returning Crusaders brought the idea back from the Middle East. Eleanor of Aquitaine is credited with inventing dental floss.

50 Reasons to Hate the French, or Vive La Difference by Jules Eden and Alex Clarke, Quetzal Publishing, 2006, page 53.

Rusk – Best-Tressed List

No wonder TV hair stylists love working with **Rusk** products. Rusk's amazing collection allows stylists to use innovative and imaginative techniques, to offer clients everything from runway looks to the next "must-have" hair trend. Two to try: Rusk's new Sensories Wellness Shampoos and Conditioners. Do you know why you will love them? They are free, free, free of sulfates, parabens, petrochemicals, and phthalates. (If you have had your hair Keratined, like I have, this type of sulfate-free shampoo and conditioner is a must.) The Bedew collection contains oil of the Tahitian tiare flower, while the Reflect collection uses soybean oil that is rich in Omega-3 and jojoba oil. Finally, there's the Heal ensemble using Moroccan argan oil that is all the rage now. Other showstoppers I love to use are the Str8 Anti-Frizz Lotion that is greaseless and makes frizzy or curly hair look like silk. Finally, there's the W8less Plus-Hold Hairspray; what makes it so marvelous is that it contains Thermplex, which means that you can use it on wet or dry hair (imagine that!) and it leaves hair completely brushable. Just use the heat of a blow-dryer to activate. This is a two-for-one product, and convenience-in-a-can, which every traveler will love (www.rusk1.com).

Sheer Cover – Leeza Loves It

If you've seen Leeza Gibbons on TV, you've seen her sing the praises of **Sheer Cover** mineral makeup. And what's not to love? The Mineral SPF Foundation is a 4-in-1 formula that works overtime to be your sunscreen, foundation, finishing, and anti-aging treatment. You'll not only love what's in it, but what it does without – no mineral oil, talc, fragrance, pore-clogging ingredients or harmful chemicals. The benefits are awesome – you'll hide visible capillaries; since it's sweat-proof it's ideal for your workout; it won't settle in wrinkles and fine lines (and make you look older); and it's ideal for dry and sensitive skin. In your black-patent leather pouch you'll receive the mineral makeup; concealer; eyeliner; lipsticks; an array of brushes; and more. Clearly, it's terrific. You cat-walk cutie, you! (www.sheercover.com)

Superlative Skin Organics

I discovered **Skin Organics** at Whole Foods and instantly fell in love with the Coffee Cherry Moisture Drench Cream, containing shea butter (to add extra moisture to your skin), argireline (a peptide that softens facial muscles), and cocoa (an emollient to lubricate the skin). Yes, it smells just like delicious chocolate! Apply it to your skin – and it'll make your day, as the delectable aroma travels to your nose. It's also free of parabens, gluten, and is vegan. Other standouts in this line include a Pomegranate Protection Moisturizer with transparent zinc oxide and micronized titanium dioxide (to block sun rays), the Apple Berry Clarifying Serum with a cornucopia of fruit oils and extracts, and the Olive Eyes Hydration Therapy for your peepers. It contains pure squalene, an emollient derived from Spanish olives. This organic skincare brand was created by aesthetician Ann Webb, so she would have an affordable treatment line for her wellness clinic in Austin, Texas. The products are beautifully designed, appealing to the eye, and attractive to your wallet (www.skinorganicsaw.com).

Get Your Start With Tarte

What sets **Tarte** apart? For one thing, CEO Maureen Kelly set out to create a cosmetic line that would prove that glamour can be good for you. She dubbed it "health couture," after the marriage between fashion and nature. Today, Tarte is beloved by fans near and far, including celebrities such as Carrie Underwood, Kristen Bell and Denise Richards. Tarte has won awards too numerous to mention, and it's no wonder. The products offer healthy ingredients, innovative packaging, portability, and cheeky names such as Lash Hugger – a natural mascara packaged in a metal tube composed of post-consumer recycled aluminum.

But let's not forget about Tarte Flush – not a day goes by that you don't hear about some celebrity who loves this natural-looking cheek gel. A little dab'll really do ya. Tarte holds a trademark on its "skinvigorating" ingredients, including its "t5" super fruit complex containing – are you ready? – acai, goji, maracuja (passion flower), acerola and pomegranate, which are said to deliver refining anti-aging and skin-restorative benefits. There's also MultiplEYE, a lash enhancer with a proprietary HydroPlant Peptide, to naturally give the appearance of longer, thicker lashes. It's free of just about everything: parabens, petrochemicals, phthalates, sulfate, glycol, fragrance, oil, gluten, dye, talc and lots more. And if you're just dying to get the look of Paris Hilton, try the Celebutante: a moisturizing dry-oil shimmer spray. Now, go pose for the cameras! (www.tarte.com)

Weleda – Lay Some Organic Farming On Me

If I told you that I'm just plain nuts about **Weleda** (Wa-lay-da) you'd have to believe me. Reason One? Since its inception in 1921, Weleda has been a pioneer in Biodynamic and organic farming, which, as company spokesperson Jennifer Barckley told me, is a "holistic way of farming as one eco-system where everything can be recycled." Second, "All the ingredients of this skincare and medical line, developed by Dr. Rudolf Steiner, come from Weleda's own gardens in Germany. In fact, the production facility is *right next door* to the gardens." Third, Weleda, known for its medicinal compositions, uses pharmaceutical practices and standards for its beauty creams and lotions. Fourth, any of the products can be injested, such as the Calendula toothpaste (a delicious, fennel-based paste that tastes like black licorice) and all are kosher. There's a lot to love: just the packaging will entice you: aluminum tubes in perky colors that will liven up any bathroom from the Marriott to Motel 6. But the biggest reason you'll love Weleda as much as me is that it's so darn affordable – here's a prestigious skincare line of beautiful products, and you can buy a large tube of say, a facial cream, for just $18 a tube. $18!! And now the line is also available in that purveyor of all-things-chic, Target, to make it even more accessible to the general public (even though it is also available in 50 countries and of course, at Whole Foods and health-food stores).

You'll love the Weleda almond cream that smells like marzipan and comes in an adorable pink tube, as well as the sweetly fragrant iris cream in purple packaging. For just $3.50, you can even get a **travel size** of the bestselling Skin Food (which Winona Ryder loves) that's packed with calendula, pansy, chamomile, sweet almond oil and rosemary, and it's great for hands, body, and feet. In fact, there are wealth of Weleda items that come in **travel sizes** – including the yummy Calendula toothpaste, Almond Moisture Cream, and Rose Day Cream. For $14.99 you can also purchase kits of the Almond Facial Care for sensitive skin; the Wild Rose Facial Care Kit for regenerating; and a Body Oils Kit of six types. No wonder, then, that celebrities such as Brooke Shields, Kate Hudson, Liv Tyler, even Adrian Brody love this European brand. I'm so pumped up about Weleda, it puts me into a cosmetics coma (www.usa.weleda.com).

Yon-Ka: The Sweet Smell Of Success

Madonna and Jennifer Lopez all love, love, love **Yon-Ka Paris**, which is a French family-owned company. "The formulations are astonishing," says Ido Kadman, spokesman. Indeed, one whiff of any of Yon-Ka's products and you're sure to be hooked (as I am). You'll also reap the benefits of aromatherapy, phytotherapy (from plants), marine therapy (from seaweed) and fruit acid therapy (from fruits, silly!). "Yon-Ka is known for its great aromas – and Yon-Ka is an experience," says Ido. I wholeheartedly agree. Its bestsellers include the Pamplemousse (grapefruit) moisturizer, made with grapefruit extract and essence, along with pumpkin seed oil, olive oil and citrus oils. Its most unusual product is a shimmering Tan Prolonger, a super hydrating cream that gives a gradual tan plus an immediate shimmer. It also smells wonderful, since it's not made with the DHA typically used in other self-tanners. Yon-Ka, a while back, introduced **travel sizes** of its most popular products. These include Lait Nettoyant ($14), a two-in-one cleanser and eye makeup remover; Gel Nettoyant ($14), a cleansing gel which uses red algae and iris extracts; the absolutely gorgeous Tonic Spray with essences of lavender, rosemary, cypress, geranium and thyme – the five essential oils the company is famous for ($15) – and Lait Corps, a velvety soft body lotion. My dear traveler, Yon-Ka will transport you (www.yonka.com).

If you just can't get enough beauty stuff, read Chapter Nine on gorgeous products from around the world, made with local, indigenous ingredients. They're your ticket to inspired international beauty.

CHAPTER NINE
C'mon Baby, Do The Local Potion

If you're like me, you travel the world and scour all the great places for fabulous and unusual souvenirs. I'm always on the lookout for locally made beauty products and cosmetics that I can bring home with me – as the ultimate souvenirs – all of which will neatly fit into a slim suitcase. You know how some people travel the world to eat regional foods? I globetrot to load up on regional *cosmetics*.

Are you perhaps interested in some unusual goodies with that certain *je ne sais quoi*? These regional cosmetics companies, from around the world, are cleaning up with distinctive soap, cosmetics, creams and toiletries – and now so can every gorgeous globetrotter. Check out these indigenous inspirations from local beautymakers who use their country's natural resources and ingredients. They're your boarding pass to international beauty, and your first stop when it comes to foreign exchange.

ARUBA

Here's how you can take the Caribbean home with you in your handbag.

Aloe manufacturing is the oldest industry on Aruba. Back in 1840, sailors from Africa left behind a powerful plant that has left an indelible mark on the island of Aruba, its people and its culture. For more than 160 years aloe has spread over the island, influencing everything from art and architecture to health and healing. Within decades, Aruba became the world's largest exporter of aloe – earning it the name, "Island of Aloe." Aloe's power springs from the fierce southern Caribbean sun and now you can purchase it directly from **Aruba Aloe**.

Bestseller: Aruba Aloe Suntan Lotion – it's Aruba in a tube-a!

What Gives Me Goosebumps: Burn Balm, the ultimate healing product for every traveler's first aid kit.

Interesting Fact: You can take a FREE factory tour at Aruba Aloe's headquarters in Oranjestad. The list of products you'll find there – all made with the island's aloe – include day and night creams, an intensive facial treatment, shampoo, conditioner, tanning lotions, and of course, after-sun repair.

Website: www.arubaaloe.com

AUSTRALIA

Now when you're flying up, you can enjoy something from Down Under. Would you be interested in a fabulous product line that has its own Biodynamic farms that span over 153 acres; uses no pesticides; prefers natural compost mixed with mature herbs and minerals; with all farming and weeding of its plants and flowers done by hand? And, to add even more attractiveness to the mix – is a product line that is clinically proven? Then you want **Jurlique.** "We have an incredible history for 25 years, and we were green when it was 'hokey' to be green," says Amanda Dawson, Executive Director. (Indeed, Jurlique was founded by a chemist and horticulturalist, before there was global buzz about the benefits of organics.) In fact, Amanda told me, "We are a step beyond organic. We do all we can to enrich the soil, such as using companion planting instead of pesticides. It's a beautiful way to grow things, with no chemicals. It harnesses what organic farming does, and we also put back into the soil." The result? Jurlique goes straight from the farm to the bottle – it creates a proprietary "Biodynamic Blend" of herbs and plants grown on its farm in Adelaide, South Australia, then infuses it into all of its legendary lotions and potions. "The Biodynamic Blend is the heart of every product," Amanda adds. For example, the Purely Age-Defying Facial Serum contains the Biodynamic Blend of black elder and licorice (to combat puffiness); beech tree buds, blue algae and hibiscus (to firm the skin and reduce the appearance of fine lines and wrinkles); and chamomile, pansy and violet. In addition, it contains marshmallow, which is a natural humectant. Jurlique is clinically proven to reduce the major signs of aging; in just six weeks, participants in a study experienced visible lines and wrinkles reduced by 34%, while 77% of users noticed firmer skin and 73% cited smoother skin. All you gorgeous globetrotters out there, take note: there's even a starter kit of Jurlique **travel sizes.**

The Jurlique collection includes the age-defying line; plus facial skincare; holistic body care; haircare; babycare; and essential oils. I'm especially fond of the facial Citrus Purifying Mist that contains essential oils of tangerine and lemon and adds a little zest to your complexion. I'm addicted to spraying it on, slathering it all over my face, neck and décolletage, and then adding a topcoat of day cream or night cream.

Bestseller: The Herbal Recovery Gel, which I call Gee, My Skin Looks and Smells Terrific. Containing rose, lavender, chamomile and marshmallow, the fragrance is a sensory showstopper that will leave you Waiting To Inhale. Also a bestseller is the Rosewater Mist that's cultivated from Jurlique's 4,500 rosebushes, as well as the Rose Handcream.

What Gives Me Goosebumps: The Citrus Handcream that contains tangerine, mandarin and lemon, offering an exhilarating, unparalleled aroma. I put it on my hands and just can't stop sniffing myself.

Interesting Fact: All of Jurlique's harvesting is done by hand, and it might take five people half a day, kneeling, just to pick tiny purple viola flowers. Even Jurlique's logo reflects its mission; the tiny tail on the "q" evokes the roots of its herb and plants, and the dot of the "i" is a little bud about to bloom.

Website: www.jurlique.com

CANADA

Here's how to add a bit of joy to your time on the jetway. Chemist Ben Kaminsky – creator of cult product line **B. Kamins Chemist** – had an "aha" moment one day while ice-fishing on his annual trip in Northern Quebec. While sitting on the frozen lake, Ben pondered why the hearty maple trees all around him survived the brutal cold weather, and then flourished again each spring. He brought the maple sap back to his lab in Canada, and discovered that the serum from the maple trees was especially rich in life-sustaining materials like polysaccharides, antioxidants, minerals, natural moisturizers ("It attracts water molecules to your skin," Ben says) and alpha-hydroxy acids. "It became intriguing to me," adds Ben. Additionally, the base was aqueous and non-greasy, making it an ideal compound for skincare. Ben purified the maple serum into an all-natural, non-toxic skin-penetrating additive – and the patent-pending Bio-Maple compound was born, which is today used in all of B. Kamins products. The Bio-Maple also became the basis for the cream that Ben created for his wife more than a decade ago, when she was

The Egyptian Modern-Day Miracle

More than a decade ago, plastic surgeon Dr. Stanley Jacobs became intrigued by an ancient Egyptian scroll that had been discovered in the early 1900s, but only partially translated. The Egyptians, who were known for their highly advanced civilization, were master chemists and physicians who mixed medicines and performed surgeries. Guided by their belief in everlasting life, these early pharmacists to the queens and pharaohs formulated a royal ointment to keep skin smooth and youthful. Their secret was buried on a papyrus scroll of hieroglyphic text that ends with the words, "proven good a million times." Dr. Jacobs, after 10 years of travel and research, solved the mystery of the scroll, and discovered the serum's active ingredient – mandelic acid, an alpha hydroxy acid derived from almond extract and a close cousin of glycolic acid. The result is **Stanley Jacobs' Visco-Elastic Transforming Serum.** Besides mandelic acid, it also contains the potent antioxidant resveratrol, glucosamine, licorice and other ingredients, and is non-irritating to the skin. In Dr. Jacobs' clinical study with 16 patients, deep wrinkles and lines were visibly diminished as the elastic properties of the skin were restored by 51% on the average, and often by as much as 86%. Coming soon: other Dr. Jacobs' signature products including moisturizer, eye cream, night cream and sunscreen. Nefertiti would approve! (www.stanleyjacobsmd.com)

going through menopause and nothing on the market would help her changing, hormone-deprived skin. This cream, known today as the Menopause Skin Cream, transformed Mildred's skin and gave her back her radiant complexion; it contains a wealth of goodies including, of course, Bio-Maple compound, sugar cane, sugar maple, horse-chestnut extract, bilberry and salicylic acid. Too good to remain a family secret, the cream quickly evolved into the legendary Menopause Skin Cream that put B. Kamins on the map.

Bestseller: Menopause Skin Cream as well as the peptide-rich Diamond Radiance Cream. "It's a new generation of topical preparation," says Ben.

What Gives Me Goosebumps: B. Kamins also makes a Therapeutic Anti-Aging Wrinkle Lift, formulated with amino zinc oligopeptides, which helps improve and stimulate collagen production and creates an instant tightening "lifting" sensation, making wrinkles appear to lift and soften.

Interesting Fact: Today B. Kamins is available worldwide, not just in Canada and the USA.

Website: www.bkamins.com

B. Kamins' secret is the sap found in maple trees.

FIJI

When traveling in today's environment, your skin and hair take a beating. Now you can discover the South Pacific's secret for keeping skin and hair beautiful: extra virgin coconut oil from Fiji, made by **Pure Fiji.** The coconuts are cold-processed locally, to retain their vitamins and minerals. (This hand-operated process of pressing nuts into oils, also limits the carbon impact on the environment while creating employment opportunities for the rural community.) In addition, sugar cane, pineapple, papaya, and passion flower are also freshly harvested and processed within hours to preserve their fresh bounty of naturally occurring nutrients. What also makes Pure Fiji distinctive is that it is owned by two women: Gaetane Austin (known as "Mom") and her daughter Andree – who employ locals. Products include Passion Flower Bath and Body Massage Oil, Frangipani Body Lotion, Coconut Body Butter, and Coconut Cream Scrub. An ancient blend of exotic drift nut oil and powerful plant actives are also used in targeted facial care solutions that include day and night cream, serum, purifying cleanser, toner, and facial scrubs. Other products include spa soap, shampoo and conditioner, diffusers, candles and room sprays (which are great in any hotel guest room from the Ritz-Carlton to the Red Roof Inn) in scents that include mango, frangipani, white ginger lily and coconut-and-honey, all which bring Paradise a bit closer to home. All of these exquisite products also carry the "Green Earth" logo, as the company is committed to sustainable manufacturing and reducing its carbon footprint. Botanical ingredients, for example, are wild-harvested, to reduce the requirement for energy-dependent irrigation and fertilization methods. Bottles used generate 40% less solid waste than glass bottles, and gift packaging is made by hand using natural fibers such as handmade papers or woven baskets.

Bestseller: Coconut Body Butter And Body Lotion, and the sugar rub made with local sugar cane.

What Gives Me Goosebumps: Products made from the local Dilo tree, known as the "beauty leaf," which has the ability to heal and nourish skin. The locals call it "the tree of a thousand virtues," for it possesses an unusual capacity to enhance the skin's own repair mechanism. Also, all the Pure Fiji packaging, in pastel colors, is gorgeous – and the candles are beautiful. For example, the frangipani **travel candle** comes in a hot-pink box with an adorable bow – it's darling. When I got my box of goodies, I immediately lit the passion flower candle, which made my office smell like the South Pacific.

Interesting Fact: Puri Fiji has won numerous awards including several "Exporter of the Year" awards and three "Excellence in Tourism" awards.

Website: www.purefiji.com

FRANCE

Caudalie

Even if you feel like Gerard Depardieu, you can look like Catherine Deneuve. Here's how. The **Caudalie** cosmetics venture started in September 1993 when Mathilde Cathiard-Thomas and her husband, Bertrand, were taking part in the harvest at their winery, Smith Haut Lafitte in France. One day the two met with the head of the Bordeaux Pharmacognosy Laboratory, who was visiting their chateau and their estate. When he saw the mountain of grape skins and seeds the couple was throwing away, he remarked that they were wasting a veritable treasure. Grape seeds contain polyphenols – active substances capable of fighting free radicals much more effectively than Vitamin E. Thus, in 1994, Mathilde and Bertrand launched Caudalie – a term borrowed from wine-tasting, to describe the persistence of a wine on the palate. Today, there is not only a prestigious line of Caudalie cosmetics, but a Vinotherapie Spa in Bordeaux, and yet another Les Sources de Caudalie Spa at The Plaza Hotel, in New York City. (Other Caudalie spas are located in Italy, and in the Rioja region of Spain.) "We are the pioneers in knowing about resveratrol and polyphenols, and the strength of their antioxidant powers," Joyce Davis, spa director, told me. Have a glass of wine – and here's looking at you!

Bestseller: Vinoperfect Serum, which softens and bleaches out white spots. "It penetrates and evens out skintone, from the cell itself. It corrects from within," Joyce says.

What Gives Me Goosebumps: Pulp Friction (don't you love that name?), the sculpting massage served in Bordeaux, made with fresh grapes. First runner-up: The Cabernet Crush, which slathers you with grape seeds and local Gironde honey.

Interesting Fact: The most popular treatment at Les Sources de Caudalie Spa in New York is the Grand Facial, an antioxidant blast lasting 50 minutes, which includes a generous 20-minute facial massage.

Website: www.sources-caudalie.com

Dior L'or de Vie

Traveling saps you. Now the real sap can restore your skin.

A little drumroll please. When I received my bottle of **Dior's L'or de Vie**, it certainly merited some fanfare. The white box opened to reveal a crystal glass bottle, with gold top, set into in a mirrored-gold compartment. It looked like an award I would set on my desk – not a superlative cosmetic. Here's why it's so special: the serum, or should I say the regenerating sap – the color of white wine, with a delicate sweet perfume – is made with the extracts from Sauvignon vines, one of the two varieties on the lands of Chateau d'Yquem in the heart of Bordeaux. Founded in 1593, Chateau d'Yquem produces wines that have been revered and respected for centuries. The secret of this unmatched wine? The power of the Yquem lands to produce vines with incomparable regenerating power.

Dior scientists discovered a precious vital ingredient in the heart of the vines that revealed a potential source of new life for the skin. To release the skincare miracle, the vines must be hand-harvested and aged for six months before the extraction can take place. With patented, Dior technology, a composition of ten molecules are extracted and the "precious essence" is transformed into what they claim is the most potent antioxidant ever discovered. The result is that L'Or de Vie preserves the skin from the effects of free radicals, while a study has demonstrated that the antioxidant power of this super serum is highly superior to that of the usual antioxidant ingredients – Vitamins C and E, and idebenol. It will more than surpass your grape expectations.

The secret to the high dose of powerful antioxidants found in L'Or de Vie is the polyphenols derived directly from the fruits of the French vines. *A votre sante!*

Bestseller: N/A

What Gives Me Goosebumps: I first tasted Chateau d'Yquem years ago when I was an Editor at ***Robb Report – "The Millionaire's Magazine."*** To this day I can only describe this "liquid gold" as "an elixir of the gods." I crave every rare opportunity I have to taste this sweet, delectable sensation that costs a small fortune.

Stick With Solid Perfume From The Crazy Sticks

Who in their right mind travels with *bottles* of perfume? The better solution is to take your cue from the French company Crazy Libellule and the poppies, who make **Crazy Sticks** – adorably packaged solid forms of French fragrance that weigh less than one ounce and are great for your carry-on. Glide them on and it will feel like a caress. One thing's for sure – they'll add *joie de vivre* to your journey. The range of scents include Presque Nue (almost in the nude) featuring lily of the valley; ginger-kumquat; another bursting with lilac (which you rarely find in other fragrances); pineapplelime; hazelnut vanilla; vanilla and red fruits; gardenia; passion fruit; and many more in this gorgeous garden. You'll be further delighted by what's not included: no coloring agents, alcohol or paraben. As the flamboyant marketing materials say, "Kiss my skin!" We couldn't say it any better (www.crazylibellule.com).

Interesting Fact: L'Or de Vie – L'Extrait sells for $370 (I used up the entire bottle in just one week, I was so addicted to it.) A L'Or de Vie **Travel Collection** is available for $215.

Website: www.dior.com

La Compagnie de Provence Marseille

When I visit Provence, I have my shopping down to a science. In Nice, for example, I make a beeline to the Cours Saleya street market, to purchase anything made with violets, one of my favorite flowers. These include Flavigny Violet Pastilles (delicious violet candies) and Violet perfume made by Monsieur Poilpot on the Rue St. Gaetan. I also love to buy any scent of Provencal soaps, such as those made by **La Compagnie de Provence Marseille**, which produces some of the world's finest skincare and products for the bath and the home. The collection combines the purity of gentle Mediterranean ingredients with a high design aesthetic. French fashion designers Philippe Boigeol and Pascal Bourelly founded the company, put their own spin on the traditional Marseille soap, and re-envisioned it by offering it in packaging that is sleek and elegant, packed in wrapping paper, and tied with hemp rope and a small wax seal. It's a first-class addition to your flight bag.

Bestseller: Liquid Marseille soap in olive lavender and fig.

What Gives Me Goosebumps: The soaps in the lemon verbena and fig scents, which I love displaying in my French country kitchen. These are souvenirs that I love looking at – and using – every day.

Interesting Fact: Marseille is the second-largest city in France, and is best-known for the oversized olive-oil based soaps that have been crafted there for more than 1,000 years.

Website: www.lcdpmarseille.com

Mistral

Let a tail wind take you – to the Mistral. During the winter and spring, the Mistral wind sweeps down from the Alps across the storied landscape of Provence, leaving behind luminous, deep blue skies. **Mistral** is also the name of a personal-care products company that offers more than 30 soap fragrances. It all started when Matthew Tilker, Mistral's founder and president, was study-ing alternative cancer therapies in Europe. During a stay in Provence, he met a 70-year-old master soap maker who, in a family factory, still crafted soaps according to a 300-year-old traditional French triple-milling process. After completing his studies, Matthew imported soaps directly from Provence and sold them out of his mother's home, then opened the first Mistral boutique in Solana Beach, Calif. His scents are intoxicating; there are eau de parfums, for example, in Balinese vanilla, grapefruit, red currant, verbena flower and wild blackberry. Handcreams, all containing olive oil, glycerin, calendula and chamomile, include gardenia, melon-pear, orange blossom, green fig and va-nilla apricot. **Travel-sized** handcreams, in gorgeous metallic silver tubes, are also available, in lavender, milk and verbena. They're like a stay in the glorious Hotel Negresco in Nice – but without spending expensive Euros!

Bestseller: Shea-butter bars of soap in lavender, verbena, South Seas, milk, and vanilla apricot.

What Gives Me Goosebumps: The soaps are made with shea butter and come in scents that include gardenia, lavender, lemon ginger, lilac, rose petal, sandalwood hazelnut, and wild blackberry. Some of these come in a luscious soap box containing nine one-ounce soaps.

Interesting Fact: At the heart of every Mistral product is a fragrance crafted in Grasse, the famous area of Provence known for its perfume-making.

Website: www.mistralsoap.com

L'Occitane En Provence

The name **L'Occitane** means "the woman from Occitania," with Occitania being the region we today know as Provence. And what a great place it is! The company's founder, Olivier Baussan, at age 23, in 1976, created a cosmetic company based on essential oils and natural ingredients found in the region – and area rich with lavender, luscious green plants, sage, juniper, thyme, lime blossom and narcissus. When the brand was created, Olivier distilled raw materials himself (using ingredients such as lavender and rosemary) using his still, and sold the resulting essential oils in the markets of Provence. In addition, L'Occitane claims it was the first company to use shea butter, an incredibly moisturizing and nourishing ingredient derived from the African shea tree, obtained from the Burkina Faso community in Africa. Today the entire line includes skincare, fragrances, bath and body products, makeup, hair care, soaps and an extensive home collection. Stepping into a L'Occitane boutique is like stepping into the heart of Provence – the fragrances are charming and the colors are warm and welcoming.

Bestseller: Shea butter hand cream.

What Gives Me Goosebumps: The lemon verbena soap, which some posh resorts (like the Four Seasons Maui) use as complimentary guest amenities in the bathrooms.

Interesting Fact: Be still, my beating heart. You can take a FREE factory tour in Provence, which includes a visit to the laboratories, to the areas where the tubes and bottles are finished, to the area where candles and soaps are manufactured. If you spend more than 30 Euros, you'll also receive a 10% discount on products.

Website: www.loccitane.com

GERMANY

Annemarie Borlind

During the course of writing this book, I tested A LOT of products. One of the products I tested on my face was a highly potent Vitamin C serum (whose brand shall go unnamed). Oh, it was powerful. So much so that it burned my face – it swelled up like a cantaloupe, with big red blisters. For a week. In the course of trying to heal myself, I put on plenty of aloe – along with **Annemarie Borlind's** ZZ Sensitive Series Day Cream. It worked like a charm.

Founder Annemarie Lindner was born and raised in Leipzig, Germany, and developed severe acne as a teenager. After trying numerous treatments without success, Annemarie was referred to an aesthetician who treated her acne with topically applied herbal extracts. Miraculously, her skin began to clear. Inspired by that, Annemarie made it her mission to develop products to help others avoid the physical and psychological scarring she had suffered from her acne. She began extensive research into the effects of herbs on human skin. This research is the foundation of the Annemarie Borlind's natural approach to skincare. Today, the company searches the world for the most pristine, organic sources for its plant materials. The brand is one of the best-selling in Europe, and its products are sold in more than 40 countries. It has also earned numerous awards, including the Beauty World Cup in Germany. The brand is distinguished by using organically grown raw materials; using the first-pressing of botanical oils; using curative waters from a natural spring located in the spa region of Germany; and is free of paraffin, silicone and other synthetic oils. Its Naturesome "Nature Effect Fluid" won the "Cosmetic of the Year" award, in the "daycare" category, in the "Victories de la Beaute" competition in Paris.

Bestseller: The LL Regeneration series of anti-aging skincare, also made with spring water from Germany's Black Forest.

What Gives Me Goosebumps: The Anne Lind Natural Wellness Line. The Cassis body lotion is divine and smells just as wonderful as it sounds. Fresh and juicy! I also love Borlind's elegant packaging, with a leaf used as its logo.

Interesting Fact: Everything in this brand is clinically proven, dermatologist tested, and Ecocontrol certified for its purity, proof of efficacy and safety, sustainability and fair trade compliance.

Website: www.borlind.com

Babor

Achtung, Baby! Bear this in mind – having ineffective products on your pores – well, that would be *verboten*. That's why you need **Babor** in your bags. This prestigious brand has been around for more than 50 years, and is the leading professionally sold skincare system in Continental Europe. The company uses, in many of the products, thermal spring water from Aachen, Germany, as well as zeolite, a detoxifier that comes from volcanic rock and Moor mud from the Eifelfango region in Germany. "Our customers seek products that are naturally based and effective, with minute percentages of chemicals, added only to give products a longer shelf life," explains spokesperson Courtney Regan. When it comes to me and Babor, there's a whole lot of lovin' goin' on. There's Skinovage Complex C, containing C, E and A vitamins that have been stabilized. There's a Wrinkle Filler made from freeze-dried hyaluronic acid, which puffs out your skin in about one hour; regular use of it stimulates collagen and strengthens the collagen structure. Intelli-zyme is the next generation of exfoliators, which works bio-actively with live enzymes (unlike particle scrubs or chemical acid peels) to loosen dead skin cells. And from the ocean, the cradle of all life, comes Babor's SeaCreation. The Sea-Telligent Complex is formulated with Babor proprietary thermophilus, as well as precious pearl protein and sea silk. The System Gold collection is also available in **travel sets**, for four different skin types: oily, dry, combination, and stressed. There's even a Doctor Babor line; Biogen Cellular, for example, includes an ultimate repair serum that delivers healing results for postoperative wounds. (Remember this when it's time for your facelift.) And the Wrinkle Control Fluid was formulated as a reliable alternative to Botox injections. In others words (actually in German) you will be *uber*-beautiful.

Bestseller: Hy-Ol Cleanser, the signature product and water-friendly facial cleanser. It is the first product that Dr. Michael Babor created back in 1955.

What Gives Me Goosebumps: Anything in the Baborganic line (I love that name), which is made with ECOCERT-compliant raw materials, and without synthetic colorants, synthetic perfume substances, animal raw materials, paraffins, petroleum-based ingredients, and a whole lot more. Everything in the Baborganic line is formulated with pure glacier water, edelweiss, and meadowfoam seed oil from the Swiss Alps. I also love the foaming self-tanner that has a light, fresh scent and is a pleasure to use.

Interesting Fact: In the 1950s, Babor chose a unique company logo – a black rose. This symbol is associated with rare and absolute beauty around the world.

Website: www.babor.com

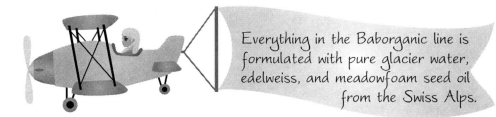

Everything in the Baborganic line is formulated with pure glacier water, edelweiss, and meadowfoam seed oil from the Swiss Alps.

GREECE

Apivita

Apivita makes the Melina Mercouri of Greek beauty products – they're beautiful, provocative, and worthy of our respect. Here's my ode to a Grecian yearn: Apivita. It was founded in 1979 by Niki and Nikos Koutsianas, a couple of pharmacists who had a passion for nature and were inspired by the bee, the flora of Greece (Europe's richest), and Hippocrates' holistic philosophy. In fact, the name Apivita comes from the Latin words "apis" (bee) and "vita" (life). Apivita combines bee products (honey, propolis, royal jelly), titrated plant extracts from the rich Greek flora, and pure essential oils to produce natural, scientifically tested and effective products. What started from a single pharmacy in Athens now covers more than 4,000 pharmacies throughout Greece, and it has also spread out to metropolitan cities in 19 countries. One of the highlight products is the Queen Bee Firming and Restoring Day Cream (SPF 15), which contains royal jelly (the exclusive food of the queen bee, often called the "elixir of life"), honey, green tea water and myrrh essential oil. All of the Queen Bee products are free of paraben, silicone, propylene glycol, and mineral oil.

Bestseller: N/A

What Gives Me Goosebumps: Three things. First, the Apivita Revitalizing Face Mask with Orange, which smells like a burst of citrus, and tones and moisturizes the skin. Similarly, the Hair Food Mask with Honey is great for dry and colored hair, and contains honey, avocado oil, aloe, and essential oils. The refreshing Cleansing Milk with honey and orange is also a great selection. Pick up all three – for a great pick-me-up.

Interesting Fact: Apivita has been instrumental in the revival of the Garden of Hippocrates on the Greek island of Kos, featuring the plants studied and used by the father of modern medicine.

Website: www.apivita.com

Apivita makes the Melina Mercouri of Greek beauty products — they're beautiful, provocative, and worthy of our respect.

Korres

Korres is the next-best-thing to the Acropolis. It's certainly one of Greece's national treasures. How did it come about? While a student, George Korres mixed natural pharmacy ingredients, to create herbal preparations, natural remedies and eventually cosmetic products. In 1996, **Korres Natural Products** emerged out of Athens' first-ever homeopathic pharmacy where George used to work. It still remains the city's biggest pharmacy of its kind, with a dedicated client following, while also serving as an intense training school for all new Korres team members. Today, the Korres portfolio includes more than 500 products, featuring a complete skin, body and hair care range, makeup, a suncare line as well as herbal preparations and nutraceutical products. You'll find unusual offerings to include Watermelon Lightweight Tinted Moisturizer, Monoi Oil Bronzing Powder, Pomegranate Cleansing Scrub, guava lipsticks, silicone-free primer, and many other indulgences that are as high-end as they are healthy.

Bestseller: Wild Rose 24-Hour Cream – one of the first-ever Korres skincare products, created when the brand was born out of Athens' first-ever homeopathic pharmacy. It's been a constant bestseller all over the world, and a favorite of A-list celebrities who include Scarlett Johansson and Angelina Jolie.

Interesting Fact: The first Korres product was an aromatic herbal syrup with honey and aniseed, a recipe inspired by George's grandfather, which he used in his hometown on the island of Naxos.

Website: www.korres.com

HAWAII

Pure Hapa

What does one do, when you're 49 years old and retired from the high-tech world?

If you're Nadyne Keala Orona, you take all of that technology experience, and you start….a skincare company? That's right. In June 2005, Nadyne was sitting on the beach, near her property on the Hawaiian island of Lanai, watching the whales and dolphins frolicking in the sea. She had already been retired for two years. "I started thinking about my Hawaiian grandmother," says Nadyne. "I'm a real girl and I love girlie products. I even designed my home's bathroom to specially display them. And I remembered how my Hawaiian grandmother taught me how to use products from Hawaii."

So she assembled a wealth of raw ingredients from Hawaii – such as noni, azuki beans, ginseng and ginger extracts – did her research, and found a lab in San Diego to create her exclusively Hawaiian product line. She calls it **"Pure Hapa."** In Hawaiian *hapa* means half, and it reflects the fact that "I'm half Hawaiian," says Nadyne "There aren't alot of Hawaiian products out there, made by Hawaiians."

Nadyne's first sale was to the new Four Seasons Spa at the Manele Bay Hotel on Lanai, close to her home, where Pure Hapa is used in manicures and pedicures. Pure Hapa is also available at Kahala Mandarin Oriental spa on Oahu, and at the 77 Maiden Lane Salon in the heart of Union Square, San Francisco. Currently, the product line includes a sugar-cane body scrub, two body creams in *haupia-* (coconut) orange and sweet pineapple, a papaya exfoliant, noni fruit extract facial serum, plus travel candles. "I simply thought my idea would be a nice hobby," says Nadyne with a laugh. But Pure Hapa has expanded on an international basis to countries like Japan, Taiwan and West Africa (Ghana). Adds Nadyne: "Everyone has commented that my Pure Hapa products exemplify the real Hawaiiana concept and especially because I am part Native Hawaiian."

"The Japanese revere their elders and they continue to be fascinated that I am now a grandmother and proud to be 53 years old. I am no different than many women in the world who have re-invented themselves in starting their own company during their prime years."

Traveling celebrities have also taken notice. ***Days of Our Lives*** star Deidre Hall buys Pure Hapa, and the line was given out in gift bags to the stars of ***Desperate Housewives, Lost,*** and at the Silver Spoon pre-Emmy parties. "I'm pleasantly surprised at my success," says Nadyne. "My Hawaiian grandmother would be very proud of me."

Bestseller: Haupia body cream, Hanalei sugar cane body scrub, and all the **travel candles.**

What Gives Me Goosebumps: Hapalicious Orange Mango Body Kit – it does for your travel-weary body what a gentle Hawaiian breeze does for your soul! Includes in a recycled box the following: Hapalicious Orange Body Wash, Hanalei Sugarcane Body Scrub, Haupia Orange Souffle Body Cream, 100% bamboo mitt glove, and Hapalicious **travel candle.**

Interesting Fact: Women in Japan love Pure Hapa and the most popular and highest-selling item is the Haupia Orange Souffle Body Cream, which they call "Happy" cream, because the scent and texture makes them happy and gets them to think of Hawaii. In Ghana, they love the Lanai Pineapple Sugar Cream and all the scented candles.

Website: www.purehapa.com

Maui Babe

Now everyone in transit can be a total babe. Here's how to put paradise in your pocketbook. Joe Rossi calls his **Amazing Maui Babe Browning Lotion** "a gift from God." The idea to create it came one day – one desperate day on Maui when he didn't know what to do next. The United Airlines strike and the Gulf War had dealt him a crushing blow to his once-profitable flower shops. His family home was being foreclosed, bill collectors were hounding him, and the future looked bleak for him, his wife and four children. Needing to be alone, to ponder his plight, Joe climbed up on the roof of his home – and took with him his coffee, plus his tanning mixture – baby oil and iodine. And, as he would tell you, he talked to God. With his hands held out, he prayed and asked God to guide him. When done praying, he got an urge to pour his Kona coffee into his tanning mixture. That night, he added fresh aloe from his farm to it, along with kukui nut oil from the Big Island, which the native Hawaiians use for sunburn. And thus he created a crazy little thing called browning lotion. A few potions later, and he perfected the formula. A few bottles later, after he had given some out, people came to his door begging for more of his tanning formula. Maui Babe was born. "It gives you the fastest, darkest tan with the least amount of time in the sun," says Joe. Off the record, he told me that it also can help with psoriasis, and is a super insect repellent. And the glowing reviews keep coming and coming in. Put it on, even use it under a lotion with an SPF (apply it 10 minutes prior) and you'll still turn a tempting cocoa tan. And it's even water-resistant. As the bottle says, everyone who has tried it loves it and returns for more!

Bestseller: Amazing Maui Babe Browning Formula – my handsome husband Bill swears by it.

What Gives Me Goosebumps: Joe has just introduced a new skin moisturizer, for daytime.

Interesting fact: Mere mortals and celebrities such as Clint Eastwood and Paris Hilton love Maui Babe, and have been photographed using it.

Website: www.Mauibabe.com

Malie Organics

Now you can perk up all your travel plans, with coffee fruit grown on the state of Hawaii. **Malie Organics** (pronounced mah-lee-ay) offers a potent, effective, natural and organic anti-aging skincare collection featuring new plant technology exclusively from the aloha state. The Hawaiian coffee fruit from Kona possesses more antioxidant power than any other fruit source – and more than other coffee derivatives used in skincare brands today. Hawaiian coffee fruit extract contains five exceptional antioxidant acids that include: Chlorogenic and Caffeic acids (anti-inflammatories); Ferulic acid (reacts against free radicals); Quinic acid (with anti-viral properties); and Trigonelline (with anti-bacterial properties). The deep red coffee fruit, which is nourished by tropical sun, abundant rain and rich volcanic soil, is hand-picked at peak ripeness. Then, using only water and no chemical solvents, the company extracts a concentrated liquid from the most valuable part of the plant – the mature fruit. The result? Malie Organics' potent Anti-Aging Firming and Elasticity cream. Also in the coffee fruit line are a body polish, clay mask and the 100% pure coffee fruit liquid extract. You'll find it in Hawaiian spas including the St. Regis on Kauai and the Halekulani on Oahu.

Bestseller: Anti-Aging Firming and Elasticity Cream with Hawaiian Coffee Fruit Extract.

What Gives Me Goosebumps: The plumeria (frangipani) collection. This is the most luscious of aromas, from the flowers that are traditionally used in Hawaiian leis. Other fragrances in the Malie Collection include coconut-vanilla, mango-nectar and maile vines. All scents are available in candles, luxurious cream soaps, body creams, mists, diffusers, and more. An organic **spa travel collection** features conditioner, shampoo, body wash and 3-oz. candle.

Interesting Fact: The delicate coffee fruit used to wind up as waste in the coffee production process – but not anymore! South American coffee pickers noticed that despite constant handling, the coffee kept their hands soft, supple and youthful even after decades of exposure to harsh conditions.

Website: www.malie.com

Hawaiian Body Products

Say aloha to some amazing products. Founded in 2006, **Hawaiian Body Products**, with its Ola brand, specializes in handmade, beautiful bath and body products made from natural and organic ingredients found on The Big Island of Hawaii. It's amazing – "We use fresh ingredients bought straight from the Hilo Farmer's Market," says Robin Williams, co-founder. The company is deeply committed to supporting local farmers, to make products "with a palpable authenticity to Hawaii," says Robin. The lilikoi, mangosteen, coffee, honey and beeswax, for example, come from local farmers. "I have many partnerships with local farmers," adds Robin. Unbelievably, the company travels nearby to Kalapana, and "we just pick noni fruit along the road." Robin adds, "We use it to make our "mother potion" distillate that includes the noni, sugar cane, aloe and mamaki (tea leaves that the company picks in the Hawaiian forest!)." Plants are put into a copper distiller and heated, to extract their "essence," which is used in all of the products. The products are incredible – and you can order them "makana" or gift wrapped, in a handwoven palm leaf sleeve with polished coconut wood charm, to impart a feeling of Hawaiiana. You'll be as excited about these products as I am. Fragrances include Coconut/Lemongrass, Pineapple/Lime, Passion Fruit/Citrus, Sandalwood/Verbena, and Ocean Essence (a mix of plumeria, lemon and green tea). The company unveiled new scents in collections this past spring, including two new intoxicating island florals and a to-die-for mango scent. The fragrance sticks – solid perfumed formulations that are **ideal for traveling**, as well as **travel candles** in all of the flavors – will absolutely change your life. There are also lip balms in lilikoi orange; mango; and banana honey. And you must try the Coffee Chocolate Crème Lotion, a seasonal specialty; this mocha mélange with kukui nut oil will definitely perk you up when the miles wear you down.

Bestseller: Anything in the Coconut/Lemongrass fragrance.

What Gives Me Goosebumps: Passion Fruit/Citrus Solid Fragrance Stick, which you can load into your Louis Vuitton luggage. The scent is delightful. Nothing to spill!

Interesting fact: "We make everything ourselves, on our farm up in Hilo," says Robin. Hawaiian Body Products is a family business.

Website: www.Hawaiianbodyproducts.com

Alii Kula Lavender

Why not reach for lavender during your layover? Nestled in the clouds, and on the slopes of Haleakala, Maui, with more than 55,000 lavender plants blooming on 13.5 acres, you'll find **Alii Kula Lavender.** If you love lavender – you'll be in Haleakala Heaven – it's the Ultimate Lavender Experience. Here, you can embark on a lavender walking tour and also visit the retail store where a wealth of lavender products are displayed – everything from cookies to candles, to soaps and sachets. In collaboration with other local businesses, the company brings new products to its customers, including – all made with lavender – chocolate truffles, lime sorbet, goat's milk soap and sweet potato/taro chips. "The products are all carefully made using natural, botanical and organic ingredients," explains Lani Medina Weigert, spokesperson. "Our lavender is grown in volcanic soil on the slopes of Haleakala – a dormant volcano. Besides the high altitude of 4,000 feet and cool nights of 40 to 50 degrees, the soil offers nutrients to the lavender that result in larger blooms and sweeter, more fragrant-smelling blossoms." You'll be surprised – and delighted – to know that you can also use lavender in a wealth of recipes – including scallops, chicken-and-feta meatballs, gravlax and even eggs Benedict. (Recipes are in *The Maui Book of Lavender.*)

Bestseller: Lavender gourmet seasoning (a dry marinade of lavender, Hawaiian salts and kukui nut); body butter cream; and the waterless handsoap.

What Gives Me Goosebumps: The lavender dark chocolate bar and the lavender fudge sauce that's sinfully delicious.

Interesting fact: Why not say "I Do" right here? Weddings are held on the Alii Kula Lavender estate.

Website: www.aliikulalavender.com

Why not reach for lavender during your layover?

Scrub Me Tender

I Came, I Saw, I Sparkled At Four Seasons Hualalai Spa

To say that my "Sparkle" spa treatment at Four Seasons Hualalai on The Big Island of Hawaii was mood-enhancing, and practically life-changing, is an understatement. It was one of those spa treatments – in a life filled with spa treatments – which I will never forget ($250 for 80 minutes).

Everything about this resort – and the spa – is to offer you a sense of place, and an understanding of your environment. Most spas offer you the standard menu of services, but Four Seasons Hualalai Spa takes it to a whole different level. What they offer is a distinctive and exclusive Apothecary of creams, oils, lotions and potions, many of them indigenous to Hawaii, so that you can have your product custommade – that's right – custommade – with a teaspoon and spatula, right before your very eyes.

I met with Lisa Chasey, who showed me the Apothecary that was inspired from the *kupuna* (Hawaiian elders), who shared their knowledge of the islands and its local ingredients, which are an essential part of the spa's focus. The resulting Apothecary features a variety of ingredients that you can select for your very own treatment. Things like Grapeseed oil. Coconut. Black lava salt. Spirulina. Pikake flowers in an almond-oil base. Green tea. Chickpea flour. And turmeric. To name just a few.

HONDURAS

We all know too well what dry airplane air does to hair and skin. Fret no more. Here's the source of hair repair for parched passengers.

Ten years ago a small jar of oil made its way to the home of a successful advertising executive with more than a decade of experience in the beauty business. A relative from Central America had visited Denis

I wanted to be uplifted, and in my book, nothing beats the scent of oranges – mix it with chocolate and I'm over the moon. So I chose moisturizing ground cocoa butter, red sea salt, lavender oil, macadamia nuts, and powdered milk (whose lactic acid is exfoliating). To these, Lisa mixed in orange essential oil. The result? A Creamsicle concoction that smelled divine.

Lisa escorted me to the wet-treatment room, where she buffed and sloughed my skin with my very own Creamsicle creation. It felt fabulous – a vigorous rubdown with an exfoliating glove that opened my pores and woke up my skin. After exfoliating me on both sides, she took the Vichy shower and hosed me off while I was still lying down. A shower while you're in repose? That in itself was relaxing. After that, she tore off the top layer of towels, and the plastic beneath it, to reveal another layer of towels on my treatment bed, where I could continue to stay still.

Then she began the awesome massage. Have you ever had a massage where your body soaked up every stroke? Where you moaned and kept saying, "Wow, that feels so incredibly good?" Where the stroking was, well, even better than sex itself? That's what this massage was like. Lisa did a great job on my body, but when she moved to my head, it was even better. For my neck and shoulders, it was complete nirvana. I wasn't just jelly, but officially Smucker's. I have to say, it was one of the best massages I've ever had in my life – and it was so fantastic, I know I'll never forget the entire experience. Afterwards, I was good to glow! (www.fourseasons.com/hualalai.)

Simioni, and left behind a baby food jar of brown oil. Calling it a "native remedy" for damaged hair and skin, Denis didn't think much about it at the time, so for two years the jar sat untouched on his cluttered shelf. One day, after coming upon the dark-colored paste again, he tried it. He found the results to be incredible. The oil was derived from the nut of the **Ojon** tree – and the oil is unique to the rainforest of the Mosquitia region of Central America. Although the Miskito Indians had used Ojon oil for centuries to condition and protect their hair and skin, it had never been exported. After Denis visited Central America, he discovered that the Miskito Indians are referred to in their native language as "Tawira," which translates to, "The people of beautiful hair." Ojon was born.

Today, Ojon provides a steady source of income for the indigenous groups that harvest and process the oil, and the Tawira are consulted on all aspects of the business – from product development to marketing. You can find Ojon at Sephora, QVC and Ulta.

Bestseller: Without a doubt the Restorative Hair Treatment ($55), a unique hair rejuvenator that hydrates and improves the condition of dry, damaged hair without weighing it down. Trust me – after just one 20-minute treatment hair is extraordinarily soft, silky and manageable. I use it on my highlighted tresses, and the results? My hair acts like virgin hair before it was ever colored – bouncy, smooth, and full of shine.

What Gives Me Goosebumps: The Rub-Out Dry Cleanser – a great dry shampoo with shea butter and sweet almond protein that is **ideal for traveling**, especially if you've had a professional blowout and want it to last. I also love the Restorative *Leave-In* Treatment that adds shine and hydration to natural or color-treated hair, thanks to passion fruit, macadamia oils and bamboo extract. And without silicones, sulfates or parabens. Who needs that?

Interesting Fact: Ojon works closely with the MOPAWI, a nonprofit group dedicated to promoting sustainable development in the Mosquitia region of Honduras; Ojon's contributions have helped build new housing and have spearheaded scholarship initiatives from local indigenous communities. Ojon continues to look for opportunities to help further support the people and ecological diversity of the region.

Website: www.Ojon.com

HUNGARY

Ilike Organic Skin Care

Now you obviate boarding the plane for Budapest.

Ilike (pronounced "Il-ee-ka") is one of the top beauty brands in Hungary – in fact, the brand has a 75% market share and is beloved by globe-hopping celebrities who include Angela Bassett, Diane Lane, Raquel Welch, Madonna and Prince. Hungary lies in the Carpathian Basin, which has long been known for being rich in minerals and trace elements found nowhere else on earth. Due to the soil, the somewhat dry climate and the abundance of sunshine, Hungarian herbs and fruits are proven to contain higher concentrations of active ingredients and aromatic agents than the world average. According to spokesperson Szilvia Hickman, Hungary was – and is – known as "the produce supplier to the monarchies of Europe." This brand is known as Ilike Skin Care in North America and Ilcsi in other parts of the world. What sets it apart from the competition is that all of the products are made with herbal pulps (not extracts) so you get the full benefits – a cornucopia of antioxidants and bioflavonoids in everything from carrots to paprika. More than 70 products are in the line, which is organically grown and hand harvested. And *anytime* is ripe to enjoy them, but especially when traveling.

Bestseller: Lemon Cleansing Milk, St. John's Wort Eye Cream.

What Gives Me Goosebumps: The Sour-Cherry Whipped Moisturizer would be right at home in a pie. And the Stonecrop Toner has a delicious minty aroma that is also good enough to eat.

Interesting Fact: The sunscreen gel and lotion are made with tomatoes.

Website: www.szepelet.com

Ilike's Hungarian Sour–Cherry Whipped Moisturizer would be right at home in a pie.

Eminence Organic Skincare

Here's your seat assignment to staying beautiful while traveling.

I first discovered **Eminence Organics** when I was in Lanai at the spa at the Four Seasons Manele Bay Hotel. What I saw – and smelled – was the Hungarian Sour-Cherry Whip Moisturizer, and I was immediately hooked. I had always looooved the sour-cherry soup at a Hungarian restaurant in Boston – and here it was, basically, in *moisturizer* form. I couldn't believe it. Since then, I've become a huge fan of Eminence products; their delightfully different cornucopia of products – more than 100 – is truly amazing. Citrus Exfoliating Wash. Pear and Green-Apple Mask. Cranberry Pomegranate Sugar Scrub. Hungarian Herbal Mud Treatment. Cinnamon Paprika Body Lotion. Eight Greens Youth Serum. Mineral sunscreens in flavors such as Cherries and Berries, and even a Cinnamon Bronzer (if you're a traveler who desires a gilt trip). Eminence Organic Skin Care is the most unusual and effective line of natural skincare products on the market today – just open a jar to find a product brimming with healing herbs, luscious fruits and vegetables, and berried treasures. You'll see the difference – you'll find whole fruit pulp, seeds and hand-harvested herbs – all of which are concentrated formulas. (If you visit the Hungarian facility, you'll also see jars of *real fruit pulps* – not extracts). The rosehips, linden, calendula, and cherries – to name a few – are still hand-picked and hand-mixed in small batches and combined with Hungarian thermal hot spring water. These formulas smell and look great, but are also effective in treating skin concerns such as aging, sun damage, wrinkling, loss of vitality, acne and rosacea. The company also uses 100% wind power energy and solar energy; packs in used boxes made from recycled materials; uses packing chips made of biodegradable corn; and hires a local courier company that drives hybrid vehicles. There's a lot to love here! Spa giants such as the Golden Door, Mii Amo and the Grand Wailea in Hawaii were first in line to incorporate this Hungarian gem into their offerings. Actresses Alicia Silverstone and Sarah Michelle Gellar are huge fans.

Bestseller: Anything in the Stone Crop collection. I adore the Stone Crop Toner. The powerful – and delicious – fragrance of the succulent cactus juice is a great pick-me-up that you'll want to use all the time. I'm crazy about it and can't wait to use it every day.

What Gives Me Goosebumps. Hands down, anything with the sour cherries in it. Macerate your entire body in it.

Interesting Fact: Hungarian skincare is legendary and has evolved from serving European royalty for centuries to the top spas and retreats around the world.

Website: www.eminenceorganics.com

ICELAND

The land of the white blondes is closer than you think. Here's why.

Like many of us, Sarah Kugelman tried to manage her stress for at least 25 years. But unlike many of us, in 1995, Sarah's doctor told her that if she didn't learn to decompress, she wouldn't live to see her 40th birthday. To add insult to injury, Sarah's stress was wreaking havoc on her skin. "I had cystic acne, scars, and incredible dehydration," she says, which is no surprise, considering the link between stress and skin.

Sarah took a leave of absence from corporate life and spent the next 18 months researching the impact of stress on skin, so she could create a skincare line that would counteract it. While in the midst of the line's development, she took a trip to Iceland. She was struck by the country's purity, cleanliness, abundance of natural resources, and immaculately complected inhabitants. "Iceland presented the ideal landscape for stress-free living," Sarah noted, and so she created **Skyn Iceland**, the only skincare line designed to treat the physiological effects of stress on skin. "I found Iceland to be an incredible untapped resource," she told me.

Think about it – it makes sense. Iceland is peaceful. It's unspoiled. And it's absolutely pure and pristine. Think clean air and water, mineral-rich hot springs, deep fjords, untouched glacial rivers, and some of the world's purest and most beneficial ingredients.

Try It, You'll Diet!

Iceland's Other Best-Kept Secret

Skyr – pronounced "skeer," is Iceland's national treasure – and the country's best-kept secret. A remarkable dairy product, skyr is unique to Iceland, is made from skim milk, and has the consistency of ice cream, yogurt and cheese together – consider it the Dairy Trifecta. It's almost fat-free and contains exceptional levels of calcium and protein. Skyr in blueberry, for example, contains just 160 calories in 6 ounces, with no fat, 16 grams of protein and only 4 mg of cholesterol. The milk is produced on family farms from contented cows who are fed on grass with no antibiotics. It's not only a great snack for travelers – but it counteracts osteoporosis – and comes in recyclable packaging. Where's my spoon? Available in the States at Whole Foods. (www.skyr.is)

Many of Skyn Iceland's products are made with indigenous ingredients that are Arctic-based, such as imported glacial water; an herb, Angelica Archangelica; cranberry-seed oil; cloudberry-seed oil; thyme extract; and butterfly bush. All of Skyn Iceland's products contain a proprietary Biospheric Complex that's comprised of stress-relieving, soothing ingredients gathered from Iceland's air, land and water. Your skin will feel cooled, replenished and pampered. It's EMT for your epidermis.

Skyn Iceland debuted with seven products, and currently there are 16 in the line, including a TSA-compliant **travel kit** of four mini products that sells for $45.

When Sarah flies on planes, she follows her own advice, mixing her own masque and applying it to her face. "I'm not embarrassed," she said.

Bestseller: The Icelandic Relief Eye Cream, which delivers immediate relief to the delicate under-eye skin, and diminishes the symptoms of chronic stress around the eyes, including puffiness, dark circles and lines/wrinkles. Also available in a convenient on-the-go treatment in a pen-tip applicator.

What Gives Me Goosebumps: The Hydro Cool firming Eye Gels, which have an enthusiastic fan base of makeup artists, actors and models who love their fast-acting, residue-free formulas for photo shoots and filming. One big fan? Actress Laura San Giacomo. The eye patches work in just 10 minutes and are great for de-puffing. I also love the Pure Cloud Cream – the cosmetic equivalent of kid gloves that's as fluffy as meringue. It's light as air! Especially good after any dermatological or surgical procedures on the face.

Interesting Fact: The word "skyn" in the Icelandic language, translates to "senses."

Website: www.skyniceland.com

ISRAEL

Did you know something dead can bring your skin to life? That's right.

The Dead Sea can bring your skin to life – in the case of **Ahava** products. Maxine Siegal, national trainer for the brand, spoke to me, explaining everything about Ahava that makes it special, unique – and dramatically different for your dermis. First, Ahava is "the only cosmetics company indigenous to the Dead Sea region," with seven unique product lines, Maxine explained. The secret behind the products? The Mineral Skin Osmoter™, which powers all the products – it is a scientifically-balanced formulation of Dead Sea minerals that works to optimize skin functioning. "It uses osmosis – the natural water-sharing process that takes place between skin cells." And of course, it all occurs thanks to location, location, location. The Dead Sea, Maxine explained, is the lowest exposed point on the planet – 1,300 feet below sea level, where you'll find the highest concentration of 21 minerals including magnesium, calcium, potassium and sodium. Even better, Ahava's factory is *right on the shores* of the Dead Sea, to easily capture the essence of the region. "When you realize that the human body is made up of 50% water, and 5% minerals in the skin, which carry oxygen and facilitate intercellular communication, that's an impressive amount of minerals," she said. "Beautiful skin is balanced skin…we harvest the magic of the Dead Sea." People travel to the Dead Sea from all over the world, but you can simply purchase any of the wonderful products – there are Time-Line anti-aging products containing dunaliella algae that's filled with vitamins, beta-carotene and amino acids; mineral body lotion and hand creams; foot and shower creams; shampoo and conditioner; even a nail hardener. *Mazel Tov!*

Bestseller: The Source Mineral Hand Cream and the Dead Sea Bath Salts that give you the pleasures of the Dead Sea, without the trip on El Al!

What Gives Me Goosebumps: The Intensive Nourishing Hand Cream is a grease-free blend of mineral-enriched mud, which works great.

Interesting Fact: Ahava is the Hebrew word for "love."

Website: www.ahavaUS.com

The Dead Sea can bring your skin to life — thanks to Ahava products.

Yes to Carrots

I'm not *meshuganah*, but I'll say yes to carrots when traveling. In fact, mark me down as affirmative for anything in this adorable line. **Yes to Carrots,** produced in Israel, is a line of face, body and hair products born of the desire to produce unique, high-quality formulas that make women feel and look fabulous. All of the items are paraben-free, and contain organic fruits and vegetables rich in beta-carotene and Dead Sea minerals. Products are never tested on animals and are housed in recyclable packaging. For example, C Through The Night is a terrific night cream bursting with beta carotene and 26 Dead Sea minerals that naturally exfoliate, detoxify and rejuvenate the skin. It smells great – thanks to ingredients that include carrot seed oil, green tea extract, orange peel oil and sweet almond oil. C You In The Morning (don't you just love that name?) is equally delightful and smells just as good. There's also Yes to Cucumbers, with special shampoos and conditioners for colored hair containing actual Dead Sea mud. You'll love the **travel sizes** – a Shower Essentials kit with daily shampoo, conditioner and shower gel; plus a Travel with C Body Essentials with moistur-izing lotion, cream, body butter, shower gel and lip butter. All of the products contain organic carrot, orange, pumpkin and melon extracts, coconut and sunflower oils, vitamin E, beeswax, cocoa butter and green tea – whew! Add them all up, and they'll put your attractiveness on auto-pilot.

Bestseller: C Through The Dry Spell Body Butter.

What Gives Me Goosebumps: I'm partial to the candy-colored lip glosses; the beeswax used is sourced from the Tung Teya community in Africa, and all of the proceeds from the sale of the beeswax are channeled into the community to build schools, enhance health care and improve overall quality of life.

Interesting Fact: A portion of the proceeds from Yes to Carrots is dedicated to the Yes To Carrots Seed Fund, a nonprofit organization created to assist communities in need to develop self-sustaining, organic food sources. Impressive.

Website: www.yes-to-carrots.com

ITALY

The original **Santa Maria Novella** apothecary is in Florence (the oldest continually-open and most prestigious pharmacy in the world) and is almost 800 years old, having been established by the Dominican Fathers shortly after 1221. The products that customers find in this pharmacy have a long and illustrious history. Take the Santa Maria Novella Eau de Cologne signature scent (a mix of citrus and bergamot first concocted by the monks at Santa Maria Novella). This is a classic cologne with a citrus base, which was created for Catherine de Medici, who, when she went to France to marry Henry II, brought her personal perfume-maker with her. In fact, there are various versions of the legend that explain how the "Acqua della Regina" (Water of the Queen) came to be commercialized as a cologne. Still hand-formulated in Florence, this remarkably light and fresh scent combines provocative citrus and bergamot with subtle white flowers and deeply exotic spices. Coveted by men and women alike, it's a unique aroma that's timeless and perfectly modern, and includes rosewater made by roses grown by Santa Maria Novella in their own gardens outside of the city. In fact, all of the products at Santa Maria Novella are made with indigenous ingredients and crafted on-site.

Bestseller: The handmade, handstamped Pomegranate Soap, as well as the Gardenia-And-Rose Body Milk, Lemon Hand Cream, Almond Foot Cream, and classic 100-gram bag of Signature Potpourri.

Interesting Fact: The delectable goods of Santa Maria Novella were brought to the United States exclusively by LAFCO New York (Luxury Articles & Fragrance Company). Today there are official SMN boutiques in New York, Bal Harbour, and Melrose Place, along with the products being available at the LAFCO boutique in Dallas.

Website: www.lafcony.com/smn

JAPAN

Who knew that sake could be so great for your travel-stressed skin? But it is. When a Japanese monk visited a sake brewery in Kobe more than 25 years ago, he was surprised, by chance, to discover that the brewery workers had extraordinary hands – soft and youthful. Even an elderly worker with pronounced wrinkles on his face had the silky smooth hands of a young man. This amazing observation prompted the monk to share his findings with a group of scientists who conducted a series of experiments. They discovered a clear, nutrient-rich liquid that could be extracted at the peak of the yeast fermentation process. It's called Pitera – the magic ingredient of all of **SK-II** products. Its spokesperson is actress Cate Blanchett, whose complexion Dame Judi Dench famously compared to a white peach.

Bestseller: The Facial Treatment Essence.

What Gives Me Goosebumps: The Facial Treatment Essence that contains more than 90% pure Pitera, which helps to promote a 28-day renewal process of the skin's outer layer. Can also be used on your elbows, décolletage and hands. Great for tired eyes too!

Interesting Fact: Pitera is a singular blend of vitamins, amino acids, proteins and organic acids, which work together to produce a seemingly miraculous re-birth of the skin.

Website: www.sk-ii.com

Sake is the secret behind Japan's SK-II skincare.

KOREA

Coffee? Soda? Here's how green tea can re-fresh you on the road, in more ways than one.

For six decades, global skincare brand **AmorePacific** has utilized a holistic ap-proach to health and beauty. In fact, it has the distinction of being the first skincare com-pany to use its own green tea extract, from its own green tea gardens. These protected gardens are located at the foot of Halla Mountain on the Pacific isle of Jeju, off the coast of Korea. The gardens are nourished by fresh spring water and mineral-rich, volcanic soil, which are the ideal conditions in which to grow green tea. All AmorePacific products blend Asia's age-defying botanicals with cutting-edge technology. In addition to the green tea, formulations include Korean ginseng, mushrooms and nutrient-rich bamboo sap.

Bestseller: Time Response Skin Renewal Crème, a powerful anti-aging therapy that contains EGCG, a potent polyphenol from AmorePacific's own green tea gardens.

Korean Cosmetics

Sulwhasoo is a Korean herbal, medicinal cosmetic brand that is rooted in the principles of Korean medicine. In fact, all of the products are based on Korean herbology, as recorded in a medical encyclopedia by a royal physician in 1613. The literal meaning of Sulwhasoo is "a frail branch covered in snow-white flowers." Its philosophy inherits Korea's long-held belief that "a beautiful face represents a beautiful heart." Soyoung Park, a young exchange student from Korea, who recently stayed as a guest in my home, raved to me about her use of Sulwhasoo. "My skin is dry, but Sulwhasoo keeps the moisture in. I use their cleansing foam, oil, essence, skin cream, and lotion." She also swears by Hera Korean Cosmetics, especially its DermaSonic facial massager, used with a Hera clear serum and cream. She added: "Women in Korea really enjoy makeup." (www.sulwhasoo.com)

What Gives Me Goosebumps: The new **travel size** of the Moisture Bound Skin Energy Hydration Delivery System. This take-away spray combats thirsty skin and contains bamboo sap, mushroom, water lily and ginger root.

Interesting Fact: AmorePacific has its own Beauty Gallery and Spa in New York's SoHo.

Website: www.amorepacific.com

MOROCCO

Here's how to get a taste of La Mamounia — without a travel agent. Self-described skincare junkie Katharine L'Heureux began her search for the perfect skincare regime at the age of 12, while rummaging through her mother's cluttered bathroom cabinet in San Francisco. Her search ended more than 30 years later, on a journey to Morocco, which has led to the creation of **Kahina – Giving Beauty**, her organic skincare line. Kahina products are all based on 100% organic argan oil sourced from the women's cooperatives of Morocco. In Morocco, home of the argan tree, law dictates that the Berber women who live in the argan region are the only ones allowed to extract the oil from the nuts of the tree. (It can take up to a day to produce a single liter of oil.) For most of these women, this work is their only road to financial and social independence. Argan oil is the beauty secret Moroccan women have used for centuries to combat the harsh effects of the desert sun, and to reverse the signs of aging. The four Kahina products are a facial cleanser; serum that also contains organic sea buckthorn seed oil and organic coffee oil; facial lotion that contains organic shea butter; and the jewel in the crown, the 100% pure argan oil. This multipurpose wonder can be applied to the face after cleansing to replenish moisture; used as a body oil; put on the hair to restore shine and relieve frizz; used as a hand treatment; and as a treatment for acne and other skin conditions.

Bestseller: 100% argan oil that most women fall in love with after just one date with it.

What Gives Me Goosebumps: Argan oil is extremely rich in Vitamin E and antioxidants, and is known to flight free radicals, reduce inflammation, minimize the appearance of wrinkles, and protect the skin from environmental factors. Wowza!

Interesting Fact: Kahina-Giving Beauty never uses parabens, synthetics, sulfates, petroleum, GMOs, animal byproducts, artificial colors or fragrances. The company also donates 25% of its profits to the Berber women of Morocco who hand-extract the argan oil, using centuries-old techniques passed down through generations.

Website: www.kahina-givingbeauty.com

NEW ZEALAND

From a former flight attendant comes a skincare line to soothe you.

Kati Kasza, a former flight attendant on Air New Zealand, knew all too well the dehydrating effects of long-distance air travel on the skin. Frustrated, she began experimenting with natural ingredients in her kitchen; it didn't hurt that Kati's mother is a horticulturist and herbalist. Soon, the plant-derived lotions and potions, all made with New Zealand spring water and pure essential oils, plant and marine extracts, found a following with Kati's fellow flight crew, and **evolu Botanical Skincare** was born. (Yes, the product doesn't capitalize the first letter of its name.) In fact, many of evolu's ingredients are sourced in New Zealand, including the kiwifruit seed oil, kawakawa oil, Manuka honey and oil, avocado oil, and grapefruit and lavender oils, as well as 100% New Zealand water sourced from a deep artesian spring.

The delicious Healing Lip Treatment contains New Zealand Manuka honey; relaxing Crème Cleanser also makes a great eye makeup remover; and the Moisturizing Day Cream bursts with kiwifruit extract, a natural antioxidant. The evolu **Travel Tower** is an ingenious solution to the space problem. It contains six evolu botanical products suitable for all skin types, in a twist-together stack of pots cleverly sized to fit in your handbag, carry-on or briefcase. An additional lid is included so the stack can be divided in two if you wish, and you can refill the pots for endless re-use. Think of it as the beauty equivalent of Russian nesting dolls. It's a group of essential potions - cleanser, eye gel, day and night moisturizers, a postflight mask and handcream. Endlessly refillable, the stack comprises six 10 ml. (0.34 oz.) compartments, which lands it well below airlines' 100 ml. (3 oz.) limit for carry-on cosmetics. It's your travel triage and your kiwi cure.

The company's amenity products are featured in some of New Zealand's leading five-star retreats and lodges including Kauri Cliffs, Cape Kidnappers, The Spire, Millar Road, Huntley House, Select Braemar Lodge and others. Consider it your passport to complexion perfection.

Bestseller: The Travel Tower.

What Gives Me Goosebumps: Manuka Honey Healing Lip Treatment – your lips will crave it. Also: the Facial Serum – it's liquid gold, loaded with antioxidant bio-actives of rosehip oil, jojoba oil, rose absolute and neroli essential oils. It smells heavenly and is good enough to eat.

Interesting Fact: Kati's father was a winemaker. Her parents' appreciation of fine natural ingredients and the power of nature were passed onto their daughter at a young age. Plants and herbs uncommon in New Zealand at the time were part of the daily fare in the Kasza household.

Website: www.evolu.com

Farmaesthetics

A trip to the farm has never been more luxurious. It all started in 1999, when Brenda Brock began selling her hand-made skincare products at an organic farm stand in rural Rhode Island. The orders kept coming…and coming, and since then, **Farmaesthetics,** in Portsmouth, R.I., has taken off and become the darling of the spa industry and the favorite new kid in town. The daughter of a 7th-generation farming family from Texas, Brenda blends the "kitchen chemistry" of her rural farming heritage with the modern science of cosmetic manufacturing. "Using the garden as a medicine chest is an

Tahitian Treat

Monoi Tiare Tahiti is a French-Tahitian cosmetic oil consisting of pure coconut oil and the fragrance of tiare, the gorgeous Tahitian gardenia. The product is a refinement of an ancient Polynesian beauty secret and has been manufactured commercially since 1942. No one knows who first thought of combining local tiare flowers with coconut extract to obtain a mixture just as exotic as its Polynesian name, MONOI, which in r'eo-maohi, their ancient language, literally means "scented oil."

What we know for sure is that several ancient documents dating as far back as the 18th Century, when the first Europeans navigators like James Cook came to visit the Polynesian Islands, already mention monoi and its regular cosmetic use by the natives. Today you can purchase monoi and bring a little bit of the South Pacific home to your powder room. There are soaps that include coconut and vanilla, and oils in fragrances such as plumeria, ylang-ylang, coconut and vanilla. (I like to brush the oil through my hair and sit in the sun, to give myself a conditioning treatment.) They're like a trip to Bora Bora – without the heavy baggage (www.monoi.com).

ancient practice and something that comes completely natural to me," says Brenda. Noted as a trailblazer in the industry of "green" manufacturing, the company only uses organic herbs and flowers from small organic American family farms, with no artificial preservatives, synthetics or dyes. Brenda's products are now available in high-end spas such as The Golden Door, Four Seasons Spa in Santa Barbara and Palm Beach, and the exclusive Mayflower Spa in Washington, Conn., for which Farmaesthetics created seasonal facial and body treatments.

At the brand new Goosewing Spa at the Stone House in Little Compton, R.I., "We're doing a very high-end amenity for all the rooms," says Brenda. "I created a Rainwater and Sea Rose Bath and Beauty Bar," she adds. Farmaesthetics' luxury line-up of products include the popular Sweet Milk and Lavender Bud Exfoliant...Rosehip and Clay Mint Mask...Nourishing Herbal Cream made with sweet almond oil and lavender...which come in recyclable packaging bearing Farmaesthetics' homespun handwritten labels. In October 2008, it partnered with Macy's Beautiful Planet – a green cosmetic boutique within the cosmetic department. "We've never been able to afford a PR firm," Brenda says, and all sales and buzz has been generated through word-of-mouth. "Consumers are stepping back and looking at the whole picture," she says. "They are responding to the complete holistic approach to staying beautiful while traveling, which is why Farmaesthetics is resonating."

Bestseller: Nourishing Lavender Milk Face And Body Lotion.

What Gives Me Goosebumps: Midnight honey, an organic bath and beauty oil for massage, bath and face – a lush warm honey oil. Seaweed and Rosehip Scrub and Mask. Also, the Vapor Bath Elixir – a chlorophyll elixir that creates a vapor steam for opening sinuses, and a bath that is used in foot treatments.

Interesting Fact: Treehugger.com, in April 2009, named Farmaesthetics the "Best of Green."

Website: www.farmaesthetics.com

Cape Cod Soap Company

Now you can nix the harsh hotel soaps. Pat Thrasher makes her **Cape Cod Soap Company** soaps in small batches with pure, natural ingredients. In June, she even gathers rose petals on the beach, and then uses them in her Rosa Rugosa soap. Pat starts with a natural oil base and adds cocoa butter, essential oils, milk, honey, herbs and exfoliants. Soaps are available in 16 scents including honey almond, orange peel and in the spring and summer, lilac. She grows her own lavender, and uses local bayberry and strawberry that she gathers and dries herself. The olive oil soap contains calendula petals that she gets from her own garden.

Bestseller: Cranberry soap made with berries from local growers. "When I'm desperate, I'll pick up a bag of cranberries at the market," says Pat. The oatmeal soap is also a bestseller.

What Gives Me Goosebumps: The honey-almond soap smells like marzipan, contains bits of almonds, and I wanted to smother it in chocolate and eat it. Other scents I love: the lilac, and the orange-peel soap with cinnamon.

Interesting Fact: Winterberry is popular at Christmastime, thanks to a holly-like berry that is used. It smells like Santa Claus.

Website: www.capecodsoap.com

Cape Cod Concoctions

A trip to Cape Cod just wouldn't be the same without lobster. Lighthouses. Superlative sunsets. And a trip to the **Beach Plum Spa,** located at the Daniel Webster Inn in Sandwich, Mass., the Cape Codder Resort in Hyannis, Mass., and the John Carver Inn in Plymouth, Mass. Owner Debra Catania did her research, and incorporated products containing beach plum – also known as rose hips – into her spa's organic product line. The beach plum, which varies from white to purple, is found naturally on Cape Cod beaches, and historically has been used in jams, jellies, teas and soaps. The fruiting shrub is rich in Vitamins A, C, E and promotes blood circulation. At the Beach Plum Spa, you'll find high-end treatments using beach plum, along with take-home products such as scrubs. The spa also offers a range of facials, massages, manicures and pedicures, using organic oils, Cape Cod cranberries, and – let me dish the dirt here – sea mud. Yes, here's mud on your thigh! (www.beachplumspa.com)

Deal Farm Soap Company

Enjoy a trip to the farm – without setting a toe on the tarmac. Renee Deal is a former industrial designer – and Saucony footwear designer – who also started out as a hobbyist. Today, her **Deal Farm Soap Company** in Boxford, Mass., carries 20 products including soaps, creams, shea butters, lip balms and milk bath. All 12 soaps are made with goat's milk that is supplied by a farm in Rowley, Mass. "Goat's milk works wonders for the skin," says Renee, because the naturally occurring caprylic acid in the milk gives the soaps a pH level close to that of your skin, she explains. "It's extremely compatible with your skin. I have customers with eczema, psoriasis and post-menopausal breakouts, who won't use anything else." Products are available online.

Bestseller: Goat-milk soap, four types: unscented Pure and Simple, and Soothing Oatmeal plus Lavender-Cream and Lavender Oatmeal. All wrapped in printed fabric, for a homey touch.

What Gives Me Goosebumps: Rose-Clay, Geranium and Bergamot soap, in a pink color, which smells divine. Also, a Dead Sea Salt and Mud Swirl soap.

Interesting Fact: Renee also makes a dog soap, also made with goat's milk plus essential oils to repel insects, which gives Fido something to pant about.

Website: www.dealfarm.com

Wine Country Naturals

Here's how to add *joie de vivre* to your journey. Another new kid on the beauty block is **Wine Country Naturals**, a startup company based in Marin County, Calif. – wine country. Currently the company makes four products with Napa, Sonoma and Lodi grapes. These are a Chardonnay-Pear Essence Body Butter; a Zinfandel-Currant Essence Mud Masque; Cabernet-Plum Essence Salt Scrub; and Chardonnay-Honey Essence Hand Lotion.

Bestseller: Chardonnay-Honey Essence Hand Lotion.

Passport to Pretty

That's Just Nuts

The rich soil of Oregon's Willamette Valley produces a whopping 99 percent of all hazelnuts grown in the United States. Until now, you'd have to get your fill by eating, say, a jar of Nutella. But now the state's AAA-rated Four Diamond Sunriver Resort offers a 50-minute, $100 **Oregon hazelnut body scrub** at its Sage Spring Club and Spa. Nuts are pulverized, drenched with moisturizers, then massaged into moist skin. The results produce a healthy glow faster than you can say, "filbert." Kids, you **should** try this at home; you can purchase the scrub, made with hazelnut oil at www.sagespringsspa.com, www.sunriver-resort.com.

The private-label, travel-ready scrub, made in Bend, Oregon, is made by Angelina Organic Skincare, whose products are so impressive they were given out in the Gifting Suites at the 2009 Oscars in Hollywood. Owner Angelina Swanson is a botanist, whose line includes about 150 products. She actually goes to the local forest and hand-picks many of her ingredients herself. "We wild-harvest a lot of our own ingredients right out of the forest," she said. "I also wild-harvest the St. John's Wort – we just rip it out of the ground in the forest in the Oregon Cascades." The bestselling product is Skin Doctor for cracked hands and feet, which is filled with calendula that Angelina has a local farmer grow for her. She also makes a Sore Muscle Rub used by athletes, which is like Tiger Balm but is made with arnica and St. John's Wort. Bruises, be gone! (www.angelinaorganicskincare.com)

What Gives Me Goosebumps: The Chardonnay-Honey Essence Hand Lotion. Non-greasy, this light, lovely lotion smells fantastic and is the next-best-thing to nibbling on a bunch of frozen grapes. Contains grapeseed oil, grape extract and aloe vera. Put it on your hands, hold your hands up to your nose and inhale deeply!

Interesting Fact: The company is currently making a Vino Bella product line that will be available in spas.

Website: www.winecountrynaturals.com

Make Way For Medical Tourism

Want to travel and get younger the fast way? Now there's no need to spend a small fortune on a facelift in the United States. Medical tourism makes it possible for you to go abroad, have a surgical procedure, and even get a leisurely vacation in the process – for a fraction of the cost. Take a look at this information, which was posted on CNN.com on 3/26/09.

Brazil is emerging as a niche market for plastic surgery. In Brazil, Dr. Ivo Pitanguy is legendary for his face and neck lifts.

Singapore is an established center of biotechnology, with a strong niche in stem cell and regenerative therapies.

Central America is known for its dental procedures – the countries of Mexico, Panama and Costa Rica offer proximity to U.S. citizens – and low prices. In Costa Rica and Panama, facelifts are available for less than a quarter of U.S. prices.

South Africa is where you'll get a "scalpel safari" – a cosmetic surgery procedure followed by a relaxing recovery in the sun. You can get a facelift for $2,500 versus $12,000 in the States. Also known for good dental care.

Malaysia is where knee replacement surgery goes for $4,500, compared to $30,000-$50,000 in the States. Cardiac and cosmetic surgeries are also a big draw.

South Korea is the destination of Japanese patients, who travel there for eyelid surgery, nose jobs, facelifts and skin-whitening.

Hungary's low prices and high-quality care make it a dentistry hotspot. Dental implants are from $775, a third of their U.S. prices.

For more information, read ***Patients Beyond Borders*** by Josef Woodman.

The Boy From Brazil

In Brazil, people are nuts about plastic surgery. Now, from the legendary clinic of prominent plastic surgeon Ivo Pitanguy in Rio de Janeiro, comes Beauty by Clinica Ivo Pitanguy. The knowledge of the Clinica's world renowned aestheticians, dermatologists, nutritionists, biochemists, and surgeons is now available in a jar. PreVious Lifting Serum is a concentrated liquid gel to be applied morning and night to tone, rejuvenate and smooth the skin.

Here's what's in it. Peptide technology targets lines and wrinkles due to aging. Extract of Centella Asiatica minimizes wrinkles, increases firmness, and naturally moisturizes the skin. Organic silicium and Vitamin E protect the skin and enrich the formula for longer-lasting results. Contains extract of aloe to moisturize without oil.

The cost? $225 for one ounce at Bergdorf Goodman. That's *a lot cheaper* than the trip to Rio on Varig Brazilian Airlines. (www.pitanguy.com.br)

New York's Temple of Beauty

What if you wanted a whiff of Italy, Paris, and Ibiza – all in one place? You'd find it at **Aedes de Venustas,** which is Latin for "Temple of Beauty," one of the most lust-worthy boutiques in the world. Located on Christopher Street in New York, the 550-sq.-ft. shop carries cult perfumes, home fragrances and little-known skincare products, which sometimes aren't even on the radar screen of beauty insiders. There's the signature perfume of the Ritz Paris; Hierbas de Ibiza, an aroma made from the herbs and plants of Ibiza; the scent of Paris' famed Hotel Costes on the rue Faubourg St. Honore; and Eau d'Italie, which is like flinging open a window in Positano. Here's where to also find crave-worthy creations from Serge Lutens, Diptyque, Carthusia, L'Artisan Parfumer, Lalique, Jurlique and Annick Goutal. All the merchandise comes in a black Aedes box wrapped in satin ribbon and embellished with a fresh flower arrangement. It's nirvana for your nose (www.aedes.com).

Whew, after all that armchair traveling around the world, you might like some added diet and beauty tips from executive, professional women around the globe, who travel for business. That's the subject of Chapter Ten.

CHAPTER TEN
Business Class

If anyone knows about traveling, it's business women in today's world. In fact, research shows that the number of female travelers is skyrocketing. You're invited to meet some of the following high-profile business women, in all industries, and get their take about being a gorgeous globetrotter. You'll find all kinds of gems from these business-minded beauties who travel for work, and make "the ride" as relaxing and as refreshing as possible. So put your tray table in the upright position, and get ready for a terrific take-off.

Nicole Hage, Professional Golfer on the LPGA

Nicole loves to be comfortable in all of her travels, as she's on the road 20-25 weeks during the year. Because of that, she tends to overpack, to make sure that's she got everything she needs, and all the comforts of home. "I always pay overweight fees at the airport," she says. She stuffs it all in her OGIO "9800" Bag, which she loves. "That suitcase is unreal. I love it. I need clothes for eight weeks in a row, and I don't like to wear the same golf clothes twice." (www.ogio.com)

She's never without a few key items: her Homedics rain machine, for one. "I got one at Walmart. It's small and lightweight and I love it." She's also never without her eye mask for sleeping –"I got it – it's part of the Lambie collection at Bath and Body Works." (www.bathandbodyworks.com)

There are also some essential cosmetics she loves to pack. "I swear by Bare Minerals, with SPF of 15. It's good for my face (www.baremineralsmakeup.net). Diorshow mascara in black is unbelievable (www.dior.com). Benefit liquid blush is awesome. Your cheeks look kissed (www.benefitcosmetics.com). But I don't wear lipstick or gloss. I'm not a lipstick person. I also use Pro-Activ solution on my skin. It's amazing. It changed my life." (www.proactiv.com)

Another huge thing that has transformed her life: a professional Keratin Complex straightening treatment on her frizzy tresses. "My Keratin treatment in my hair lasted five months, because I also used the special Keratin Complex shampoo, and I did the Infusion once a week. I wanted it to last as long as it could. My hair is typically frizzy and really dry – crunchy! – with a light wave, and it's really humid in Florida, where I live. I used to blow-dry and straighten it every day. Now, I rarely use my straightening iron. If I blow-dry my hair, it looks like I spent hours on it. It's a miracle. It takes me 10 minutes to blow-dry and I have long hair. It makes life a lot easier. And people keep telling me how great my hair looks. When the Keratin wore off, I was miserable. I said to myself, 'How did I ever live without it?' It's worth every penny. It changed my life." (www.keratincomplex.com)

Traveling takes its toll on Nicole, and she tries to make herself as comfortable as possible. On the plane, "I chew gum. Or I sip on 7-Up or water. I don't like flying. I'm always so uncomfortable. I take a blanket I bought at Brookstone, and I'm normally wearing sweats with a hoodie – it makes me feel more protected. I worry about traveling on planes and getting germs. I like to lean against the window and cover up."

Since Nicole doesn't eat on planes, she dines beforehand. "I might have a chicken wrap or even a Taco Bell once in a while. It's hard to eat healthy on the road. I have had to run in nearly every airport in this country, to make it to the gate on time after I get something to eat."

Nicole also proudly announces that she just stopped wearing acrylic nails, which she has done since the 6th grade, as she was a chronic nail-biter. "In September 2009 I stopped biting my nails. Finally. That's big for me, as I did it ever since I was born."

Georgette Mosbacher, CEO of Borghese Cosmetics, www.Borghese.com

Georgette is the CEO of Borghese Cosmetics, and while she prefers to use her own brand in her travels, she has tremendous other top tips to make travel a breeze.

First thing? "Use baggies. I have all five sizes, and I use them for shoes, bras, scarves, handbags. They make it so easy to pack and unpack – they're a dream. It takes me three minutes to pack. I order them online, directly from the company."

Curl, Interrupted

How do I manage my wavy tresses now? Keratin Complex Natural Keratin Smoothing Treatment by Coppola, which I get a Salon Acote in Boston (www.salonacote.com). This incredible process infuses natural keratin into the hair cuticle, to eliminate up to 95% of frizz and curl, making hair healthier, shinier, smoother, more manageable and easier to maintain. It has changed my life. Unbelievably, I had wash-and-wear hair when I recently went to Hawaii – I simply washed my hair after working out, and went to dinner with a wet head of straight hair that looked fantastic. How did I manage, for all those years, without it? There's even a special formulation just for blondes like myself. With Keratin, waves will disappear like magic, and you can kiss straight hair hello! (www.keratincomplex.com).

Georgette also lives – and travels – in just one pair of lovely, custommade black-velvet shoes, from Shipton and Heneage in London (www.shipton-usa.com). (These slippers are sold to royalty, aristocracy, and if you remember, the late Dean Martin!) "I have these custommade for me, with my initials in gold on the front. I literally wear them with everything, year-round. They're $400 a pair but they're worth it. They will last you three to four years, and they're fabulous. Buy them a half-size larger than your normal size. I wear them with socks sometimes. They're great with everything from jeans to a silk dress."

Buy custommade black-velvet slippers from Shipton and Heneage in London with your own initials on them, to wear with everything. An indispensable investment!

Georgette also has a baby comforter that she travels with, as well as a pillow. "I'm known for my baby comforter," she told me. But this first-class flier doesn't carry the same stuff that you and I do. She has her comforter and pillow custom-covered in specially made linens, of "the best Egyptian cotton. Then I roll them up and put them in a canvas tote bag." These two little luxuries are so impressive, people always ask her where she got them. "I bring these with me, along with a sleeping pill, and that's the trick. I wear a tunic and leggings or change into a caftan in the plane's bathroom. I don't like sleeping in my clothes. Changing on the plane makes the experience like night and day. So I feel refreshed when I land."

She has yet another custommade trick: she purchases special luggage tags measuring 4" long and 3" wide, embossed with her contact info, from the King Ranch in Texas, which is known for its saddle shop (www.king-ranch.com). "They're HUGE, one-of-a-kind and fabulous."

"I don't carry a purse, ever," says Georgette. "But I'm never without my cell-phone, iPod, with a Swarovski crystal cover for it – I'd never travel without it."

On the plane, Georgette doesn't eat anything except a box of Wheat Thins that she takes with her. "Or I eat beforehand – something filling like pasta."

Niki Leondakis, COO
Kimpton Hotels,
www.kimptongroup.com

As the Chief Operating Officer of Kimpton Hotels and Restaurants, Niki spends much of her time in the sky. "Oh my goodness, I travel for business 60% of the time," says Niki. "My husband and I...both suffer from wanderlust. About 70% of my time is spent traveling personally and professionally."

"On the plane, if I get upgraded – which is often – I travel United Airlines – the food is better in First Class, with salad, fruits and veggies. I always carry almonds and whole fruit in a Ziploc. My Kimpton profile says that I like fresh fruit and water, so those are always in my room. I throw the fruit in my carry-on. My other fallback? Luna bars tucked in my suitcase. It's a good source of nutrition."

To keep her skin soft and supple when flying, Niki swears by Fresh air travel masks (www.fresh.com). "It's clear and comes with wipes. I put the invisible mask on, to moisturize and protect my face. It's herbal and wonderful. I take it off before landing and put on Fresh moisturizing cream that contains caffeine. I love to do that. I also love to carry, on short flights, mists for my face, such as those by True Cosmetics (www.truecosmetics.com) and by Caudalie (www.caudalie.com). Both come in travel sizes. I love to mist mid-flight. Another ritual is that I travel with my own tea bags,

The Sensational "Oh Dear!" Cupboard at Four Seasons Hotel Boston

It happens to everyone. You're on a business trip and you forget your reading glasses. Hair gel. Pantyhose. Adapter. Well, there are no more worries at the Four Seasons Hotel in Beantown, because the crackerjack concierges there have an entire CUPBOARD filled with things business travelers might forget. All of the above, as well as phone chargers, eyeglass repair kits, and for men, yarmulkes, cufflinks, ties, black socks, and even a selection of shoes! And much more. "I can't tell you how many times we open the cupboard on a daily basis," says Kristan Fletcher, Director of Public Relations. In addition, on our recent stay, when we forgot a few items, the hotel gladly assisted with complimentary workout gear, sneakers, and even disposable swimsuits, so we could swim in the 82-degree pool. These savvy concierges have earned their membership in the phenomenal "Clefs D'Or" (golden key society) and then some! (www.fourseasons.com)

in chamomile or mint. I use Mighty Leaf tea sachets (www.mightyleaf.com). They're beautiful and it's the most wonderful tea. It's a sensory experience. The flight attendants always say, 'That smells so great.' I bring extra so I can give them one or two bags, along with my leftover magazines."

Niki is a runner, so she's good to go upon arrival, provided she's brought her sneakers and running gear. But get this – she also loves to hula hoop! "I also recently developed an appreciation for hula hooping," Nike explains. "Mine breaks down into four parts and fits into my carry-on. We like to have fun at Kimpton, and we hula hoop at company meetings. All the new General Managers and Executive Chefs do it at our annual meeting. We do a 'hoop off' to the tune of "Wipeout." Being silly…humanizes people and says, 'Don't forget to have fun.'" When she's not running or hula hooping, Niki might do Pilates, push-ups and stretches in the privacy of her hotel room.

Her favorite brands of luggage are Mulholland (www.shopmulholland.com) and Bric's. Both brands, she says, are understated yet beautiful, and since they're pretty uncommon, they're not apt to be mistakenly taken off the luggage belt.

Niki is also a savvy shopper – and you'd be wise to follow her advice. She is a regular at boutiques such as Susan in San Francisco, and when she finds something she loves, she tells a salesperson, and then states, "Tell me when it goes on sale." "I've gotten to know a particular salesperson there, and I have her tell me when it goes on sale. You can do the same at Saks and Nordstrom. At TSE Cashmere, near my office in San Francisco, they know what I love. They call me when it goes on sale, before the "Sale" sign hits the window. They notify me so I get first choice."

Victoria King, President, Victoria King Public Relations, a boutique public-relations firm specializing in luxury resorts and destinations, www.vkpr.com

"If you take care of yourself on the ground, it's easier to do it in the air," advises Vicky, whose firm is in Los Angeles, and represents luxury airlines, hotels and destinations. She takes about 50 trips per year. "I don't eat much on the plane, although I do low-sodium or vegetarian, ordered in advance. I may only eat the salad and fruit. I always bring raw almonds, sunflower seeds and Power bars."

Vicky exercises every day, regardless of where she is in the world. "I give myself one-half to a full hour of Pilates and stretching – I have my routine down. When I take the red eye to New York City, I exercise immediately when I get to my hotel. In Jordan, I took a hike immediately." What goes with her on every trip is her Burt's Bees lip balm (www.burtsbees.com). "I like Boots – their cosmetics are great. I'm a drugstore junkie when I'm in their stores. I also only do carry-on. I can go to Asia for 10 days only with carry-on. And my favorite airline is Emirates."

Ruthann Niosi, a Park Avenue Securities Defense Attorney who travels to Europe every few months

"I like Delta," says Ruthann. "They're usually on time and I also like Alitalia – I like their service and the food choice. I never order a special meal, though. I stick with cheese and crackers and fruit – usually not the entrees. I always travel with small packages of almonds, dried apricots and granola bars, which I'll eat if I get hungry – both on the plane or during the trip. Before I get on the plane, at the airport, I like to have avocado salsa, chips and a glass of wine – and then within half an hour of boarding, I can usually fall asleep. That's my routine at Kennedy Airport before I fly to Italy."

Ruthann wears no makeup when she flies, and never travels without Neutrogena Lip Moisturizer (www.Neutrogena.com). Her old reliables include Clarins Demaquillant tonic express facial cleanser (www.clarins.com), L'Oreal eye makeup remover (www.lorealusa.com), and Clinique moisture surge (www. clinique.com). "Plus I always bring my own Safeguard soap – as funny as that sounds, when you think about it, hotels in Europe usually don't stock anti-per-spirant soap. And instead of using the hotel soap for the 'perfumed scent,' I take sample sizes of Chanel body washes." (www.chanel.com). "Last, I never travel without Neutrogena Body Oil. I always use it after a shower or bath as the absolute guarantee against any irritation from a change in water softness." (www.neutrogena.com)

Her luggage is the fave of frequent-fliers: Louis Vuitton (www.louisvuitton. com). "I have one on wheels, and the big square soft one, which squishes down in the cars in Europe. I take a large Fendi totebag, plus an evening bag. My shoes? Manolo Blahnik – guaranteed comfort - that's all I wear."

She adds: "I love to clothes-shop in Paris, on particular streets. I have a route that I do all the time, I have it all written out." (See Ruthannn's route in Chapter 12!)

Ali Brown, Entrepreneur, and driving-force behind a rapidly expanding multimillion-dollar empire, www.alibrown.com

From Sydney, to Los Angeles, to Maui, self-made multimillionaire entrepreneur Ali Brown's American Express Platinum Card is as important to her as her passport. "I'm constantly working on the road, so it's worth the $500 that it costs for one year, because of the access it provides to airport lounges. Lounge access is a must for anyone who travels frequently for business!"

Ali knows what she's talking about. As founder and CEO of Ali International, a company that includes *Ali Magazine,* Ali Boutique, the Millionaire Protégé Club and SHINE, an annual live event for entrepreneurs, she's on the road for an average of four months out of every year.

"I've got traveling down to a science," she says. "When I travel, I'm usually going somewhere where I need to be at my best, so diet on the road is very important. On the plane, I've tried all the low-fat meals and snacks, but they just don't taste like real food to me! These days, I prefer raw almonds or Isagenix peanut crunch bars (www.isagenix.com). Also in her carry-on are Airborne (www.airbornehealth.com) and Emergen-C (www.alacer.com). "Travel can weaken the immune system but whenever I feel like I'm coming down with something, Emergen-C and a good night's rest seem to knock it out."

Ali has a simple on-the-go beauty regimen. "I always make sure to bring eye drops, hand lotion, and Evian water. And I can't leave without Klorane dry shampoo (www.laboratoires-klorane.com). It's a great fix if you don't have time to wash and blow-dry your hair. And, if you can't find a good dry shampoo, baby powder is a perfectly fine backup."

Where does she stash all of her travel supplies?

"Big Ziploc bags. I buy them from Drugstore.com. They even make 10- and 20-gallon bags with zippers, which are great for packing clothes, so your nice garments don't get wrinkled or stained. Anything white definitely goes in a Ziploc bag." The last must-have item, she admits, is a little 'dorky.' "I bring a little folding footrest from Magellan's. It saves your legs and it's definitely worth it," says Ali.

All carry-on items get placed into her Jamah travel bag (www.jamah.com). "It's a line by a friend of mine. I bought the 'Elizabeth' style in three colors, and it's the best travel bag in the world." On that note, she's a firm believer in looking good on the plane: "Have some pride, people!" she recommends. "Wear jeans with a heeled shoe, then change into slippers on the plane. A little tip I've learned is that when you dress nicely, you attract better service."

Of all the places she travels to, she swears by the Four Seasons Maui Resort at Wailea. "I just read (founder) Isadore Sharp's biography, which is fascinating. In Maui, they really pamper you - they greet you by name, remember your favorite drink at the pool. And those beds – wow! It's a home-away-from-home. I once went there all by myself for 10 days on vacation, and had a great time." (www.fourseasons.com/maui).

Carol Brodie, President and CEO of Carol Brodie and Company, Luxury Brand Advisors, Designer and Face of Rarities Fine Jewelry by Carol Brodie, seen exclusively on HSN, www.carolbrodieandco.com, www.hsn.com

If her name sounds familiar, that's because you've probably seen Carol on TV, promoting her luxurious line of jewelry on HSN. And that's just one of the ventures she's got going. Carol says she travels about 22 weeks a year, promoting her exclusive line of Rarities Fine Jewelry by Carol Brodie, and working on other business projects. To make her journeys more enjoyable, she never flies without Airborne (www.airbornehealth.com) as well as Crème de la Mer moisturizer (www.cremedelamer.com) and June Jacobs facial spray (www.junejacobs.com). Her Tumi luggage is always also filled with Tarte eye-color boxes (www.tarte.com), Laura Mercier tinted moisturizer (www.lauramercier.com), and Lancome Definicils mascara (www.lancome-usa.com). "I used to travel with four cosmetic bags," Carol says. "But now everything goes in quart-sized Ziploc bags. Plus I always use tissue paper and plastic to pack my clothing, and I put my purses and shoes in special bags."

On the plane, she finds that eating something nice helps with boredom. "I might bring a hummus and veggie plate on the plane. At my destination, I order out and am able to order things the way I like them – such as egg whites, seven-grain bread, entrees grilled dry, and made with no fat. At home, I tend to eat off my kids' plates. I'm not diet or fitness obsessed. I make smart choices and I don't deny myself."

On the plane, comfort is key for her. If she's traveling on a night or weekend, she's outfitted in Juicy Couture, Lululemon and Converse no-lace sneakers – "They're my favorites," she says. But if she's traveling during the day, she wears "my Glamazon business outfits" and plenty of stilettos by Jimmy Choo and Christian Louboutin. And make no doubt about it – this trend-setting New Yorker never travels without bejeweling herself in her Rarities collection, and also carrying a stash of inventory in her purse. "After all," she says, "I am a walking model for my brand, so every flight gives me the opportunity to host my own trunk show right on the plane!"

Carol walks for exercise at her destination, and along with that, always makes sure that she looks just right. "I'm obsessed with my hair and makeup when I travel. I also make sure that my clothing is perfectly steamed – I hate the look of wrinkled clothes."

One great tip, to make your travels terrific: Carol always packs a fabulous-smelling sachet in her suitcase, "so that when I open up my luggage, everything smells beautiful."

Pack a pretty sachet or soap
in your suitcase, so that when you
open your bag, all you smell is
a delicious aroma.

Elizabeth Bard, Journalist and Bestselling Author of *Lunch in Paris: A Love Story With Recipes* (Little, Brown and Company)

Elizabeth's memoir is like biting into a sweet and airy *chouquette*: crisp, tantalizing and full of the very essence of life. She's an American living in Paris, and she has some wonderful tips to feel great when traveling. "I put on expensive eye cream in the duty-free cosmetic section. You get to try all those products you've been reading about in magazines," she explains. "At my destination I hit the pharmacy on arrival and buy an exfoliating product for my body – it just seems easier in the hotel bathtub. For my face, I use Annick Goutal's hydrating mask (www.annickgoutal.com). When I'm on my own, I can slather it on and leave it to soak overnight – but it would get sticky with my husband around!" She's also partial to Eucerin Shower Oil – "It's 20% oil, so you don't need to use much body cream when you dry off." (www.eucerinproducts.com)

On planes, Elizabeth is never without nuts, raisins, and a bag of Swedish fish. "I NEVER eat airline food. I don't even let them put it down in front of me (boredom kicks in and you'll eat it anyway). I pack my own meal – chicken breast, veggies, maybe a couscous salad, and a bag of dried apricots."

Elizabeth recommends to other travelers that the best way to explore a city is to visit the local marketplace where you can sample a variety of produce, spices and meats. "It's the best way to discover a country's cuisine!"

Favorite destination? "My husband and I have a secret village in Crete that we escape to – we swim, we read, we eat grilled octopus, we swim some more. It's like Canyon Ranch, but for only 60 Euros per night!"

Visit the duty-free cosmetics sections of airports to try the testers of the latest and greatest beauty products.

Betty Spence, President, National Association for Female Executives, www.nafe.com, and author, *Be Your Own Mentor* (Random House)

"We do events all over the country," says Betty. "At times I'm on six planes a week. It varies. I took nuts with me when I went to South Africa. I always buy water and bring a sandwich from home – unless I fly First or Business, in which case I'll eat on the plane. I sometimes order a special meal, or vegetarian plate. I don't like to buy at the airport. I don't eat fast food. I bring turkey on whole wheat bread. I'd rather not eat, than eat fast food."

Betty has a terrific daily routine. "I step out of my bed every morning, throw down a towel, and do Pilates for a half-hour while watching the news," says Betty. "It saved my life. I used to have back problems."

"I carry my cosmetics in tiny bottles. Now I use Jurlique (www.jurlique.com). I walk back and forth on the flight, doing whatever I can on the flight. My luggage is Tumi." (www.tumi.com)

Cathy Hughes, Founder and Chairperson of Radio One, Inc., the largest African-American owned and operated broadcast-company in the nation, www.radio-one.com

Cathy Hughes travels, she says, 65% of the time, mostly in the United States – "and I just returned from a contract in Bermuda," she told me. "On the plane I usually eat nuts. But I'm strange. When they have linens and china, I enjoy airline food – eating it makes the time pass. I always carry trail mix with me, and I've started buying individual snack packs, to give to small, hungry children if the flight's delayed and we're stuck on the jetway."

Cathy is faithful about using sanitizer – "Anytime I use the airline blanket or pillow I get sick. Airplanes are the perfect incubators for disease. How bad it had to be when people could smoke? I sanitize even when reading the magazines, before and after. I also stay very hydrated and drink a lot of water – I drink 16-24 ounces before I even get on the plane. And I carry a spray bottle of rosewater for my face, because I can feel my skin drying."

For exercise, Cathy explores destinations by walking although she's partial to "fidgeting," because she once asked actor Jamie Foxx how he watches his weight, and that was his answer. "Yet, it's easy to discourage me from exercise," Cathy admits. When she does make the commitment, she swims – "I even pack webbed gloves for resistance in the water. They make your fingers look like a duck's, but you can really feel the difference."

Since Cathy makes many TV appearances – including her eponymous TV show on TV One – she always travels light but makes sure to take "six pairs of shoes. I like a lightweight bag – I take a Delsey." (www.delseyusa.com)

Two beauty product lines that she swears by are Carol's Daughter and Pooka (owned by five African-American women). (www.carolsdaughter.com, www. pookapureandsimple.com)

"Bargain-lover" also ought to be Cathy's middle name. "I try to find bargains everywhere I visit," she said. In Paris once, she overheard some hotel employees discussing their finds – and learned about a Paris flea market. "I could not believe what I found," she says. "Flea markets are my thing in every city. Plus Native-American crafts in the Southwest. I love things that are unique to their geographical area. You'll find great bargaining in abundance at flea markets and vendors markets. Everyone teases me about it – but it's my favorite hobby. From my excursions I also provide lots of things to families who are helped by Habitat for Humanity. It helps them to decorate their homes. After I retire I want to provide home decorating services for people who can't afford it….It's very enjoyable, walking the through Goodwill stores picking up something I know someone needs. When I travel, I'm always *looking,* you know."

Susan Bixler, President and CEO of Bixler Consulting, www.bixlerconsulting.com

When I interviewed Susan, she had just returned from a trip to Venice and Florence with her niece, Larissa Bixler, a lawyer. Susan's been traveling for business for 30 years. Here are some of her best travel secrets:

♦ Roll up your items tightly and put rubber bands around them for overseas travel. It's amazing how much you can fit into a suitcase when items are compressed.

♦ If you travel a lot, have a duplicate toiletries bag packed with small sizes of makeup, hair products and cleansing items that you use at home. Keep this only for travel. While it is an additional expense upfront, if saves so much time when packing. You won't wind up in a hotel room without your favorite mascara, moisturizer, or mousse.

♦ Do something fun and adventurous on every single business trip. I used to bring my roller blades and tour the city. Now I just look for live performances or cool shopping.

♦ Schedule a car service, not a rental car, when it is going to be a jammed-packed and stressful trip. Renting a car and figuring out a new city is so much work, and can significantly detract from being fresh and on your game when you get in front of clients. Always use a car service or a reliable friend or family member when getting back from a Pacific Rim or European trip. Reflexes are not to be trusted after 20 hours on the plane.

♦ Get massages on the road.

♦ Bring a bathing suit so you can swim at night. Bring yoga pants to do some stretching in the hotel room.

Susan also makes sure to travel with fruit, nuts, and chia seeds and uses Bose noise-reducing headphones to listen to music (www.bose.com). In her seat, she might also do "squeeze-and-release" isometric exercises, or head to the back of the plane for some toe touching and arm stretches. And she recommends to other business women to only travel with costume jewelry, because you never know if your luggage will get lost. And when it comes to luggage, she swears by the Kirkland brand found at Costco. "It's roomy, soft, sturdy and lasts for years – I've tried everything – and I like Kirkland the best." (www.costco.com). Also, "Pick one hotel chain and stay loyal. Use a credit card that provides points to your honor program. It is amazing how quickly those points add up."

Mary Richardson, former "Chronicle" Anchor on WCVB-TV5

"I love to travel," says Mary, whose work on the hit TV news-magazine show, *Chronicle,* in the Boston area, has brought her to far-flung locales including China, Egypt, France, Italy, Ireland and all the Caribbean islands. "It's one of the joys of the job," she said. "If you gave me a bus ticket to Fresno, I would go." On the plane, she munches on trail mix and fruit. "If I'm stuck at the airport, I get granola and fruit along with my Starbucks – that can carry me across the country." She takes her shoes off on the plane and wears warm socks, especially as she likes to get up and move around as much as possible. "I go in the back and talk to all of the flight attendants. I've met more nice flight attendants that way. It's good to get out of your seat."

Her swear-by lotions and potions include the new Cetaphil dry skin cream (not the lotion) that you can purchase at the drugstore. "I slather it on my hands and face," says Mary. "Before this I used to need a prescription for my face, my skin was so dry." Her other must-haves in her bags include E Phyto-Erba hairspray; L'Oreal Voluminous mascara ("It's the best," www.loreal.com) and Jane Iredale mineral makeup base in Golden Glow (www.janeiredale.com).

Mary is a runner, so her carry-on always contains a leotard, bike shorts, and T-shirt. She wears her running shoes to the airport. In her Tumi go all of her clothes, left in their dry-cleaning bags. Attached to her luggage is a separate Tumi bucket bag that functions as her purse. "It's the world's best invention," she says.

Mary is eagerly awaiting a trip to Arizona, to visit Nordstrom's Last Chance store in Phoenix. "My friend left there the other day with 11 pairs of designer shoes at bargain prices." (It's a great place for true bargain shopaholics.) For a vacation, Mary adds: "My very favorite resort in the world, though, is the Pasadena Langham Hotel, formerly the Ritz-Carlton, Pasadena. It's located in one of the most beautiful neighborhoods in America. Service and food are divine...and it's the most peaceful spot. I like to stay in the wing at the back of the hotel right next to the swimming pool. Total relaxation and only about 20 minutes from LA!"

Astrid Merriman, Property Manager

"My love of travel was jump-started when I married a 'gypsy,'" says Astrid. "I was not a traveler and my husband had already traveled around the world...so he turned me into the vagabond that I am today. The only continents that I personally have not visited are Japan, Indo-China and the Antarctic. We take three to five trips per year; at least two of those are to Europe."

Astrid always packs a yoga mat that she uses for stretching, and always does floor exercises at her hotel. One of the savviest things she's done is to buy both a European hair dryer, and a heating pad, which are always at the ready. "That way I don't have to worry about voltage when I travel to Europe," she says. She also uses a travel plug adapter made by Kensington, into which she plugs a voltage converter. "I use this for charging my Kindle, iPhone, iPod and laptop."

Beauty products that she swears by include Cellcosmet (no website found). (Cellcosmet is a skincare line from the Cellap Laboratoire SA., Switzerland. Products are created with marine extracts and with pure or natural oils.) "Cellcosmet facial products are available pre-packaged for travel. I also love Doctor Babor facial products (www.babor.com) – I can't live without them! After your first night's rest, get a facial and massage as soon as you can."

She also can't live without her Louis Vuitton luggage, which she describes as "indestructible," (www.louisvuitton.com) and Easy Spirit walking shoes (www.easyspirit.com).

Sylvia Weinstock, "The Leonardo da Vinci of cakes," New York City, www.sylviaweinstock.com

Sylvia Weinstock loves, loves, loves Continental Airlines. And why not? After all, Continental is the airline that constantly ships her gorgeous, one-of-a-kind cakes without a hitch. "Continental gives great service. I constantly write to their president to tell them about how great their service is." Sylvia, like her cakes, is constantly traveling around the globe, to create cakes for some high-profile clients and celebrities.

"In First Class, I might have a vodka cocktail, and I might just eat and deconstruct something," she told me. "After all, we all want to fit into our clothes. I eat fruits and salads. I put on a Donna Karan Cashmere facial lotion (www.donnakaran.com), or one by Oil of Olay (www.olay.com) or Estee Lauder (www.esteelauder.com). I also use a lot of Nars lipsticks (www.narscosmetics.com).

Sylvia almost always travels with Longchamp luggage (www.longchamp.com) plus a Tumi on wheels (www.tumi.com). "I hate waiting at the carousel for my luggage. In terms of shopping, "You must remember, I'm a New Yorker," she says. "I just go to Neiman-Marcus when I'm in any city."

Vivian Deuschl, Corporate Vice President of Public Relations, Ritz-Carlton Hotel Company, www.ritzcarlton.com

Vivian takes five to eight overseas trips per year, and sometimes as many as 30 domestic trips annually. She's an intrepid traveler, who has much of it all figured out. "My favorite airline is Delta. I'll never take anything but the Delta shuttle from Washington to New York," she told me. "On Cathay Pacific, the service is impeccable. What I love is that as a female business traveler, they treat me with respect, from the moment I check in. They don't ever say 'No.' Service is very important to me. The food is very good, and there are impeccably groomed young men and women on staff who look like they just stepped off a bandbox."

When it comes to dining, "I usually yield to temptation," Vivian admits. "I'll get to the airport three hours before a flight, and I'll get pizza or a hamburger at the airport. I also bring emergency snacks such as cheese and crackers, and candy bars."

Vivian says "I like to look tan," and so she's never without her Guerlain terra cotta blush (www.guerlain.com). "It's the one thing I always buy. I have tried everything from La Prairie to Lancome. And I take a nice lipgloss by Shiseido (www.shiseido.com). They have a great makeup remover too. I used to bring a cosmetic bag on board. I would clean my face and brush my teeth. I try to arrive with some lipstick on and a little blush."

Exercise at her destination? "I hate it," she says. "I'm an early riser. If I'm in a city and it's safe, I'll put on tennis shoes and walk. In Beijing I did a bike ride for three hours, but I don't use the gym at the hotel. I like to walk in any city, and I usually stop at a patisserie for a croissant and hot chocolate."

She carries a Louis Vuitton satchel that her husband gave her, along with Delsey luggage that she always buys in the latest color. Her newest addition? Five pieces in royal blue (www.delseyusa.com). "I also love to collect great luggage tags, and I have one that says, 'Not Your Bag.'"

Vivian is also a big shopper. "I always hit Lord and Taylor, and Saks in New York. I often have my clothes made in the Orient. I have some Shangai-Tang-like showstoppers that I had made for less than $100 apiece. Make sure you always have *three* fittings, because two are never enough."

In Berlin, she never fails to visit KaDeWe, a seven-story department store that is the largest store in Europe, carrying more than 3 Million products. "I love to go there, especially to the huge cosmetics floor and food emporium."

Nancy Michaels, President, www.suddenlysinglenow.com

"The secret is to have a great hairstylist in every city you're in," explains Nancy. "Before I had my Keratin treatment on my hair, I would arrive in Florida and immediately have to get a blow-dry. I used to go every week and get my hair done, like my grandmother. Now, after my Keratin treatment everything has changed for the better (www.keratincomplex.com). The true test of this treatment is vacationing in the tropics and by God, it stood the test of time and climate change. Given my kinky lock of curls – winter in New England is my kind of good hair locale. However, my 'do' held up in St. Martin perfectly for the first couple of days and after swimming, boating, and sunbathing, I washed it, blew it out and flat ironed it, and was up and running again. Keratin is a miracle cure. I'm not sure how I survived my high school and college years without it."

Nancy relies on Legal Seafoods for a meal at the airport. On the plane, she will bring mixed nuts, cheese, salad and sushi, "although I hate carrying a lot of stuff through security." For cosmetics, "I have travel sizes that I constantly replenish. John Frieda moisture barrier is the best hair spray out there." (www.johnfrieda.com)

"I also carry elastic bands – My personal trainer mapped out a whole exercise routine for me, which I can do with them."

Deepika Gehani, Creative Head, Genesis Luxury Fashion, www.genesiscolors.com

Deepika is a fashion designer who heads the creative part for India's biggest fashion conglomerate. Her company pioneered luxury retail in India, and introduced premium Indian labels to the world.

Her exercise when she travels? Yoga and lots of window-shopping. "As a creative person in the fashion industry, I can absorb varied influences and keep energized." She eats at an airport lounge before boarding, and has a list of swear-by cosmetics she uses in her travels. All of her facial products are custommade for her skin in Mumbai by Dr. Dinyar Boxwalla; these include a collagen gel; brightening skin pack; and almond-based night cream. She especially loves to spritz her face with rosewater, to seal moisture into her skin. And she never goes anywhere without Sephora's travel-proof cosmetic bottles.

Deepika's luggage, purse, and shoes, all come from one purveyor – Bottega Veneta (www.bottegaveneta.com). "Bottega ballerinas make up my day wear," she told me. And she loves the comfort and food of just one airline – Emirates.

Mary Cantando, Author, *The Woman's Advantage: 20 Entrepreneurs Show You What It Takes To Grow Your Business* (Kaplan Publishing), Speaker, Professional Facilitator, www.womansadvantage.biz

Mary travels 40 weeks out of the year, and when I spoke to her, she had just returned from Belarus on behalf of the U.S. State Department. For exercise, she does Pilates two times a week while at home, and yoga three times a week – and she aims to keep to the same schedule when traveling. One great tip: To avoid those desserts that she often finds on the table when she sits down at luncheons and dinners, Mary sprinkles them with a lot of salt and pepper, "so they won't taste good." She also typically orders half an entrée, and when she travels on cruise ships as a public speaker, "My goal is to never step on the elevator. I always climb the stairs." On the plane, she typically eats Quaker granola bars and wears compression socks to avoid blood clots. As an intrepid traveler, she loves Chico's in-house private-label brand called 'Travelers' – "It's very comfortable, and I can step off the plane and on stage to give a speech, and look good." In fact, Mary so loves this brand that she makes it a point to visit Chico's outlet stores when she travels, especially the one in Charlotte, N.C., which she visits once a month (www.chicos.com).

If you have children, you'll love Mary's tips on raising them to be savvy travelers. "When my kids were 7 and 8 years old, we traveled a lot. We would put one of our children in charge as the navigator, as soon as we got to the airport – in charge of tickets, luggage, keys, you name it. He would lead the way, get us to the gate, make the connection, everything. That child was responsible." She explained that even, at times, when they were headed in the wrong direction at the airport, yet still had time to make their flight, they let their child take charge and learn from his mistakes. The resulting advantage? "By the time my kids were 15 they could travel comfortably and confidently to international destinations by themselves, because they knew how to do it. We aggressively taught our kids how to travel. My son went by himself to Norway when he was 16, and we were perfectly comfortable with it."

Chico's has a special in-house, private-label clothing brand called "Travelers," which is ideal for business women on the road.

Meredith Oden, Dallas Cowboys Cheerleader

Meredith certainly travels for business – and what a business it is, being a beautiful, fit, Dallas Cowboys Cheerleader. "We do a lot of appearances, charity events, media tours, USO Tours, and swimsuit calendar photo shoots. As a cheerleader, I can travel up to one to two times per month."

"I usually pack my own snacks," says Meredith, "so I'm not tempted to eat peanuts and pretzels," she adds. "I carry fruit, almonds, and 100-calorie packs. I retain water when I fly and getting off the plane with a swollen face or ankles is ugly….so I always drink lots of water, carry moisturizer, and use lipgloss."

One of her favorite beauty tricks is to use Bedhead Rockaholic dry shampoo on the road (www.bedhead.com). "It soaks up the oil and makes your hair look brand new – it's one of the best things ever." She also is a firm believer in flexible hair spray – "I don't want crispy hair – I like it to brush out easily, especially after a long day of traveling."

At dinner, her strategy is to splurge on a dessert, but it's complemented by eating fresh seafood, a small cup of rice, and fresh vegetables as her main meal.

And believe it or not, exercise, when Meredith travels, "is at the bottom of my priorities. As a cheerleader, we're go-go-go. Our practice every night is four hours of cardio, five times a week." When traveling, therefore, Meredith simply walks everywhere, and does 100 crunches at night, and another 100 in the morning. "And if I need to go to the bathroom, instead of walking across my guest room, I'll do a lot of lunges, all across the floor," she says. "It works big muscles and gets your heart rate up – it gets your glutes and quads going, that's for sure."

Joelle Jenson, Las Vegas Showgirl and Performer with "Vegas The Show"

Joelle traveled extensively when she worked for 18 years with magician Lance Burton, and also enjoys singing and acting gigs on the side. "I am very busy," she told me. Joelle loves Four Seasons hotels anywhere in the world. When traveling, the first thing she does is to make sure her booked hotel has a gym. "If they do then I hit the gym when I get up and go to the treadmill for maybe 20-30 minutes. Then I do some light weights and squats for the thighs, and then stretch."

On the plane, she relies on "water, water, water," as well as fruit and salads, and Power bars. She brings a travel pillow with a satin pillowcase. Always in her suitcase are flip-flops, and a photo of her son. "It makes me feel closer to them," she says.

 Joelle also always keeps a travel case packed and stocked with small sizes of her favorite cosmetics, especially Mary Kay products (www.marykay.com). "It has everything in it from face products to creams." And her preferred carrier of choice? Japan Air Lines, whenever she can fly them.

Maria Manrique-Rosa, Financial Analyst, Fidelity Investments

Maria is my beautiful next-door neighbor, and as long as I've known her, she's been jetting off to Paris and Madrid for business. How does she do it and still look so lovely? "I stay at hotels that have gyms but I rarely have time to enjoy them. I get workouts in by walking instead of taking a taxi or the subway. Or I climb stairs. At the airport I skip the escalator and the moving walkways." On planes, she brings nuts, a large bottle of water, and if she's craving something sweet, a bottle of diet Snapple. "Once at my destination I order at restaurants – without looking at the menu. I invariably order mixed greens, broiled chicken or steamed veggies and the catch of the day. If I look at the menu, I might be tempted to order the lasagna!"

In Maria's Longchamp bag she packs silk tunics from Belle & Bunty (www.belleandbunty.co.uk). "I love these as they are lightweight, fold small, don't crease and look amazing." To keep her skin looking supple, she swears by Kiehl's avocado facial moisturizer (www.kiehls.com). She says, "It's the best cream to rehydrate with after a flight." She also makes sure to take her Optrex eye drops for hydration during the after the flight (www.optrex.co.uk). "My eyes get red even on short-haul flights."

Karen Asp, Fitness, Health, Nutrition And Travel Writer for national publications, *Woman's Day* Contributing Editor, Fit Travel blogger for AOL, and Certified Personal Trainer, www.karenasp.com

"I'm gone every six weeks," says Karen, who's a vegetarian. "I eat very little on planes. I am a huge fan of Lara bars. I pack nuts, carrots, and string cheese. At the airport I might grab a yogurt parfait." She also always travels with a BPA-free water bottle that she fills up, after going through security.

Karen is a self-proclaimed fitness fanatic, and so tries to log a workout at her destination – and even on the plane. "I'm always up on the flight, every hour. And I stretch in my seat. I wear a pedometer when I travel. I've logged tremendously high step counts, especially during long layovers." She also packs resistance bands with her, so she can do strength workouts in her hotel room.

She admits that part of the pleasure of traveling is the food. "At home I have dessert once a week, but on vacation, I have dessert and drinks more frequently. I keep portion sizes in check, which is why I'll split a meal with my husband, or only choose two appetizers or an appetizer and salad. But I love the bread in Paris."

Janet Wolfe, Ph. D., President and Founder of Wolfe Laboratories in the Boston area, www.wolfelabs.com

Janet travels at least once a month all around the United States and to Europe. "I make sure I have fruit on hand on the plane, because airline meals are disgusting," she told me. "I also bring a sandwich on long flights. I drink lots of water.

On the plane I stretch – small stretches so it's not invasive to the person seated next to me. And I watch a good chick flick, which I never get to watch at home. I swear by Chanel and Lancome and Estee Lauder products. All the samples go into my travel bag – it's a complete second set of everything, which is always packed. When I buy cosmetics and they load me up on samples, I always ask for more." (www.chanel.com, www.lancome-usa.com, www.esteelauder.com)

"For exercise," she continued, "I walk everywhere. I love touristy stuff. I only need my sneakers. I walk at 5 o'clock in the morning. I was in Vienna a few weeks ago and found myself on a corner where four composers had all lived simultaneously…I've discovered I also like the local markets in Europe and in cities like Seattle. They open early and I can squeeze it in before I walk. I might buy cool pieces of art, wall hangings, scarves, or soaps. I have bought a lot of olive-oil-based soaps in Paris."

Andrea Reese, Actress and Playwright, www.jackieoshow.com

New York actress Andrea Reese is a dead ringer for the late Jacqueline Onassis. So much so, that she wrote and stars in her own play based on Onassis' life, called *Cirque Jacqueline,* which she performs in various venues around the country.

To stay in shape on the road, Andrea does Tae Bo every morning for 45 minutes in her room, no matter where she is in the world. Before boarding planes, "I take 1,000 milligrams of Vitamin C. I'm vegetarian, so I pre-order the vegetarian meal and eat the nuts. I don't eat the whole desserts they give, except for the fruit. Sometimes I bring Clif bars and cashew nuts. I have a big appetite, so am always careful that I have enough food," she explains. For ultimate comfort, Andrea wears Allegria clogs and takes extra socks to stay warm.

Andrea has a great beauty secret that she found in the health-food store, which her hairstylist, who works on everyone at the *Good Morning America* TV show, now uses on everyone. "It's called Naturcolor. I have some gray in my hair, and found this Italian natural hair dye that is so incredible that my hairstylist/cutter now uses it with all her clients. It actually improved the health of my hair. I get it in New York at Fairway." (www.naturcolor.com; It has no ammonia and was created for people who are chemically sensitive.) On her hair, Andrea also swears by Pantene Pro-V Deep Fortifying Ultra-Fortifiant Rinse-Off Treatment. "My hair is so dry, and when I used this, it felt like a sponge was just sucking it in. After, my hair is completely shiny and soft." Her other fave product is Burt's Bees Marshmallow Cream (www.burtsbees.com).

"I love Morocco," Andrea told me. "That's where my mother worked for three years in the Peace Corps. I visited her on Air Maroc, which had amazing food and service. I don't like flying and I felt completely at ease. I visited Paris recently and had a wonderful time. I also love Italy and lived in Florence for six months."

She continued: "I'm known for being a bargain queen. In New York I shop at the thrift shops. I'm also a big eBay person – a lot of the costumes and props for *Cirque Jacqueline* came from eBay."

Well, it's almost time to check in. In the next chapter, you'll learn how to pack so you travel easy, breezy and beautiful.

..

CHAPTER ELEVEN
Leaders Of The Pack

I don't know about you – but I just can't seem to fit all my travel needs into one carry-on. I guess that's one of the drawbacks to being a gorgeous globetrotter – I want all my lotions, potions, notions and nostrums with me – as well as a winning wardrobe, great jewelry and sexy shoes. It's hard, now that most airlines are charging you $25 for each checked bag – that's skyway robbery. Come take the luggage tour with me, and discover some of the beautiful bags you'll covet, as well as packing tips galore, to make your travels easier. Yes, you can take it with you!

Pack Like A Travel Pro

How could the Three Wise Men have made their travel easier? They should have taken their cue from Robert Plath. Robert, a former pilot for Northwest Airlines who founded **Travelpro,** changed the physical orientation of luggage from horizontal to vertical, when he added wheels and an extension handle and thereby invented the Rollaboard®, an entirely new way to transport personal belongings while traveling. Fellow crew members saw Bob's invention and immediately wanted a rolling bag like that for themselves. From these humble beginnings, Bob founded Travelpro, and began providing Rollaboard luggage to airline flight crews and pilots across the country. The idea was so successful with the airlines that Travelpro launched the product commercially through retail outlets. Robert's invention forever changed the economics and ergonomics of travel, as more passengers opted to fly with only carry-on luggage. He sold his business in 1999, and semi-retired. Travelpro has continued to grow and expand to become one of the leading luggage brands and the choice of flight crews and frequent travelers worldwide.

Today, Travelpro offers the Walkabout Lite 3, offering the ultimate in value and versatility. The Walkabout Lite 3, which comes in black and forest-green fabric, features a honeycomb frame that is lighter yet stronger than frames found on traditional luggage.

This lightweight bag can be expanded on demand to gain up to 35% more packing capacity.

It's available in duffel bag, rolling tote, four Rollaboard suiters, two rolling duffels and rolling garment bag. The 22" Expandable Rollaboard Suiter is the most common carry-on size suitcase.

If any of the luggage looks vaguely familiar to you, that's because in the hit movie *Up In The Air,* George Clooney travels from city and city and lives out of his Travelpro luggage. Travelpro partnered with Paramount Pictures to supply the film's luggage needs (www.travelpro.com).

Award-Winning Landor & Hawa

With more than 40,000 products on display at the 2009 Travel Goods Show, competition was fierce for the Travel Goods Association's 2009 Product Innovation Awards. In the end, the winner had no trouble rising to the top – it's **Landor & Hawa's** ultra-light luggage line that's half the weight of typical luggage. This brand lays claim to the world's "lightest luggage" title, with the IT-0-1 Collection of featherweight wheeled luggage. The largest piece is a massive 30" tall rolling bag that weighs just over six pounds – whereas typical 20-22" carry-ons tip the scales at almost 14 pounds. "Packing light matters now more than ever, with airlines strictly enforcing overweight fees for checked bags," explains Michele Marini Pittenger, president of the Travel Goods Association. No doubt about it – a lightweight bag has serious sex appeal.

Ken White, Managing Director of Landor & Hawa, told me that Landor & Hawa, which has been in business in the UK since 1985, is the third-largest luggage company in Europe, and offers great value for affordable pricing. The IT-0-1 collection comes in red and black as well as a multi-circle print, has a Fiberglas structure, and is fully lined. The company also makes an EVA Frameless line of luggage with a 20-year-guarantee against airline damage. "We felt so confident in its ability to withstand repeated airline flights under all types of adverse conditions, that we made the decision to back it up with a guarantee against airline damage – and not just a standard five-year guarantee – but a bold 20-year guarantee." He added: "We were the first to introduce zippered expandable polycarbonate luggage in the USA – a plastic space-age material used in the insides of aircraft."

I'm in love with the purple and white polka dot "Shiny Dot" collection that includes a darling 14-inch vanity case. This is one time where I really do want to be left holding the bag (www.landor-hawa.us).

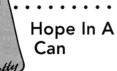

Hope In A Can

Does this ever happen to you? You purchase a new pair of crisp white shorts or slacks, or a lovely white-cotton blouse. Then you wear them once, whereupon, like a magnet, they immediately attract dirt and stains, and they're ruined. Here's what to do: Immediately after purchasing light-colored clothing, protect it with spray-on Scotchguard. It will add years of use to your garments, and keep them looking pristine, no matter where your travels take you. One can is an indispensable investment.

Gown Control from WallyBag

Worried about carrying your bridal gown or evening gown on the plane? You need **WallyBag's** Destination Bag Style 410 – the 66" Destination Bag. It features:

♦ The WallyLock that holds up to six garments with room for a wedding gown and tuxedo

♦ Broadened bottom for voluminous gowns

♦ Fully lined interior

♦ Pockets with room for shoes, accessories and other essentials

♦ Velcro closures for easy carrying

♦ Comfortable shoulder strap

♦ Padded roll bars to secure clothing and prevent wrinkles

♦ Side release buckles to hold the bag together when folded

It fits easily in overhead compartments and meets carry-on requirements for most airlines. If there are formal nights on your cruise, you want this bag. Don't miss the boat (www.wallybags.com).

Ghurka: Age-Old Craftsmanship

Seeking a large leather jewelry box for about $2,795? Or a $6,500 leather golf bag? Then look no further than **Ghurka,** who has refined the centuries-old craft of leather-making to where it is an art. The artistry of Ghurka begins with the most luxurious materials on earth, where the famously supple hand of the leather originates from the most desirable hides. Sourced at tanneries in Italy and Spain, these natural hides are scrupulously inspected to ensure that they're good enough to become Ghurka. Making the brand even more distinctive, old-school artisans and pattern-makers at the brand's factories worldwide cut and stitch, while distinctive Ghurka details are often rendered completely by hand. "It's one of the last brands hand-made in America, in Norwalk, Conn.," explains Colette Krahenbuhl, spokesperson. The quintessential bag – and the bestseller – is the Cavalier, a weekender bag available in three sizes; the smallest retails for $695. Every bag is stamped with the Ghurka crest, bag name, and a unique registration number, before being released for sale. Ghurka focuses on strategic partnerships, including the

Carry It Off, Beautifully

What's my No. 1 packing secret? I re-purpose plastic bags that are used to package sheets and pillowcases. I looooove these huge plastic bags with zippers. Do what I do: First, arrange and fold your items into the bags – use separate bags for sweaters, evening wear, underwear, etc. Second, put the bags into your suitcase. This has numerous advantages: If your luggage gets wet or something leaks, your garments are protected. You can simply pull out the bags and hide your luggage in the closet or under the bed. Many times, I simply put the bags on the floor of my hotel room, instead of wasting time packing things into drawers. Third, everything is all arranged for you – the bags act as clear plastic "drawers" and store your things tidily and neat, instead of them being scattered in a suitcase. And you're reusing and recycling all that plastic! If you prefer something more high-tech, try Travel Storage Bags that are airtight and watertight. The green plastic bags are damp-proof, dust- and insect-proof, and have a wide opening. A real space-saver! (www.vacuum-storage-bags.com)

sponsorship of the luxurious Concours d'Elegance in Pebble Beach, Calif., as well as support of community charitable efforts such as the Joslin Diabetes Center Annual Gala. Ghurka is strictly a cult brand for those in-the-know, and is esteemed by many A-list celebrities. You can find it in the Ghurka Boutique at the Plaza Hotel in New York and at specialty retailers worldwide. No doubt about it – these are sophisticated, stylish goods for discerning customers who demand craftsmanship and quality.

Hey, Take A Look At Heys Luggage

The **Heys** brand was born in 1986, three years before the invention of upright rolling luggage. Since then, Heys USA has concentrated on its niche market

Princess Diana's Luggage Of Choice

I just couldn't write a book about being a gorgeous globetrotter, without mentioning luggage with the same name! (They just spell their brand a bit differently.) The **Globe-Trotter** line of luggage was founded in Saxony, Germany in 1897 by an Englishman, and the company has since been termed "the quintessential British suitcase." Just how British is it? Well, many members of the Royal Family love this luggage line; HRH Queen Elizabeth chose it for her honeymoon luggage, as did the late Princess Diana. Sir Winston Churchill always used the 18-inch suitcase, and Sir Edmund Hilary took his Globe-Trotter up to the first base camp during his conquest of Mt. Everest in 1951. Globe-Trotter suitcases and trunks were also widely used on the great steam liners including the *Titanic.* Nowadays, other iconic names favor this British brand, including Sofia Coppola, Kate Moss, Dita von Teese and Bjork. The company is famous for its Vulcanized Fibreboard, which is used to make the luggage, along with leather trimmings, and everything is handmade. In fact, many of the craftspeople who handmake the luggage in Hertfordshire have been with the company for more than 40 years. You can find styles in the original dark blue, black or brown, although there are more modern versions in ivory, red, green and burnt orange. Baby, it's hue! (www.globe-trotterltd.com)

of fashionable hard-sided travel goods – all the while focusing on innovative manufacturing methods to make the most durable and lightest weight product for the traveling consumer. In fact, the company bills itself as offering "the world's lightest carry-on," which weighs in at just 5.1 pounds – the xCase. Every fashion color it makes is popular with women – zebra and leopard are the most popular exotic prints; polka dots are the most popular pattern; red, yellow and green are the best-selling fashion colors; and silver is the best basic color. In 2009 Heys USA introduced the Britto Collection, designed with art by the celebrity Brazilian artist Romero Britto, a pop culture artist. His vibrant images appear on Heys' four-piece Britto Collection luggage sets that include 20-inch, 24-inch and 28-inch upright hard-sizes, plus a beauty case (needed by every gorgeous globetrotter). In 2010 Heys introduced two more companion pieces to the collection: a computer case and a business case/overnighter.

If you're still not convinced this is a great brand of luggage – take a look at some of the accolades Heys USA has received. Heys is the recipient of the 2009 Product Innovation Award by the Travel Goods Association, and its EcoCase was named by *O, The Oprah Magazine* as a favorite of Oprah and her team. Headquartered in Miami, Heys also operates a Fifth Avenue showroom in New York (www.heysusa.com).

Hartmann Has A Good History

I had a **Hartmann** Wings Luggage bag for more than 20 years. It was a tote bag; the folks at Hartmann had sent me one when I was an Editor at *Robb Report*, and believe me, I was thrilled to receive it. It was the greatest bag – it stored everything, including my lunch and my laptop, and easily fit under my seat on an airplane. After 20 years of constant use, however, it started to go, understandably, but it was great while it lasted.

Hartmann is a great line of luggage, and they still make the Wings brand, and nowadays Wings even comes in a sassy stripe. "We go back 140 years – we made field trunks for the military in World War II," says Frank Johnston, Chief Operating Officer. The company's bestseller is the "Intensity Collection," made with a coffee-color ballistic nylon. However, for my money – and yours – check out Moulin Rouge – a black-and-red mock croc collection that offers a gorgeous

It's Clear

Use the hotel's clear shower cap to wrap up your dirty shoes, to prevent them from soiling your clothing in your suitcase.

array of styles. Women will also love the Reserve Collection that is made from North American native steer hides – it's the epitome of elegance. Don't forget – there's also a beautiful line of leather totes made of belting leather, with names such as the "Palm Beach" (quilted) (www.hartmann.com).

eBags Makes It E-Z

What's the most bestselling type of luggage right now? It's the wheeled duffel bag, says Peter Cobb, Co-founder and Senior Vice President of **eBags,** www.ebags.com. "A wheeled duffel is lightweight, and great for car or air travel," Peter says. "They are our Number One luggage category."

eBags is a place where you can find 500 brands of luggage, and more than 40,000 bags plus almost 2 Million customer reviews. "Our private-label brand is a bestseller, and comes in five colors," he added. He also gives a thumbs-up to Victorinox luggage. "They are a phenomenal brand for us, especially the model with a single pull-up handle that's expandable. They have a great wheel system." Another big trend in luggage he has noticed is the colorful hardsides by Titan and Heys. "There are more fun colors out there….but lightweight luggage is the overarching trend right now."

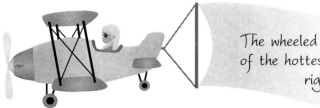

The wheeled duffel bag is one of the hottest luggage trends right now.

Flying High And Healthy

Phoenix Sky Harbor is America's healthiest airport, according to **Health Magazine.** The magazine recently ranked 10 airports, and sought amenities and services to promote healthy living and lower passenger stress. The criteria included food, relaxation zones, walking paths, music, lighting, environmental programs and safety technology. Phoenix Sky Harbor was cited for its "healthful" restaurants, video-paging system that lists and announces names, two pet parks and clean bathrooms. It's also known as "America's Friendliest Airport," thanks to its **FLY** or Friendly Let me help You program. This customer service and incentive program recognizes and rewards employees who exceed expectations and make a positive impact on the customer experience at Phoenix Sky Harbor. More than 300 employees have been recognized for demonstrating a FLY attitude, including an airline employee who helped find the owner of a lost wallet; a cab driver who helped to find a customer's lost wallet; and a city employee who assisted a woman in securing a flight and overnight lodging after her flight was cancelled. At this airport, customer service is second only to security. It even offers free fear-of-flying classes, taught by a local airline pilot with a master's degree in counseling (www.phxskyharbor.com).

Other airports on the **Health Magazine** list, in order, and the amenities cited by the rankings are:

Baltimore/Washington (a spa, and a hiking path near the airport)

Chicago O'Hare (healthy restaurant food, and the fitness facility in its on-site Hilton Hotel)

Detroit Metropolitan (healthy restaurant food)

Denver (solar energy panels, an art collection, free Wi-Fi, and healthy restaurant food)

Washington National (an art collection, a walking-and-biking trail)

Dallas/Fort Worth (healthy restaurant food)

Boston Logan (environmental initiatives)

Portland (a paved bicycle-and-walking path, covered bicycle parking)

Philadelphia (a health clinic, free Wi-Fi)

Flight 001 Makes A World Of Difference

John Sencion and Brad John were traveling for business on Air France to Paris, talking about the routine that they always went through, prior to every trip. "We'd talk about going to Duane Read for toiletries, then Barnes and Noble for a map guide or language book, then the Innovation Luggage store for a bag or luggage. We thought, 'Wouldn't it be great if it was all under one roof?'" That was the idea when John and Brad co-founded Flight 001 (pronounced Flight One), which opened in 1999. Today there are six Flight 001 stores, including one in Sydney, Australia, bringing you every travel item imaginable: organizers, passport holders, all kinds of great books, chargers and flash drives, pillows, amenity kits, luggage – and that's just the tip of the travel iceberg.

"We have paper soaps, paper shampoos, a large selection of Mario Badescu, solar chargers for your gadgets, cameras, guidebooks, luggage, travel board games – everything in our store is portable, and everything is travel-sized," says John. Bestsellers include its proprietary SpacePak system that offers maximum space and organization in your luggage – "it lets you pancake-stack your clothing," he says – as well as a Seat Pak with a loop, which you hang from your airline seat tray. There are eye masks and amenity kits galore, and if you really want one – airplane food carts. (With hope, you'll forego the airline food and whip up something really delicious.) This is anything but a fly-by-night operation. And it makes your shopping as streamlined as aircraft itself (www.flight001.com).

JetCart – The Bag That's A Seat

It's luggage. It's a chair. Actually it's both! The **JetCart** from Walkin' Bag makes for one heck of a happy traveler. Just imagine - - instead of standing in line at airport checkout for what seems like hours, you can actually sit down – on your luggage. CEO Etsuo Miyoshi, a polio survivor and busy businessman, invented Walkin' Bag with a personal need in mind. "As a polio survivor, I dreamed of having a bag I could 'lean on.' So I invented Walkin' Bag." With its patented curved handle it provides "lean on" support up to 250 pounds. As an added feature it also comes with a chair – to use it, just lift up the flip seat on the outside frame of the luggage, and set the seat into place. It will hold up to 300 pounds. And wonder of wonders, it's also carry-on compliant and will fit easily under most airline seats. Smart! (www.walkinbag.com)

Victorinox: The Sign Of The Cross

Switzerland is known for its chocolate, punctuality and precision, and of course, the iconic Swiss Army Knife, whose parent company is the same as **Victorinox** Luggage. Jason Morris, vice president of product strategy, told me that one major attribute that sets Victorinox luggage apart is its cross and shield, which offers great brand recognition. "It's one of the core attributes that makes us so good, along with our function, quality, and innovation." The company offers a range of styles, including the bestselling Werks Collection. "It's one of our lightest and has a curved rotating handle." It comes in black, red, emerald green and sapphire blue, but exclusive palettes in the colors of apple green, cayenne and cappuccino have sold at Macy's and Bloomingdale's. The 22-inch carry-on is also the bestselling case. At this writing, Victorinox is re-releasing its most premium collection, Tourbach; what's especially great about it is that this line comes with a FREE warranty program called Carry With Confidence Plus – if something happens to it, Victorinox will offer you an immediate replacement in an expedited manner – "even if you're

Load Up Your Louis Vuittons

What goes through my mind when I see a traveler toting a piece of Louis Vuitton luggage? Well, I think that person has inimitable style – and deep pockets. (A Pegase suitcase can cost almost $4,000.) No wonder it seems to be the celebrity style of choice. Now, LV offers a "Mon Monogram" service, so that Your Own Personal Monogram is actually painted onto the canvas, and then coated so that it never flakes off, and your unique piece of luggage is properly identified. After all, would a Hollywood A-lister really be caught with a Big Tag? (www.louisvuitton.com)

What Electronic Attachment Do I Take to Denmark or New Zealand?

Now there's an easy answer to that question. Just log onto www.Belle-hop.com, a great travel site specializing in travel accessories just for women. Here, you'll learn everything you need to know from the World Electricity Chart, which showcases a wealth of adapters in Standard, Universal and Grounded. You want to use your blow-dryer or your flat iron, don't you? It will also tell you everything you've ever wanted to know about using an appliance abroad. Belle-hop also carries homeopathic No Jet Lag, neck pillows, luggage tags, combination locks, and oodles more stuff, and its sister site, www.lewisnclark. com, for men, even carries GoToob plastic travel bottles that are designed for human hands.

Thank You, Samsonite!

What can you say about a beautiful 35-year-old bag that has never died? For more than three decades, I have proudly carried my Samsonite beauty case everywhere. It was a high-school graduation gift from my aunt (to whom I am eternally grateful). Knowing that she wanted to buy me something I craved, I hand-picked the bag at the best luggage store in Milford, Conn., back in 1973. Little did I know that this oversized (10" x 13" x 8") beige number, with red-, white- and blue-piping, would be my best friend and travel companion for more than a quarter-century. It cost $40 – a huge amount of money at the time. My aunt had no idea of the incredibly valuable gift she offered me – in more ways than one. Being a self-proclaimed cosmetics queen (who was even born on *Avon* Street), I loved putting all my lotions, potions, notions and nostrums into one cute little carry-on, which seemed like a pretty novel idea back then. I kept it in my Boston apartment's bathroom, packed at all times. (It also functioned as an extra drawer for all my gear-to-make-me-gorgeous. What can I tell you? I'm high maintenance.)

I used it frequently in college and graduate school, and then constantly when I was an editor at **Robb Report – "The Millionaire's Magazine."** This "little-bag-that-could" (which made an excellent footrest, by the way) made countless trips to Africa, the Caribbean, France, Greece, all the Hawaiian islands, Monaco, Switzerland, Tahiti, and throughout the United States. I'll never forget the look on my Polish cousin's face, when I arrived in Krakow and she realized that I owned such an adorable little accessory just for – gasp! – *cosmetics.* She asked incredulously, *'Kosmetyka waliska?'* "Oh yes!" I exclaimed. We both laughed hysterically at that one, and instantly bonded.

My little Samsonite's durability has amazed me even more. The crime – and pun-ishment – it has endured! It's caked with grime, the mirror is missing, and its blue silk lining is stained from years of spills. A few exterior seams ripped in Bora Bora 10 years ago, but a few drops of glue fixed that. After I realized that its days were really numbered, I started shopping around. Few could live up to the test of Little Miss Samsonite – let's face it, I also used my versatile valise as a portable chair, when desperate. However, then I discovered an apple-green Delsey doppelganger, and had to have it, even though it was smaller. I couldn't resist! I love my Delsey and its color-coordinated Big Tag nametag – yet I still couldn't say "sayonara" to my Samsonite. It sits proudly in my walk-in-closet –a pleasant reminder of my many past bon voyages. Now, with the TSA ban on any liquids over three ounces in a carry-on, and expensive luggage fees, I've had to completely give up carrying *any* beauty case whatsoever. Yet I'm grateful to these cute little cases, and the many years of happy travels that they've given me. Like old friends, we shared many, many good times!

Take The "Lug" Out Of Luggage

Pay for checked luggage? That's a pain we know all too well. That's why before any trip, I visit the free website www.LuggageLimits.com, which features baggage info for more than 125 airlines. However, you may opt to simply ship your bags beforehand – and that's where Luggage Forward comes in, for travelers seeking the utmost in convenience, reliability and predictability. Luggage Forward guarantees delivery of baggage from doorstep to destination, with its worldwide network of shipping partners. An agent will pick up your bags at home and send them on their way, no special packaging required. Rates start as low as $60. It's the smart alternative to checking and carrying bags – and breezing through security (www.luggageforward.com).

in Timbuktu," says Jason. Other Victorinox collections also come with a warranty for free repairs, no matter what. That's confidence that you can carry with you everywhere (www.swissarmy.com).

Samsonite: A Brand On The Move

When Jesse Shwayder founded **Samsonite** in 1910, early travel was once reserved for only an exclusive few – those people who had the means to see the world. Given this exclusiveness, travel was a high-quality experience from the transportation, to the attention to service, to even the accessories used to carry one's belongings. Samsonite is one of the original brands in travel, and continues to leverage its craftsmanship and heritage as an innovator. The bestseller is the Silhouette collection that comes in softside as well as a hardside, although you might also like the F'lite that comes in red, sky blue and black. The brand also employs six quality tests to make sure that each piece of luggage passes muster – these are the tests for tumbling, handling, dropping, wheeling, zippering, and locking. Enjoy the journey! (www.samsonite.com)

Tumi – At The Top

Tumi, which is known for its scores of very, very satisfied and loyal customers, is one of the leading international brands

Get In The Slim

How to stay svelte – and still look good in your travels, even if you've indulged? One of my favorite ways to look whittled down is to pack clothing from the **Newport News** catalog, which carries an astonishing array of shapewear called Shape fx ("effects"). Each item in the Shape fx line has a panel to hold you in and prevent unwanted jiggle. For example, my current catalog offers "The 10 lbs. Smaller" Velvet Tux suit, with a bandless high waist to visually slim your waist; a built-in power mesh panty to control your tummy and hips; and a boot cut to balance your hips and rear end. And it's so affordably priced, I want to shout it from the rooftops! There are pants, dresses, skirts, tops, swimsuits – all with strategic seams to shape and slenderize you. You'll also love the easy-to-fit swimsuits with BYOB "Build Your Own Bikini" separates (www.newportnews.com). And of course, what would we do without **Spanx** – the body-conscious line that is loved by Hollywood A-listers and celebrities? You'll find gorgeous swimsuits, body shapers, hosiery shapers, "Bra-llelujah" bras, and even "haute contour" high-fashion undergarments (www.spanx.com). The other catalog I like to order from is **Boston Proper,** which even publishes a special, dedicated Travel catalog of clothing once a year. You'll find beautiful sportswear, dresses, bathing suits, and much more, all affordably priced, and sleek and chic at that. One offering you may want to try: the "Not Your Daughter's Jeans" with special "tummy tuck" styling if you have real curves. Each pair will take 10 years off your life – and 10 pounds off your body! To paraphrase Rod Stewart, you'll wear it well (www.bostonproper.com). As a sidenote, please, please, *please* don't ever wear nude or beige stockings, and especially with sandals. It's unspeakably un-chic! Instead, please show off your bare sexy legs, and use self-tanner if you must!

Zoe Saldana Checks In

"My travel must-have is a cute bag. I always carry my laptop, so I need a bag where I can dump everything and it will look beautiful," says Zoe Saldana, who carries a Tod's bag. She also swears by Cetaphil facial cleanser, saying "because I travel so much and am in different climates, I keep it simple with Cetaphil, which I have been using for years."

People Magazine, Feb. 1, 2010

Belly Up To The Bar

You'll not only belly up to the bar – but you'll cover your entire body – in any of the superlative scented soaps from Magic Senses. Here's where I get on my soapbox – to tell you there's no reason to suffer with tiny hotel soaps, or even a plain old white soap. Magic Senses, a family-owned business, offers an irresistible array of beautiful handmade glycerine soaps that you can pack in your bags – so you can scent your entire suitcase just like you scent your drawers. Take the Orange Clove, for example – and please do. This smells just like a pomander ball (or Agraria potpourri) and is unique to the market. Other fragrances include luscious watermelon, lovely lime cooler, glorious gardenia – as well as plumeria, mango papaya, raspberry, green apple, grapefruit and so many more. These beautiful soaps definitely raise the bar on getting clean (www.magicsenses.com).

of premium travel, business and lifestyle accessories. Since its founding in 1975, Tumi's commitment to design excellence, functional superiority and technical innovation has made it the brand of choice for the world's most discerning and demanding travelers. What made it famous? Its ballistic tri-fold garment bag. Today, Tumi holds some 25 patents, and is known for technical innovation, excellence in design and unparalleled quality. The bestseller is the 20-inch wheeled carry-on (style 22021) (www.tumi.com).

Whether you're embarking on your first trip to the City of Light – or you've lost count – make sure to check out the bargain-shopping secrets in France, and the inimitable Guide To Paris Shopping, in Chapter Twelve.

CHAPTER TWELVE
SPECIAL BONUS SECTION:

Bargain-Shopping Secrets In France

Say "Bonjour" to French Bargains!

A budget-friendly guide to France? *Mais oui!* France is filled with oceans of opportunities to make the most of your Euros – everything from affordable prix-fixe menus to discount Metro passes and even free museum visits. With some savvy planning, travelers can indulge their dreams without paying through the *nez*.

If you like to shop – you're in luck. Surprise! The entire country is packed with retail outlets, bargain-shopping streets, value-packed stores, resale shops and flea markets offering more cachet for less cash. You'll find French foods, housewares, accessories, books, cosmetics, clothing and more, for a *chanson*. (Cue the cancan music!)

What's the secret? Travelers simply have to know where to look. Before you go, check with your hotel concierge to get the most up-to-date info on hours and directions.

But before you read on, let me say this. Much of this chapter was made possible by the incredible concierges at The Four Seasons George V in Paris. On one of my last trips to Paris, we stayed at this amazing property (in the Presidential Suite, no less), and I had drawn up a list of "bargain spots" I wished to visit. I gave the list to one of the concierges, hoping to get directions, addresses, telephone numbers and nearby Metro stops, so I could do the shopping tour all by myself. And voila! He happily obliged. As a result I had a fabulous, successful shopping experience. So, I doff my *chapeau* to these penultimate professionals, who deserve their prized membership in the Clef's d'Or (golden key society). The great thing about it, they are there to serve YOU in this capacity as well. That's what a concierge is for!

More In Store

I swear by **Monoprix** (www.monoprix.fr), a Target-type dimestore chain, for fabulous cheap chic. I've spent many a Euro on watches, lingerie, clothing, accessories, jewelry, and groceries at Monoprix, especially at the store on the Champs Elysses. I always stock up on Bourjois makeup, which is made in the same factory as Chanel – but is much less expensive. (Sometimes it's even on sale at Monoprix.) **Tati** stores (www.tati.fr) resemble a huge indoor yard sale where you'll find lingerie, makeup, clothing and much more, for much less. (It was indispensable on one trip to Paris, when my luggage was lost for a week.) They even have specialty stores selling wedding gowns and jewelry. The entire **Rue St. Placide** is chock-a-block with bargains on shoes and clothing; around the corner, **Chaussures Edouard** at 146, bis Rue de Rennes, has charming Chanel-knockoff flat shoes in a rainbow of *femme-fatale* colors. Fabrics for decorating? The entire **Rue de Rivoli** boasts numerous souvenir shops selling embroidered Aubusson-like goods and fabrics for decorations, pillows, and tablecloths. I also recommend **museum shops**; at the **Hotel National des Invalides** (Napoleon's tomb), in addition to art reproductions, I purchased adorable $20 pillows decorated with fleur-de-lis and, for $10, Marie Antoinette's favorite music on CD. (All national museums, such as the Louvre, Musee d'Orsay and the Rodin, even offer free admission the first Sunday of every month.) Or, purchase a Paris Museum Pass for two, four or six consecutive days, and you'll have FREE access while visiting more than 60 museums and monuments (www.parismuseumpass.com).

Regularly scheduled street markets offer produce, locally made delicacies, flowers, and all types of indigenous products. On Sundays, for example, food-and-cooking cognoscenti head to **Rue Cler** in the 7th arrondissement or **Rue de Buci** in the 6th, for the vast array of gourmet goodies. I get a *coup de coeur* (thunderbolt to my heart) every time I visit the **Cours Saleya** market in Nice, where fruits and vegetables are artfully displayed like Cartier jewelry. Nothing beats the bargain-basement prices I've paid on everything from lemon soaps from Menton, Provencal herbs and olive oils, and anise and violet *pastilles* from the Flavigny Abbey. (***The Riviera Times*** lists information about the local markets in 45 towns in the Alpes-Maritimes, Var region and Monaco; visit www.rivieratimes.com).

Need a fashion fix? ***Depot-vente* resale shops,** especially in Paris' 16th arrondissement, provide huge hunting grounds. At **Maison de Fanfan** at 4, Rue Mayet, I found mint-condition, First Class clothing brands at coach prices. Hermes, Chanel, Louis Vuitton, Prada – hey, the gang's all here.

Paris' famous covered passageways can also be a mecca for markdowns. Built in 1823, Vivienne Gallery, with its impressive archways and indoor topiary, is a charming arcade with shops selling old books, cartographers, and tearooms. Others to note: the passages Choiseul, and Grand Cerf, with their beautiful 19th-century skylight windows.

I've even discovered discount deals on scarves, belts and wallets in some of the underground shops within the Metro stations.

The Nose Knows

When in Paris, by all means stop by the chic boutiques housing Frederic Malle perfumes, called "Editions de Parfums Frederic Malle." Frederic Malle is the grandson of Serge Heftler – the founder of Dior Perfumes. After many years as a consultant to some of the best French and international perfume companies, Frederic was determined to create fragrances truly worthy of luxury status. So what did he do? He approached the very best "noses" in the business, who agreed to put their names on what have become some of the finest creations you'll find anywhere. These fragrances are sought-after by those in-the-know, and have something of a cult status. There are three boutique locations in Paris: 37 Rue de Grenelle; 140 Avenue Victor Hugo; and 21 Rue du Mont Thabor. (There is also a boutique on 898 Madison Avenue in New York, and the scents are also sold at Liberty in London, at Isetan in Tokyo, and at Tsum in Moscow.) The fragrance I love most is En Passant by Olivia Giacobetti, which captures white lilac, a scent that you rarely find in a perfume. It's light, delicate and delicious. Another you must try, if you love violets, is Lipstick Rose by Ralf Schwieger, who says he likes to compose out-of-the-ordinary fragrances. This is yet another of those scents, with a beautiful bouquet, which you just won't find anywhere else. In all there are 18 distinctive scents that you've been waiting for (www.editionsdeparfums.com).

Irresistible Advice

To bag more bargains, head to **flea markets**. At the **Marche aux Puces de St.-Ouen-Clignancourt** – the *mere* of all flea markets – I have scored stunning $5 glassware and $40 Limoges miniatures – exciting *bling* without the *ka-ching*! At the **Marche aux Puces de la Porte de Vanves**, I purchased a $30 copy of a 16th-century lithograph depicting Greek mythology, and came *this close* to buying a $200 miniature jewelry box shaped like an antique *chaise porter*. Shoehorn it all into your schedule with a discounted Metro pass, available in many denominations.

Savvy shoppers should also know: major sales (*les soldes*) are regulated by the French government and are held twice a year, in mid-June and in mid-January.

If you live outside the European Union, and make purchases totaling at least $215 (175E) in one day, in one department store, you qualify to receive the Value-Added-Tax (VAT) deduction. All goods in France carry a 19.6% value-added-tax, but you can get a *detaxe* refund of at least 13%. All department stores throughout Paris have VAT offices where you can process the appropriate forms; bring your passport and safeguard your receipts.

To qualify for the detaxe, you must meet the following requirements.

- ◆   You have to be at least 15 years old.

- ◆   You can't live in the European Union (EU).

- ◆   You have to be visiting the EU for less than 6 months.

If you spend the appropriate amount in the same store on the same day, on merchandise where the tax was charged, those purchases are eligible for the detaxe refund. By all means, go to Galeries Lafayette or Printemps and shop smart!

Any items you are claiming on your refund forms must be unwrapped, and in your carry-on luggage. Get the documents stamped before you leave France. *C'est tout!*

Making Their Marques

Brand names for less? *C'est incroyable* – but you'd better believe it. France offers a wealth of retail outlets where bargain-hunters can get their fill of all-things-French. Intrepid shoppers will feel a flurry of delight at the depth and breadth of bargains. There are so many patrician brands, at plebian prices, that I consider French outlets the eighth wonder of the world.

La Vallee Village, just 40 minutes east of Paris by TGV train, offers reduced prices of at least 33% on prestige-brand men's and women's fashions, shoes, accessories, lingerie, beauty, jewelry and home design. The brands you know and love – Agnes B, Celine, Charles Jourdan, Faconnable, Givenchy – they're all here. With so many selections, you can have your *gateau* and eat it too. (Other "villages" are in Munich, Dublin, Brussels, Frankfurt, London, Milan, Barcelona and Madrid.) (www.lavalleevillage.com)

For more fabulous finds, France's **Marques Avenue** outlet malls showcase hundreds of brands, from Alain Manoukian to Zapa – and everything in between – including Hugo Boss and Yves St. Laurent. In **Troyes**, 120 Marques Avenue shops offer at least 30% off original prices. Other Marques Avenues outlets are located in **Paris** at Ile St. Denis; in **Romans**, in the Rhone-Alpes; and at the **Cote d'Opale**. At Marques Avenue **La Seguiniere** stores offer even more discount designer deals. If you want First Class at coach prices – Marques Avenue is just the ticket (www.marquesavenue.com).

The **McArthur Glen Center in Troyes,** the charming capital of the Champagne region, has more than 80 factory outlet stores selling 200 luxury brands such as Armani, Courreges and Wolford, for low dough (www.mcarthurglen.com).

Craving crystal? Head to **Lorraine**, where outlets sell slashed-price Daum and St. Louis. China? Make a price-cutting pilgrimage to the Limousin capital city of **Limoges**, for outlets discounting Limoges, Bernardaud and Haviland porcelain. If you're seeking your sole-mate – look no further than **Romans**, the capital of the shoe industry, where cobblers have bent over their workbenches for generations. In the Old Town, you'll find numerous shoe outlets within a network of picturesque alleys winding around the St. Bernard Monastery; Charles Jourdan, Stephane Kelian and Robert Clergerie, at rock-bottom prices, are always a step in the right direction.

If that whets your appetite, remember: the best way to save money on French restaurants is to order a fixed-priced-menu and indulge at lunch, when prices are lower than dinner. France, with its cornucopia of cheeses, wines, and baguettes, also naturally lends itself to inexpensive picnics, even in your hotel room.

Discovering a dynamite deal is a rush and – like most French things – even kind of sexy. Just remember what a handsome Frenchman once told me. "Where is a woman's G-spot?" he joked. "It's right there – as the last letter in 'shopping.'"

More Vive La France Shopping!

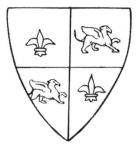

New York attorney Ruthann Niosi was kind enough to share with me some of her secrets of Paris shopping. Take a look at what Ruthann has been doing for years. Here is what she told me. "I had an apartment in Paris and this is my treasure-trove of years of going local with a 21- and a 22-year-old daughter.

"Take a map and draw with a marker a large "V," using rue de Babylone turning into rue Sevres as one side, and Boulevard Saint-Germain as the other. That will be your "V" that you'll walk.

"I always suggest starting out at **Bon Marche, 24, Rue de Sevres** (www.lebonmarche.com) and working from there. Bon Marche has the best shoe department, and Princess TamTam lingerie that is difficult to find elsewhere. If you fly into Paris and are short on time and want to shop for yourself or buy gifts, go straight to the second floor and work your way through all of the labels.

"Of course, Bon Marche is connected to the **Grand Epicerie**. I used to go grocery shopping there when I had my apartment on Rue de Babylone, but even after we no longer had the apartment, my daughter and I make it a point to go there for one evening's meal and eat in the hotel, picnic style. It is unequaled anywhere in the world, and if you are a foodie, a chef or a gourmand you will enjoy it immensely. Don't forget to weigh and price your vegetables and fruit *before* you go to the register to pay.

Stores Along the "V" include the following, says Ruthann:

Brand Bazar: 33 Rue de Sevres (www.brandbazar.fr). This store, which caters to teens, is always jam-packed with clothes. It makes a really nice visit even if you only walk away with one item because you'll feel as if you have seen a ton of clothes in the process.

Bel Air: Inexpensive chic clothes, non-US labels, 33 Rue du Four (in the 6th arrondissement). (The City of Paris is divided into 20 arrondissements, or districts.)

La Vaissellerie: 85 Rue de Rennes (www.lavaissellerie.fr). For the best kitchen little gizmos and dining things, all in bins that you will love to pick over. I never miss this stop.

Allison & Sasha: 44 Rue du Dragon 75006 (www.allisonetsasha.com). This little shop is on the left side of the street, just off of Rue de Rennes. It specializes in cotton knit dresses priced at about 42 Euros. A great place for gifts, or inexpensive dressing. The dresses go beyond being a "T-shirt dress" and are really very nice.

et vous: 69 Rue de Rennes. I will always poke my head into this store. While they are not inexpensive, they always have that little thing, whether it be a little dress or different piece of costume jewelry, which is priced very nicely and which you have not seen elsewhere. I always buy my "20-something" daughters something from this store. (*Fodors* said that "it takes its cue from the catwalk.")

Djul: 83 Rue des Saints-Peres 75006 is a wonderful costume jewelry store. Tiny, and a jewel of a find.

The BEST almond croissants in the world are in Paris at **Claude Binet Boulanger-Patissier-Chocolatier** 44 Rue de Babylone-75007 Paris. It's located on a wonderful little side street near Bon Marche where they serve giant coffees and warm soft croissants. You can sit inside at tiny crowded tables and watch the world go by. A very local place. I've never seen a tourist there. They changed owners once and stayed the same. At lunchtime the little local kids come running in to buy the long baguettes with thin slices of meats for their lunches. It makes you smile to sit there, even if you are traveling alone.

Further down the street is the finest place in Europe (second only to Corso Venezia in Italy) to have stationery made. It is called **Imprimerie Grife,** 24 Rue de Babylone. While they don't speak English they know enough about what they are doing to make sure everything is understood, and in the end they will not print anything until they email you proofs. I've placed my order there (including a wonderful oversized European business card) and they have shipped to New York for a tiny handling price.

It goes without saying that once you are done with walking the "V" you must eat at **Les Deux Magots,** 6 Place Saint Germain des Pres – 75006 Paris (www.

lesdeuxmagots.fr). Dining on their special chicken salad with curry sauce and a glass of chardonnay, while sitting inside the front glass porch in the rain in the evening, will make you feel totally Parisian. Remember, the tables are probably only 18 inches around, and you sit side by side. Eating inside is a totally different experience, in that it is more of a restaurant vs. a bistro – nothing I've ever been inclined to try.

You should always be aware that in Paris the taxis are at stands, or you can call one, or a hotel will get you one. But in an emergency, you should be aware that there is an airport **transport run by Air France** (even if you are not flying with them) and there are pick-ups about every 30 minutes at Place d'Invalides, Ave. de Triomphe and Montparnasse. The fare is about 8 Euros one way.

If you are in Paris on Sunday then you must go to the section called the Marais, as it will be the only place to shop and on Sundays it is THE place to shop. Go to **mi-va-mi,** 23 Rue des Rosiers-75004 Paris for lunch. No, it is not a dive, and yes, climb the stairs up and up and up to the top. There is waiter service at the tables and photos that tell you what you are ordering. You will probably see someone you know.

Stores in the Marais:

Maje Boutique: 9 Rue des Blancs Manteaux. They have beautiful silk day dresses that women in their 20's love.

Repetto/Pointe Shoe: Shoe store, 22 Rue de la Paix. A must-have for those "real" ballet slipper shoes, which also come with kitten heels.

Hair: Alexandre Zouari: 1 Avenue du President Wilson 75116. Cut, color, makeup, manicure, pedicure – the French way. Not a cookie-cutter place, and no tourists. A real find as it is predominately filled with very chic Parisian regulars. Cheaper than Manhattan.

Of course you have to go to **Laduree** to eat (several locations in Paris) (www.laduree.fr). Lunch and dinner is really nice for men and women; the dinner menu is quite extensive and the food delicious, and of course the long display case of every color of macaroon cannot be beat. (They once chased me out of the macaroon side for trying to take a photo of a wonderful pastry they had – so be warned, no camera allowed.). But Laduree at 16 Rue Royale 75008 Paris is where you want to go just with fellow females for lunch or tea or a sweet. It is too tiny for men and the ambiance is more for women.

Consignment/Vintage/Boutiques Known Only To French Women:

Gabrielle Geppert: Jardins du Palais Royal, 31-34 Galerie Montpensier 75001 Paris. Keep walking, it is in the gallery of tiny stores to your left, hidden. They do not want tourists to know they are there. If you want a designer anything, from any year, it will be there. It is tiny, jammed with clothes, bags, shoes, jewelry. They do not like excessive touching and the prices are inside so you have to ask. And they do not like a lot of questions. Only go if you are a serious shopper, not for sightseeing.

Scarlett Haute Couture: 10 Rue Clement Marot. And yes, they do have Hermes Birkin bags. Only real items. Don't even suggest otherwise.

84 Eighty Four Paris: 84 Rue du Faubourg Saint Honore 75008. This is the hidden shoe store that every woman wants to know about. Christian Louboutin for 100 Euros. Hit or miss, but usually something."

Merci, Ruthann!

For more information on traveling to France, visit the French Government Tourist Office's website, www.franceguide.com.

Now, what to do with all of those shopping bags? Take your cue from a good friend of mine, who had spent an entire year in Italy as an exchange student while in college – she shopped **every** day. After making her purchases, they were toted to her Italian home, in beautiful designer (paper) shopping bags from the best stores. My friend returned to the States and used these bags to decorate her Boston apartment. In one of her long hallways, she meticulously measured and hung seven different shopping bags, all in a long row, where she could enjoy them every day. That's a great way to showcase your beautiful sou-venirs – and one of the best (and cheapest!) ways for a gorgeous globetrotter to remember her travels.

Author Bio

Debbi Karpowicz Kickham is a former Editor of **Robb Report Magazine** – "The Millionaire's Magazine" (www. robbreport.com) and a current and veteran member of the Society of American Travel Writers, (www.satw.org). A professional travel journalist for more than 25 years, Debbi has criss-crossed the globe, writing travel articles for a wealth of magazines and newspapers that include **The New York Times, The Boston Globe, The Los Angeles Times, Glamour, Cigar Aficionado, InStyle Weddings, Bridal Guide** (Contributing Editor to the Travel Section), **Bellaonline**

(Hawaii and Spas Editor), *For The Bride, Destination I Do, Caviar Affair, WellesleyWeston, US Airways, Continental, Gatehouse Media, Porthole, Simply The Best, First for Women* – including custom-published magazines for ITT Sheraton and the Ritz-Carlton. She was also the "Passionate Collector" columnist for the custom-published magazine, *Sotheby's Domain.* Interestingly, she also spent two years as an amateur stand-up comedian, doing "open-mike" nights in the evening while she was an advertising copywriter by day.

Debbi says that her career began in 8th grade at St. Ann's School in Devon, Conn., when she entered her school's oratorical contest. First you had to write a speech, then become a finalist, and finally, present the speech, on stage, to the entire school. On the day that she learned about the contest, Debbi decided then and there that she would was going to win – and she did! Her speech about "Family Unity In Our Changing Times" was sponsored by the Modern Woodmen of America, and Debbi captured first prize back in 1969. This success led her to a lifetime of writing and speaking engagements.

At *The Robb Report Magazine*, Debbi was the magazine's on-air Corporate Media Spokesperson, making appearances on diverse media such as *Live With Regis and Kathie Lee*, and the *CBS Morning News*. She also created the magazine's signature tag line at the time, *"The Magazine For People With Million-Dollar Taste."* Her warm, bubbly personality, and business savvy also led her to become the national on-air media spokesperson for other businesses, including AT&T, SureFit Slipcovers (exclusively on Home Shopping Network, HSN), and VELCRO USA.

The Globetrotter's Get-Gorgeous Guide© is Debbi's third book. Her first book, *I Love Men in Tasseled Loafers: How To Judge Men By Their Shoes©*, was published in 1988 by Quinlan Press. She singlehandedly marketed and promoted the book, including sending the book to the media in Allen-Edmonds shoe boxes, and press releases rolled up and tied with actual leather laces with tassels. Her second book, *Off The Wall Marketing Ideas: Jumpstart Your Sales Without Busting Your Budget©,* was co-written with friend Nancy Michaels, and published by Adams Media in 2000. The book made *The Boston Globe's* Bestseller List in just 11 days after publication, and led Debbi to appearances on a wealth of media including *CNN*, *National Public Radio*, and articles about her in publications that include *Entrepreneur* and *Investors Business Daily*.

Debbi has made hundreds of media appearances in her career, promoting her clients, and her books, and has also been the featured guest speaker at numerous in-person speaking engagements. She is also the former Editor-in-Chief of *Mirror Magazine*, Boston's first magazine that was dedicated to beauty and well-being.

Debbi is the owner of **Maxima Marketing** in Westwood, Mass., (www. Marketingauthor.com), and provides marketing and public relations consulting to clients in all industries, especially the beauty industry. She works with plastic surgeons, cosmetic dentists, hair salons and skincare salons, masterminding strategies that include developing unusual story angles; creating marketing plans and signature tag lines; writing press releases, ads and newsletters; copywriting; media placement; and product naming. She produces for clients what Maxima Marketing's tagline promises: *"Making You Memorable, Moving You Ahead."*

Currently she is the Contributing Travel Editor and Contributing Spa Editor at www.JustLuxe.com, the leading luxury website on the internet. (Debbi has never met a luxury she didn't like, with the exception of Thai massage.)

When Debbi is not traveling the globe, getting spa treatments, shopping for bargains, writing marketing proposals and travel articles, exercising, buying cosmetics, and finding the humor in everyday life, she is watching movies, reading voraciously, flirting with her handsome husband Bill, and studying Combat Sambo (Russian martial arts), where she is an orange belt.

You can email Debbi at dkk@marketingauthor.com, and visit her website for *The Globetrotter's Get-Gorgeous Guide*, which is www.gorgeousglobetrotter.com.

COVER CREDITS

Pearl-and-gold necklace, and pearl drop
earrings by Landau, www.landaujewelry.com

Makeup

Base: Dior Airflash Spray Foundation #200

Blush: Rimmel Pink Rose

Eye Shadow: Rimmel Chocolatine Colour
Rush

Liner: Maybelline Brown Ultra Liner

Mascara: Rimmel Extreme Black Sexy
Curves (the most awesome mascara ever!)

Lip pencil: Giorgio Armani Silk pencil #10

Lipgloss: Yes To Carrots C Me Shine in
Playful Nude

Manicure: Orly Basket Case

Photographer: Paul Goldberg

THE JET-SET EXPRESS
at Boston's Salon Acote

Book your appointment for the "Jet-Set Express" and present your airline boarding pass, passport, train ticket, or subway ticket at the salon. In return, Salon Acote, Boston's Most French Salon, will offer:

- Chic haircuts with a waiting time of less than 15 minutes

- Free travel-size sets of Kerastase products ($50 value)

- Free cappuccino to-go (or to enjoy at the salon)

- Gift certificates for a complimentary blow dry upon your next visit to the salon ($35 value)

25% DISCOUNTS FOR TRAVEL PROFESSIONALS

Salon Acote also offers 25% discounts to all travel professionals around the world – flight attendants, pilots, airline personnel, travel agents, cruise professionals, even travel writers. Just give the password "travel" when you book your appointment.

Say you saw it in
THE GLOBETROTTER'S GET-GORGEOUS GUIDE!

Salon Acote | 132 Newbury Street | Boston, MA 02116
(617) 262-5111 | www.salonacote.com

As seen in:
**Lucky Magazine   LOLA Magazine   Marie-Claire Magazine
Elle Magazine   The Boston Globe Style Section**

Breinigsville, PA USA
15 December 2010
251489BV00004B/55-56/P